A book of monsters

Manchester University Press

A book of monsters

Promethean horror in modern literature and culture

David Ashford

MANCHESTER UNIVERSITY PRESS

Copyright © David Ashford 2024

The right of David Ashford to be identified as the author of this work has been asserted in accordance with the Copyright, Designs and Patents Act 1988.

Published by Manchester University Press
Oxford Road, Manchester, M13 9PL

www.manchesteruniversitypress.co.uk

British Library Cataloguing-in-Publication Data
A catalogue record for this book is available from the British Library

ISBN 978 1 5261 7087 3 hardback
ISBN 978 1 5261 9545 6 paperback

First published 2024
Paperback published 2026

The publisher has no responsibility for the persistence or accuracy of URLs for any external or third-party internet websites referred to in this book, and does not guarantee that any content on such websites is, or will remain, accurate or appropriate.

EU authorised representative for GPSR:
Easy Access System Europe – Mustamäe tee 50,
10621 Tallinn, Estonia
gpsr.requests@easproject.com

Typeset by Newgen Publishing UK

*Dedicated to Marion Wynne-Davies and Geoff Ward,
with gratitude
for supporting and fostering
the spirit of curiosity
that set me writing this book*

Contents

List of figures	*page* viii
Acknowledgements	x
1 The modern Prometheus: A brief introduction to the horror of Enlightenment	1
2 Architects of the occult: London's alternative "gothic" tradition	16
3 Gorillas in the House of Light: Inter-war Modernism as crisis management at London Zoo	45
4 Orc-talk: Spectres of Marx in Tolkien's Middle-Earth	75
5 Pandora's box: The insidious appeal of the Brutalist dystopia	111
6 The Mechanical Turk: Enduring misapprehensions concerning artificial intelligence	158
7 The Promethean altar: Prospects of atonement in twenty-first-century science fiction	198
Select bibliography	219
Index	228

Figures

2.1 The Mason's Carpet – as depicted on the apron presented to George Washington by General Lafayette in 1784. (Robert Macoy, *Illustrated History and Cyclopedia of Freemasonry*, New York: Masonic Publishing Co., 1896. GRANGER – Historical Picture Archive/Alamy Stock Photo.)   *page* 17

2.2 Sir Christopher Wren, *Ichnographia urbis Londinii (A Plan of the City of London, after the Great FIRE, in the Year of Our Lord 1666)*. Today Wren's original 1666 plan is lost. This version was drawn in 1744 by the engraver P. Fourdrinier, who claims to have replicated exactly a scarce 1724 original owned by the Earl of Pembroke. (Courtesy of Geographicus Rare Antique Maps.)   30

3.1 Tecton, model for the Gorilla House, London Zoo, Regent's Park, London (1933). (RIBA Ref, No. RIBA4769. Image courtesy of RIBA.)   45

3.2 Emmanuel Fremiet, *Gorilla Dragging Away a Dead Negress* (1859). (Photograph reproduced in Philipe Faure Fremiet, *Les Maitres de l'art: Fremiet*, Paris: Plon, 1934, 118.)   52

3.3 Emmanuel Fremiet, *Gorilla Carrying Off a Woman* (1887). (Photograph by Gustav Ollendorf, *Salon de 1887*, ed. Ludovic Baschet, Paris: Librairie d'art, 1887, 210.)   53

List of figures

5.1 Le Corbusier's Open Hand. (From Shaun Fynn, *Chandigarh Revealed: Le Corbusier's City Today*, Hudson, NY: Princeton Architectural Press/Mapin Publishing, 2017. Image reproduced here by kind permission of the photographer.) — 111

5.2 Le Corbusier's Modulor Man (1954). (From Le Corbusier's *The Modulor*, trans. Peter de Francia and Anna Bostock, London: Faber and Faber, 1954. Image reproduced by kind permission of the Le Corbusier Foundation.) — 129

6.1 The Mechanical Turk as depicted by Joseph Racknitz. (*Ueber den Schachspieler des Herrn von Kempelen und dessen Nachbildung*, Leipzig: Breitkopf, 1789.) — 163

6.2 Images of chaos. The Heighway Dragon Curve or the Harter-Heighway Dragon, also known as the Jurassic Park Dragon. First investigated by NASA physicists John Heighway, Bruce Banks and William Harter, and described by Martin Gardner in his *Scientific American* column 'Mathematical Games' in 1967. Iterations of the fractal appear at the beginning of each chapter in the novel *Jurassic Park*. (Image drawn by Dr Philip Gressman for the Internet Fractal Archive, University of Pennsylvania. Reproduced here by kind permission of the author.) — 191

7.1 Charts showing the correlation between changes in global temperatures and the percentage of carbon dioxide in the atmosphere over millions of years. (J. W. B. Rae, 'Cenozoic CO2 and Global Climate', *Annual Review of Earth and Planetary Sciences*, Vol. 49 (2021), 609–641. Image reproduced here by kind permission of the author.) — 216

Acknowledgements

This book has had an extraordinarily long gestation, and to thank everyone who has played a part in inspiring or supporting, improving, producing and promoting it would require more space than the material itself. I restrict myself here to my key sponsors.

My thanks to Rod Mengham at the University of Cambridge for encouraging this research in its formative stages, and to Prof. Marion Wynne-Davies at the University of Surrey, who founded the English department there and grew the research culture where I first began to develop the ideas expressed in this book.

My thanks to the many editors at various journals who published early drafts: in particular Geoff Ward at *The Cambridge Quarterly*, who was the first to engage with the essays now published as Chapters 3 and 6.

My thanks to Claire Mace and Owain Brown (and their cat Gajita), for their hospitality and friendship on the remote island retreat where I spent some months completing the fifth chapter in 2018.

Thanks to Richard Lansdown at the University of Groningen for his kindness and support following a devastating theft, which resulted in the loss of the laptop and back-up files containing a near complete draft of the book upon my first moving to the Netherlands: a theft that put me around two years behind schedule. Had I not had such extraordinarily supportive colleagues, I do not believe that I would have completed the book following this considerable setback.

My thanks to Frankie Mace for her help in preparing the book for publication and to Matthew Frost at Manchester University

Acknowledgements

Press for choosing to publish it. Enormous thanks to him and to his team, and in particular Kate Hawkins, Tanis Eve and Luke Finley, for the superb job they have done in editing and producing this volume.

Thanks also to the many students who have inspired and encouraged me over the years, as I presented ideas, now collected together in this book, in lectures and seminars, with particular thanks to those who took my MA tutorial on Promethean horror or kindly reviewed the book in its final stages of composition: Silvana Bogdanova, Danielle van den Brink, Tora Lyngøy, Bart Mulderij, Marijke Valk, Myrthe Voornhout, Nicholas Roberds, Joey Verhaar, Juan Florido Tormo and Floris van den Berg.

Finally, my heartfelt gratitude to family and friends who have played no small part in helping me to complete this book, against considerable odds. I wish to thank Evie Tokens and Nicholas Spicer in particular for their interest and patience as the book took shape over fifteen long years, together with my mum and dad, my sister Sarah, and my nephews Alex and Elliot.

1

The modern Prometheus: A brief introduction to the horror of Enlightenment

Autopsy

'A new species would bless me as its creator and source; many happy and excellent natures would owe their being to me', declares Victor Frankenstein, before adding that 'I might even in process of time (although I now found it impossible) renew life where death had apparently devoted the body to corruption'.[1] Only pause for a moment to process precisely what is being said here, for that one parenthesis must appear to contradict everything we thought we knew concerning the Monster – widely believed to be a thing stitched together from anatomical specimens stolen from university dissecting rooms and from dank charnel-houses, the ultimate result of 'experiments leading towards the revivification of the dead'.[2] But that would be to confuse Mary Shelley's *Frankenstein* with H. P. Lovecraft's Herbert West. Though both scientists are said to have 'dabbled among the unhallowed damps of the grave', only West would seem to have done so with a view to *reanimating* what he found there.[3] In contrast, Frankenstein collects human specimens only in order to disturb with 'profane fingers' the secrets of the human frame: 'To examine the causes of life, we must first have recourse to death', he explains. 'I became acquainted with the science of anatomy, but this was not sufficient; I must also observe the natural decay and corruption of the human body.'[4] And he is 'led to examine the cause and progress of this decay and forced to spend days and nights in vaults and charnel-houses', but he never loses sight of his primary end: not the overcoming of death (indeed Frankenstein explicitly declares that impossible) but rather discovering the cause of generation and life: 'I became myself capable of bestowing animation upon lifeless matter.'[5] Certainly, a great many details in the description of the reasoning behind the construction of the Monster must preclude the idea that Frankenstein is contemplating a mere collation and arrangement of corpses. 'Although I possessed the capacity of bestowing animation, yet to prepare a frame for the reception of it, with all its intricacies of fibres, muscles, and veins, still remained a work of inconceivable difficulty and labour', he reflects:

> I doubted at first whether I should attempt the creation of a being like myself, or one of simpler organization; but my imagination was too much exalted by my first success to permit me to doubt of my ability to give life to an animal as complex and wonderful as man.[6]

But why should Frankenstein feel that materials thought to be derived from human remains should be unsuitable to the latter project ('The materials at present within my command hardly appeared adequate to so arduous an undertaking'), given that constructing a human from humans would essentially constitute a form of reverse-engineering?[7] The answer is that what Frankenstein creates cannot consist wholly of those human materials furnished by the dissecting rooms because it is on too large a scale: he simply cannot possibly have fashioned a Monster eight feet tall from the remains of humans of between five and six feet tall. 'As the minuteness of the parts formed a great hindrance to my speed, I resolved, contrary to my first intention, to make the being of a gigantic stature, that is to say, about eight feet in height, and proportionably large.'[8] Indeed, were any reader in a position to approach the first description of the Monster without the preconceptions which we inevitably bring to the book, they might well wonder whether the creature delineated here were a *Blade Runner*-style "synthetic human", or a cyborg, or even a robot:

> His limbs were in proportion, and I had selected his features as beautiful. Beautiful! Great God! His yellow skin scarcely covered the work of muscles and arteries beneath; his hair was of a lustrous black, and flowing; his teeth of a pearly whiteness; but these luxuriances only formed a more horrid contrast with his watery eyes, that seemed almost of the same colour as the dun-white sockets in which they were set, his shrivelled complexion and straight black lips.[9]

Would a reanimated corpse really be the first idea that sprang to mind? 'A mummy again endued with animation could not be so hideous as that wretch,' says Frankenstein; a similitude that would be entirely redundant were the Thing actually that to which it is being compared.[10]

A mis-reception history

Many readers will surely find it hard to shake their preconceptions concerning the Monster. How might one account for this certainty? Certainly, the cultural tradition that has grown up around Mary Shelley's original novel is an important factor. Over the past centuries the story has itself come to embody precisely what is popularly understood by the term "Frankenstein's Monster": having long outlived its creator, this undying organism is now the product of no one mind, perpetually returning in a series of (often very loose) film adaptations that revel in the gruesome opportunities presented by body horror and grave-robbing. Director James Whale's *Frankenstein* (1931) begins with Henry Frankenstein and his young assistant Fritz watching a funeral like jackals, cutting recently hanged men from the gallows, before combining these body parts with a 'criminal brain' stolen from Dr Waldman's laboratory. In *The Horror of Frankenstein* (1970), a coolly psychopathic Ralph Bates cuts up and sews together fresh corpses with all the finesse of a tailor, displaying impatience and sloppiness (again) only when it comes to the brain: the jar containing the brain of Professor Heiss is dropped and the brain mangled by a shard of glass, but the brain is inserted regardless into the head of a highway robber played by David Prowse (a.k.a. Darth Vader) – with predictable results. Even the ostensibly faithful *Mary Shelley's Frankenstein* (1994) reiterates this macabre trope: in this adaptation the brain of Dr Waldman is reanimated inside the body of his murderer (played by Robert De Niro). Needless to say, there is no basis for any of this in the original novel, but Mary Shelley's story, like the Monster itself, has proven to have a life all of its own.

But it is Shelley herself who produced the first, most influential accretion that set the Frankenstein story on its path to becoming a modern myth – in her 1831 preface to the novel. In this evocative piece of writing, the author remembers how she, Percy Bysshe Shelley, Lord Byron and John William Polidori had taken to reading 'ghost stories' in the course of one long, wet, ungenial summer: 'We will each write a ghost story,' said Lord Byron, and Mary Shelley refers to her own novel as such, though no ghosts actually appear in the text.[11] From the very start, Frankenstein's Monster was thus associated with the undead. Indeed, the first modern vampire tale would emerge from this same parlour game: unholy twins, it is unsurprising that Polidori's *Vampyre* and Mary Shelley's *Frankenstein* should have developed intersecting mythologies over the following century at Universal Pictures and Hammer Studios. The impression of affinity between Monster and Undead is reinforced by the famous passage wherein Shelley recalls a discussion concerning 'galvanism' and appears to relate this to the prospect of reanimating the dead. 'Perhaps a corpse would be re-animated,' writes Shelley; 'galvanism had given token of such things: perhaps the component parts of a creature might be manufactured, brought together, and endued with vital warmth'.[12] The final clause in this sentence has been interpreted, ever since, as an expansion upon the first, rather than as an *alternative* application of the new electrical technology referred to in the clause immediately preceding: the implication would appear to be that the component parts have been acquired at "second hand" rather than being "purpose-built". In fact, there is nothing anywhere in the preface to support a literal (rather than figurative) reading of Shelley's description of the Monster as a 'hideous corpse'.[13] Indeed, a reader in a position to approach this text without the prevalent preconceptions concerning it would certainly regard as perverse the popular interpretation of the following line as a *reanimation* of *once-living* matter. 'The Creator' writes Shelley:

> would hope that, left to itself, the slight spark of life which he had communicated would fade; that this thing, which had received such imperfect *animation*, would subside into *dead* matter; and he might sleep in the belief that the silence of the grave would quench for ever the transient existence of the hideous corpse which he had looked upon as the cradle of life.[14]

In fact, Frankenstein is deliberately vague concerning the technical basis for his experiment (explaining that he wishes to prevent anyone from attempting to repeat it), and so over subsequent centuries well-meaning editors have attempted to help readers fill in the blanks, with notes concerning Italian physicist Giovanni Aldini (and the twitching bodies of recently deceased malefactors in Newgate); or his uncle Luigi Galvani (and the twitching amputated legs of frogs); or Byron's remark, in his poem *Don Juan*, that 'Galvanism has set some corpses grinning'.[15]

The homunculus

In truth, the inspiration for Shelley's tale would appear to be ... *somewhat older*. 'When I was thirteen years of age', recalls Frankenstein, 'I chanced to find a volume of the works of Cornelius Agrippa.'[16] The discovery of the German occultist is likened to a new dawn, and these volumes are soon supplemented with those of Renaissance alchemists Paracelsus and Albertus Magnus. 'I read and studied the wild fancies of these writers with delight; they appeared to me treasures known to few besides myself.'[17] Disillusioned with the limits of natural philosophy, Frankenstein concludes that these men had penetrated deeper and knew more: 'I took their word for all that they averred, and I became their disciple', he declares, though it 'may appear strange that such should arise in the eighteenth century'.[18] Indeed, Frankenstein's professors at Geneva are horrified to learn that he has burdened his memory with exploded systems and useless names: 'In what desert land have you lived, where no one was kind enough to inform you that these fancies which you have so greedily imbibed are a thousand years old and as musty as they are ancient?' asks M. Kempe: 'I little expected, in this enlightened and scientific age, to find a disciple of Albertus Magnus and Paracelsus.'[19] Preferring chimeras of boundless grandeur to realities of little worth, Frankenstein continues to mingle, 'like an un-adept, a thousand contradictory theories and flounders desperately in a very slough of multifarious knowledge, guided by an ardent imagination and childish reasoning, till an accident again changed the current of my ideas'.[20] It is Professor Waldman who persuades Frankenstein that while the ancient teachers of this science promised impossibilities and performed nothing, the modern masters, promising very little, have indeed performed miracles: 'They penetrate into the recesses of nature and show how she works in her hiding-places', Waldman declares. 'They ascend into the heavens; they have discovered how the blood circulates, and the nature of the air we breathe. They have acquired new and almost unlimited powers; they can command the thunders of heaven, mimic the earthquake, and even mock the invisible world with its own shadows.'[21] But if the procedures that Frankenstein will now study with rigour are those of eighteenth-century natural philosophy, there is no implication that his objective is anything other than that he had previously sought to achieve through the study of his old alchemists: not the discovery of the philosopher's stone, nor the raising of ghosts and demons (though he tries his hand at this), but the creation of an elixir of life; it is this that had first obtained his undivided attention. 'Wealth was an inferior object, but what glory would attend the discovery if I could banish disease from the human frame and render man invulnerable to any but a violent death!'[22] Indeed, if the materials furnished by the dissecting room *and the slaughterhouse* be not items required for study but actual component parts in the Monster, the latter provenance might suggest that not merely the end but even the means have remained unchanged from those set out by Paracelsus and Cornelius Agrippa, with Luigi Galvani providing only (quite literally) the Vital Spark. '[Let] the sperm of a man be putrefied by itself in a sealed cucurbit for forty days with the highest degree of putrefaction in a horse's womb, or at least so long that it comes to life and moves itself, and stirs', writes Paracelsus in *De Natura Rerum* (1537):

> If, after this, it be fed wisely with the Arcanum of human blood, and be nourished for up to forty weeks, and be kept in the even heat of the horse's womb, a living human child grows therefrom, with all its members like another child, which is born of a woman, but much smaller.[23]

Reflecting Aristotelian misconceptions concerning reproduction and spontaneous generation, the reproductive or digestive organs of animals are integral to such alchemical recipes for the creation of artificial life: 'there is an art', writes Cornelius Agrippa, 'wherewith by a hen sitting upon eggs may be generated a form like to a man, which I have seen and know how to make, which magicians say hath in it wonderful virtues, and this they call the true mandrake.'[24] Both Paracelsus and Cornelius Agrippa use the term *mandragora* or *mandrake* to describe these creatures, perhaps casting a new (and disturbing) light on precisely what Frankenstein is attempting to acquire from the dissecting rooms and public gallows – for according to science historian William Newman, this root was for many centuries thought to be generated by the sperm ejaculated by hanged men: 'in honor of its provenance, the *Alraun* [*alreona*] was also called *Galgenmann* or *Galgenmännlein* ("gallows man")'.[25] The mandrake root was in fact regarded as a naturally occurring example of the spontaneous generation that Paracelsus and Cornelius Agrippa were attempting to emulate through artificial means, albeit on an altogether much more ambitious scale: 'the distilled essence of masculinity', writes Newman, 'concentrated and purified of its material dross'.[26] Having received their life from art, these creatures are said to have wonderful strength and powers as a result, such as the ability to defeat enemies with 'great, forceful victory' (*grossen, gewaltigen sig*) and to know 'all hidden and secret things' (*alle heimlichen und verbogne ding*). 'Through art they are born', declares Paracelsus, 'and therefore art is embodied and inborn in them':[27] a fact that might account for the exquisite sensibility and eloquence that is displayed by Shelley's Monster – entirely at odds with what one might expect either from a lumbering reanimated corpse or from a student educated inadvertently, eavesdropping in a shepherd's hut – a problem that later filmmakers have sought to circumvent (as noted previously) by means of Dr Waldman's brain. In fact, no retcon of this sort is necessary, for we can surely conclude with Paracelsus that this is what we call a *homunculus*,[28] and, further, that *that* is why Frankenstein's Monster *should* have been educated (as the old alchemists instructed) with the greatest care and zeal: 'They have reason in common with man (except in regard to the soul)', observes Paracelsus. 'They have knowledge and intelligence of the spirit (except in regard to God).'[29]

Defining Promethean horror

Having identified Frankenstein's Monster as a *homunculus*, we are in a position to suggest that Shelley's novel might well constitute a belated contribution to a body of writing that had flourished centuries earlier, in the Renaissance, and that I term *Promethean horror*: cautionary tales in which promises of vastly increased power over natural limits are countervailed by fears about being overwhelmed by the products of our own ingenuity – the homunculus of Paracelsus and Cornelius Agrippa; the Jewish golem of Prague; the inhuman servants conjured in Shakespeare's *Tempest* (1611), Marlowe's *Doctor Faustus* (1592) and Robert Greene's *Friar Bacon and Friar Bungay* (1595). 'These tales, in other words, are about being blinded by our intellectual enthusiasm to the danger of our intellectual products, about becoming enslaved by those things which are meant to serve us, about being bound rather than liberated by the ambitions that produce them', writes Kevin LaGrandeur, in his groundbreaking study *Artificial Slaves: Androids and Intelligent Networks in Early Modern Literature and Culture* (2013). While we are 'just beginning to realize the aim of creating humanoid servants in our own time', LaGrandeur demonstrates that 'dreams of such servants have been surprisingly common throughout history – including ancient history'.[30] In the eighteenth book of Homer's *Iliad* we read that the smith-god Hephaistos has fashioned a number of intelligent serving tripods that can roll themselves in and out of the banqueting room (like R2D2 serving drinks), as well as metallic serving-women that 'worked for him, and were like real young women, with sense and reason, voice also and strength, and all the learning of the immortals'.[31] In Book 4 of Aristotle's *Politics*, the philosopher would refer back to Hephaistos' intelligent artefacts and argue that 'if, in like manner, the shuttle would weave and the plectrum touch the lyre, chief workmen would not want servants, nor masters slaves'.[32] Conflating human servants and slaves with artificial prosthetic labour-saving devices in this way, Aristotle established the theoretical basis for all subsequent discussion concerning the promise and peril of artificially intelligent servants.

> Aristotle's use of a ship's rudder and human lookout as examples of the kinds of tools he is speaking of is revealing, because the pilot uses the rudder and the lookout as different types of sensory and manipulative tools and because, since they are classified as part of the master's body, they are in fact prostheses: the rudder acts as a modified extension of the pilot's arms, and the lookout acts as an enhancement of his eyes.[33]

Indeed, it is from the Greek word for *pilot* in this passage (*kubernētēs*) that the term '*cybernetics*' would be derived by pioneering computer scientist Norbert Wiener. Contemporary fears regarding computing technology that find expression in science fiction such as Isaac Asimov's *I, Robot* (1950), Capek's *R. U. R.* (1923), Heinlein's *The Moon is a Harsh Mistress* (1966) and Clarke's *2001: A Space Odyssey* (1968) are thus seen to have very long roots in classical fears concerning the potential reversibility of the master–slave relationship: 'in Aristotle's formulation the master exists in a virtual network comprising his tools, animate and inanimate, upon which he depends to control or, indeed, to supersede Nature's limits', explains LaGrandeur. 'Though he might be initially at the center of this network of prostheses (or "tools"), the attachment to an overly-potent tool could conceivably cause the prosthesis–master status to reverse.'[34] The relevance of this to *Frankenstein* need hardly be stated, and LaGrandeur is surely correct to suggest (as he does in passing) that the Monster might well be 'the first android of the industrial era'.[35]

How to account for this resurgence of Promethean tropes from the Early Modern in nineteenth-century gothic horror? As its very name would suggest, the gothic genre has, from the beginning, been associated with a negative (mis-)conception of medieval Europe as a "Dark Age". Horace Walpole's *Castle of Otranto* (1764), Ann Radcliffe's *Mysteries of Udolpho* (1794) and Matthew Lewis's *The Monk* (1796) each play upon liberal British fears of a past that will not remain buried, of a return to a Roman Catholic Europe definitively rejected only with the Stuart dynasty. Headless horsemen, the Spanish Inquisition, Jesuits and ghostly nuns, the prospect of atoning for the sins of the fathers: it was the revenant or spectre that initially preoccupied writers of gothic fiction, and still does to a significant degree, to the extent that one is hard pressed to speak of the subject being broached here without recourse to terminology that must be entirely misleading. (Even Mary Shelley was compelled to speak of her Promethean fable as a "ghost story".) One might have thought Early Modern alchemy an unlikely subject for an early nineteenth-century gothic horror. I believe the answer lies in the parallel tradition of gothic horror that had emerged in contemporary German-speaking Europe, part of the Romantic reaction to the French Revolution, widely perceived as the culmination of eighteenth-century rationalism. In Friedrich Schiller's *Der Geisterseher* (1787), the agents of the Inquisition (Jesuits) are presented as being on moral par with the agents of modernity (Freemasons and Illuminati) – and subsequent works in this German gothic tradition present nearly the mirror image of their British counterparts. In *The Necromancer* by Carl Friedrich Kahlert (trans. 1795), *The Victim of Magical Delusion* by Cajetan Tschink (trans. 1795) and *Horrid Mysteries* by Karl Grosse (trans. 1796), the natural philosophers and Freemasons integral to Britain's experiment with empirical science and Liberal government are presented as terrifying magicians, psychologically manipulating the populace with technology, including magic lanterns, magnets, electrical devices and gunpowder. 'Once the mind of initiates had folded under the stress of inexplicable mysteries', explains Robert Miles, in his survey of this literature, 'their minds would be putty in the hands of their masters, who plotted the overthrow of monarchies across Europe.'[36] Translated into English, these German tales of terror enjoyed a brief vogue in the UK but no imitators. Shelley's novel might now perhaps be recognised as Britain's first significant contribution to this alternative "gothic" tradition. (It is certainly interesting to note that Ingolstadt, the site of Dr Frankenstein's experiments, is said to have been the birthplace of the Illuminati.) Participating in the broader questioning of pre-Revolutionary Enlightenment values that had brought about a shift to Burkean conservatism in politics and Romanticism in literature, Shelley's novel is the first in English to exploit fears not of medieval revival but of modern innovation, not of the undead but of new creation, not of the Holy Inquisition but of the coming revolution, not irrational faith but forbidden knowledge. No terror of a so-called Dark Age but, rather, a horror of Enlightenment.

The plan of this work

Philosopher Jurgen Habermas once observed that Masonic lodges were central to the development of European civic society. To see freemasonry now being represented emphatically as an agent of horror in late twentieth-century English psycho-geographical fiction, by authors such as Iain Sinclair and Alan Moore, would seem to suggest that a sea-change has taken place, vindicating Habermas's suggestion that post-modernism must be understood as a reiteration of the Romantic reaction against Enlightenment ideas. This book will endeavour to discover how Modernism (a phenomenon that, in architecture, for instance, typically defined itself against neo-gothic irrationality, aligning itself with neo-classicism) has been demonised by post-modernists, imbued with uncanny horror, in an eclectic body of writing that constitutes a belated but substantial contribution to the alternative "gothic" tradition outlined above.

The next chapter begins by engaging with some of the most prominent anti-gothic gothic fiction created over the past century: paranoid psycho-geographical fantasy in poems by Iain Sinclair, novels by Peter Ackroyd, essays by Stewart Home and graphic novels by Alan Moore. The potential for such provocative misreadings of the English baroque is shown to have a basis in the architecture itself, and it is suggested that the scope for uncanny sensations opened up by the structures might have much to tell us about the post-modernist baroque revival, the fiction of Sinclair and Moore having as much to do with the Thatcherite renovation of the metropolis as anything in the theory and practice of Nicholas Hawksmoor.

The third chapter traces this "architectural uncanny" back to London's earliest inter-war Modernist architecture, showing that this "functionalist" architectural aesthetic is as ripe for uncanny sensations as the eighteenth-century "rationalist" architecture considered in the previous chapter, and for much the same reason: being committed to an act of dissimulation in order to see off a perceived threat to Enlightenment values posed by the evolutionary theory of Charles Darwin and the psychoanalytical theory of Sigmund Freud, the rival tradition of Modernist theory and practice that emerges from what one might call the radical empiricist or Romantic tradition of Western philosophy.

The fourth chapter shows how the tradition of Modernism in which one might place Lubetkin (with writers T. S. Eliot, Ezra Pound and Wyndham Lewis) would itself be demonised by writers within the Romantic-Modern tradition, exploring how fear and hostility provoked by the Promethean energies of the USSR (and by the New Linguistic Doctrine of the Soviet linguist Nikolai Marr in particular) manifest themselves in perhaps the most memorable demonisation of a symbol of Enlightenment: the all-seeing Eye of

Sauron on its pyramid. Deeply committed to the discipline of philology that had inspired Schopenhauer (and the radical empiricism that followed), J. R. R. Tolkien is revealed to be an unlikely combatant in the great culture war between these two estranged philosophies that defined the era of High Modernism.

The fifth chapter considers the third-quarter-century synthesis of the two rival "Freudian" and "Marxist" Modernisms considered in the preceding chapters, and ways in which post-war theory and practice designated "Late Modernist" would be (very successfully) demonised by successive waves of post-modernist critics, particularly in relation to architecture. This chapter considers the profound reaction from Brutalist architecture that anticipated the general turn to post-modernisms in other disciplines, and questions many of the widespread assumptions that have developed with regard to this. The ferocity of the debate suggests that the issues at stake here are not merely practical. Those for and against seem to share an irrational faith in the power of the buildings to exert control over the communities they contain, whether for good or for ill, in a manner that must recall the fantastically weird responses to Hawksmoor's baroque churches in psycho-geographical fiction of this era. The underlying causes of this uncanny effect are identified, analysed and traced back to the architectural theory that designed such spaces and to the economic theory that required their production. Finally, a peculiar subgenre of the anti-socialist dystopia is defined that is, specifically, anti-Keynesian.

The sixth chapter traces the persistence of Promethean horror tropes beyond the apparent collapse of the Late Modernist paradigm, into the neoliberal and post-modernist era. Expanding on issues relating to the crisis in Enlightenment humanist thinking raised in preceding chapters, and addressing concerns central to post-humanist theory relating to the consequences that must follow for human identity arising from the development of artificial intelligence, this chapter instead outlines an entirely new approach, suggesting that the famous "Turing Test" has been consistently misinterpreted, and that we are now in a position to see that it is designed to gauge an "uncanny" effect; that is, the extent to which a system for modelling social behaviour can outperform an older, tried-and-tested system for producing such models (i.e. human personalities: a social construct that each of us attempts, with varying success, to perform). The consequences for failing to recognise this are that we are likely to remain "taken in" by such models when they are applied to other aspects of our lives, limiting our freedom of action. While systems for predicting political and economic phenomena are widely believed to have fallen out of favour in the final quarter of the twentieth century, this chapter demonstrates that such systems actually remain integral to our contemporary economy in the form of scenario planning and computer modelling, with the failure to recognise this having often devastating effects.

The final chapter will examine twenty-first-century novels by Reza Negarestani, Stephen King and Nnedi Okorafor, in order to assess whether the "turn" towards Enlightenment horror identified in this book is likely to prove an enduring phenomenon or whether its moment might now already have passed, as memories of the hopes and fears provoked in equal measure by the Promethean ambitions of Modernist practitioners and theorists begin to fade with time, with the Golden Age of Western capitalism (as the historian Eric Hobsbawm termed it) receding ever further into the past.

It is hoped this book will present an overview on what Walter Benjamin would have called our collective "dream-work", in the decades since the dreams of the nineteenth century were realised in Modernism, by tracing the inception and outlining the potential consequences of the post-modernist literary fantasies here analysed. I conclude with a prospect of Mount Kazbek, where the Georgian Prometheus, Amirani, is said to be chained, and of the Promethean Fire Temple in Baku, in Azerbaijan, to reflect upon what the myth of the rebel Titan might teach us today, as we seek to reconcile a culture that remains bitterly divided over the legacies of Modernity, and the post-modernist reaction: brief centuries in which humanity has witnessed, after so many long millennia, the full glory and terror of Prometheus unbound.

Notes

1 Mary Shelley, *Frankenstein; or, The Modern Prometheus* (London: Penguin Classics, 2003), 55.
2 H. P. Lovecraft, 'Herbert West – Reanimator' (1922), republished in Stephen Jones (ed.), *Necronomicon: The Best Weird Tales of H. P. Lovecraft* (London: Gollancz, 2008), 38.

3 Shelley, *Frankenstein*, 55.
4 *Ibid.*, 52.
5 *Ibid.*, 53.
6 *Ibid.*, 54.
7 *Ibid.*, 54.
8 *Ibid.*, 54.
9 *Ibid.*, 58.
10 *Ibid.*, 59.
11 *Ibid.*, 7.
12 *Ibid.*, 8.
13 *Ibid.*, 9.
14 *Ibid.*, 9.
15 Lord Byron, *Don Juan*, I: 130, Ernest Hartley Coleridge (ed.), *The Poetical Works of Lord Byron* (London: John Murray, 1905), 794.
16 Shelley, *Frankenstein*, 40.
17 *Ibid.*, 41.
18 *Ibid.*, 41.
19 *Ibid.*, 47.
20 *Ibid.*, 42.
21 *Ibid.*, 49.
22 *Ibid.*, 42.
23 Paracelsus, *De Natura Rerum* (1572), A. E. Waite (trans.), *The Hermetic and Alchemical Writings of Paracelsus* (London: James Elliott and Co, 1894), I.124.
24 Cornelius Agrippa, *De Occulta Philosophia* (1533), James Freake (trans.), *Three Books of Occult Philosophy* (London: Printed by R. W. for Gregory Moule, 1651), I.36.
25 William Newman, *Promethean Ambitions: Alchemy and the Quest to Perfect Nature* (Chicago: University of Chicago Press, 2004), 215.
26 *Ibid.*, 6.
27 Paracelsus, *De Natura Rerum*, II.317.
28 *Ibid.*, I.124.
29 Paracelsus, 'A Book of Nymphs, Sylphs, Pygmies and Salamanders, and on the Other Spirits' (1566), Henry E. Sigherist (trans.), *Four Treatises of Theophrastus von Hohenheim Called Paracelsus* (Baltimore, MD, and London: Johns Hopkins University Press, 1941), 239.
30 Kevin LaGrandeur, *Androids and Intelligent Networks in Early Modern Literature and Culture: Artificial Slaves* (New York: Routledge, 2013), 1.
31 Homer, *Iliad*, XVIII: 410–425, Samuel Butler (trans.), *The Iliad of Homer* (London: Longmans, Green and Co., 1898), 312.

32 Aristotle, *Politics*, I: 4, B. Jowett (trans.), *The Politics of Aristotle*, Vol. 1 (Oxford: Clarendon Press, 1885), 6.
33 LaGrandeur, *Androids and Intelligent Networks*, 10.
34 *Ibid.*, 11.
35 *Ibid.*, 160.
36 Robert Miles, 'The 1790s: Effulgence of Gothic', Jerrold E. Hogle (ed.), *The Cambridge Companion to Gothic Literature* (Cambridge: Cambridge University Press, 2003), 51.

2

Architects of the occult: London's alternative "gothic" tradition

Memory palaces

The temple is perfected in the killing of the architect. The master-word being withheld, the assailants strike the skull three times, with plumb rule, level and maul. In recoil, passing from south to north, between pillars of brass (each bears a ball: the giving and receiving of strength), to the east, he collapses to a pavement (chequered, white and black flag). The body is buried on top of a hill. The grave is a secret marked with a sprig of acacia.

This is the third degree. To acquire the name of master mason, the initiate must proceed through a diagrammatic map or plan; the story of the architect plays out on a schematic representation of the temple complex, a mnemonic device surely inspired by the *method of loci*, or *memory palace*, spoken of in the *Rhetorica ad Herrenium*. 'Persons desiring to train this faculty [of memory] must select places and form mental images of the things they wish to remember', wrote Cicero.[1] In so doing, practitioners produce an imaginary architecture that they can enter at will, a series of spaces that contain objects. In order to recall the content of, say, a speech, a speaker proceeds from room to room, revisiting the memorial placed in each.[2] To enact the pattern on a Mason's Carpet is to reactivate a sort of memory board; lost to Western Europe for several centuries, artefacts like this were the information technology of the ancient world. Apparently introduced into Masonic practice by James Anderson in the years between 1723 and 1729, the image of the 'Legend of the Temple' does not merely signify but realises the resurrection of classical learning taking place in that period. In practising the narrative space mapped out upon the floor, the man is reconfigured as architect, the mind is

MASONIC APRON, WROUGHT BY MADAME THE MARCHIONESS LAFAYETTE.

Figure 2.1 The Mason's Carpet – as depicted on the apron presented to George Washington by General Lafayette in 1784. (Robert Macoy, *Illustrated History and Cyclopedia of Freemasonry*, New York: Masonic Publishing Co., 1896.)

restructured in line with new – or rather, revived – conceptions of classical space that members of the group were then producing in London; the topographical and psychological spaces of the city that rose from the ashes of the Great Fire converged upon the monumental.[3]

Given this last point, it is unsurprising that the Brotherhood of Free and Accepted Masons have figured so prominently in that body of London writing since labelled *psycho-geographical* – a term coined by Guy Debord of Lettrist International in 1955 to describe the study of the precise laws and specific effects of the geographical environment, consciously organised or not, on the emotions and behaviour of individuals. From the beginning, in texts such as Iain Sinclair's *Lud Heat* (1975), Peter Ackroyd's *Hawksmoor* (1985), Stewart Home's *Mind Invaders* (1991) and Alan Moore's *From Hell* (1989), the spaces of this secret society have been central to psycho-geographical literature in the UK; the extent to which Masonic theory and practice have produced the physical and psychological spaces of the modern metropolis has been a recurring theme. In Peter Ackroyd's *Hawksmoor*, for instance, the churches of the Freemason Nicholas Hawksmoor are explicitly identified with contemporaneous transformations in literary form that would ultimately result in the novel.

> I have finished six Designes of my last Church, fastned with Pinns on the Walls of my Closet so that the Images surround me and I am once more at Peece. In the first I have the Detail of the Ground Plot, which is like a Prologue in a Story; in the second there is all the Plan in a small form, like the disposition of Figures in a Narrative; the third Draught shews the Elevation, which is like the Symbol or Theme of a Narrative, and the fourth displays the Upright of the Front, which is like to the main part of the Story; in the fifth there are designed the many and irregular Doors, Stairways and Passages like so many ambiguous Expressions, Tropes, Dialogues and Metaphoricall speeches; in the sixth there is the Upright of the Portico and the Tower which will strike the Mind with Magnificence, as in the Conclusion of a Book.[4]

But what to make of the fact that Hawksmoor's *neo-classical* buildings are the subject of what is unmistakably a *gothic* narrative? For this is a book of uncanny doubling. Hawksmoor has been reimagined as a police officer stalking the dark phantom of himself, as he attempts to solve a series of ritualistic murders, while the architect, renamed Dyer, is represented as the Shadow to the Enlightenment. Having been commissioned to build monuments to the new rational religion, championed by his master Christopher Wren, he has produced structures that incorporate satanic secrets: 'I, the Builder of Churches, am no Puritan nor Caveller, nor Reformed, nor Catholick, nor Jew, but of that older Faith which sets them dancing in Black Step Lane.'[5] In fact, the whole body of psycho-geographical literature on Masonic architecture could be characterised as a subgenre of the gothic. Sinclair's study of Hawksmoor draws heavily upon the fiction of H. P. Lovecraft, and Moore implicates the churches in the Ripper murders that took place two hundred years after they were built. But on the face of it these uncompromisingly neo-classical buildings are not what one might consider an obvious setting for a genre of literature that has (from its inception) been inextricably bound up with the architectural style known as gothic revival. Horace Walpole – the creator of *The Castle of Otranto: A Gothic Story* – also commissioned the original gothic folly: the suburban castle up on Strawberry Hill. Indeed, according to one critical introduction to the genre, the most obvious justification for the use of *gothic* as a literary term was by analogy with the movement in architecture, which also began in the mid-eighteenth century.[6] The existence of a significant contemporary subgenre that situates gothic narratives in Enlightenment forms of thought, investing neo-classical space with gothic gloom, cuts straight to the heart of the suspicion now surrounding the term: the recognition that 'Gothic as an aesthetic term has been counterfeit all along'.[7] In seeking to explain how Hawksmoor's churches – and neo-classical spaces more generally – became generators for everything the New Architecture was meant to exclude, the following chapter must cast light on questions that continue to animate gothic studies. I begin with a consideration of Nicholas Hawksmoor's life and work; rejecting the idea that either are inevitably grist for a gothic mill, I situate his church project within the context of the rebuilding and expansion of London after the Great Fire, and consider the impact that some of the more peculiar aspects of the New Architecture might have had on a contemporaneous redevelopment project, whereby the romance became novel. The neo-classical spaces explored in much recent psycho-geographical fiction were produced in the decades immediately preceding the taste for gothic, or rather neo-gothic, in literature and architecture, and the present study should therefore be helpful in the ongoing attempt to establish that process whereby the gothic became gothic.

The magician's apprentice

It is the prototype of the Ripper tour. The fourth chapter of Alan Moore's *From Hell* takes the reader on a coach ride across London, offering insights into the murders that took place in the autumn of 1888. But this tour is set before the event – and is conducted by "Jack the Ripper". 'We must consider our great work in ALL its aspects', explains the killer to his coachman. His commission to remove certain women who threaten the crown is merely occasion for a creative engagement with the pattern of history and myth that makes up the modern metropolis. Beginning at King's Cross, where Queen Boadicea died in battle with the Roman empire, the tour proceeds to Hackney, where Saxons toasted Ivalde Svigdur, the man who killed the moon, then Bunhill Fields and the obelisk on the grave of Daniel Defoe. In the course of this, the guide will interpret London's built environment as a monument to the primordial rebellion of men against matriarchal power:

> Back in the caves, life hinged on childbirth's mystery and we served mother goddesses, not father gods. 'Twas thus for several million years. Then men rebelled, perhaps a few at first, a small conspiracy ... who by some act of social magic, politics, or force, cast women down that man might rule.[8]

This revolt is said to have involved a psychological repression on the part of the men themselves, an act that necessitated an internal war on those aspects of the mind that had been designated feminine. 'All human brains ... have two sides: the left is Reason, Logic Science; our Apollonian skills. The right is Magic, Art and Madness ... the Mind's unconscious hemisphere, whose symbol is the Moon.'[9] In the view of Jack the Ripper, "Tis in the war of Sun and Moon that Man steals Woman's power; that Left brain conquers Right ... that reason chains insanity'.[10] This misappropriation of prophetic power finds its most forceful expression in those five chains set into the stone about the dome of St Paul's Cathedral. Formerly the site of a temple sacred to Diana, the current structure is now said to be a temple to the sun, named after that 'staunch misogynist' beaten by the goddess at Ephesus. 'Here is DIANA chained, the soul of womankind bound in a web of ancient signs.'[11] The city's architecture emerges as a centuries-long conspiracy on the part of the male principle, involving the manipulation of stone and symbol. The violence that follows later in the graphic novel will therefore not admit of only one solution. As in a detective story, everyone in the region is a suspect, having both motive and means (the entire city has been exposed as a systematic form of misogyny), but in contrast to, say, Agatha Christie, Moore's graphic novel refuses to resolve the ontological uncertainty that the genre opens up, stating that the Ripper must be recognised as a super-position: the sum of all the possibilities presented by London in 1888.[12] The Ripper ultimately turns out to be not William Gull but the single point upon which the oppressive energies generated by the architectural structures mapped in chapter four converge. The tour concludes in the centre of the mosaic of the sun beneath the dome of St Paul's. Having marked on a street map each building visited in the course of their journey through London, the Ripper asks his coachman to join the dots – and discovers an 'earthbound constellation'.[13] The pattern is the five-pointed star, 'pentacle of Sun God's obelisks and rational male fire, wherein unconsciousness, the Moon and Womanhood are chained'.[14]

Most of the points on this map refer to the churches of Nicholas Hawksmoor, and his 'cheerless soul', his 'personality encoded into stone', emerges as the moving spirit behind the Masonic conspiracy.[15] Even its design, built by the original Grand Master of the Lodges, Sir Christopher Wren, seems to have been included in Moore's pattern because Hawksmoor is known to have assisted with St Paul's.[16] Moore acknowledges that the musings on alignments that make up so much of this chapter have their basis in a meditation on the psycho-geographical properties of the Hawksmoor churches, the narrative poem *Lud Heat* by Iain Sinclair. In this, Sinclair develops Alfred Watkin's theory of ley lines: his belief that prehistoric landmarks of the British Isles are aligned in a such a way as to produce huge invisible networks, and that such alignments are still there even in urban landscapes: 'There are curious facts linking up orientation with the ley system illustrated by some London churches.'[17] According to Sinclair, each of Hawksmoor's 'great churches' is 'an enclosure of force, a trap, a sight-block, a raised place with an unacknowledged influence over events created within the shadow-lines of their towers'.[18] If one were to mark out the total plan of churches on a map – like that provided in the book by Sinclair's friend and fellow poet Brian Catling – one could trace 'lines of influence, the invisible rods of force active in this city'.[19] This would produce a triangle in the east. If churches to the west and south are included, the result is an irregular polygon. Sinclair likens this to the 'symbol of Set, instrument of castration or tool for making cuneiform signs'.[20] The pattern is further complicated by subsystems of obelisks (towers at St Luke, Old Street, St John and Horselydown, and the obelisk of Thothmes III on the Embankment). This network of ley lines is rather less spectacular than the pentacle star discovered by Moore, and one can detect a shade of frustration, in his appendix to *From Hell*, at the often arbitrary nature of the map produced by Sinclair and Catling.

> After weeks of research and a day-long trip around key points of the diagram, only one point eluded me, this being the point on Sinclair's map that is labelled "Lud's Shed". Even though I knew that the spot must be somewhere in the suburbs of Hackney, near to the London Fields, I could locate no reference to any such place as Lud's Shed. Finally, in despair, I contacted Mr Sinclair himself, who informed me that the inclusion of Lud's Shed at that point in the diagram had been a personal reference shared between himself and Mr Catling.[21]

In later editions of *Lud Heat*, this mysterious spot, marked on the chart with the Eye of Horus, is rather more clearly designated: it is Iain Sinclair's house on Albion Drive. In contrast, Moore is at pains to stress that every one of the points on his Ripper trail has a historical rather than a merely personal significance: has been 'verified'.[22] But this serves only to highlight the extent to which one must struggle to elicit any pattern – occult or otherwise – from the alignment of Hawksmoor churches alone. 'He was the force behind the operation, the planning was in his hands', insists Sinclair: 'So that what we are talking about is not accident'.[23] But this faith in the strategic capacity of the architect is simply not compatible with the historic background on his church project, given at the start of *Lud Heat*. Here Sinclair notes that the Act of Parliament of 1711 provided taxes for the acquisition of sites, burial grounds and parsonages, and that there was the round notion of fifty churches – but when the Commission of the Building of the New Churches discharged the Surveyors, Hawksmoor and John James, in 1733, only a dozen had been completed.[24] If the occult network of sight-lines Sinclair describes truly were intended by the architect, it was far indeed from being realised! How, then, is one to explain the tenacity of this myth in the psycho-geographical fiction of the UK? In part its existence must be seen to testify to the overwhelming illusion of power and mystery projected by the architecture of Nicholas Hawksmoor. His brief was to achieve 'the most Solemn & Awfull Appearance both without and within'. And it is worth noting in this context that, contrary to suspicions entertained by the psycho-geographers, the nature of this project, thus defined by John Vanbrugh, must have displeased Hawksmoor politically because (as Kerry Downes points out) the architect was an outspoken Whig.[25] The Act of Parliament in 1711 had been pushed through by the Tories, in response to the clergy's fears that the non-conformist sects that had played such an important part in the revolution of the previous century were now flourishing in the East End. The creation of Anglican church buildings in these new neighbourhoods (fifty of them!) was intended to stamp out a political threat. The churches would reassert the authority of the state religion in spaces that the government had long since lost the opportunity to shape and control. This is precisely why this aggressively expansive church-building project was so soon halted. In 1714 the return of the Whigs to power, following the succession of George I, put the project under new management, hostile to the objectives that had motivated their predecessors and determined to restrict the number of churches built to those that were already in hand. The churches began as objects that were hated by their reluctant parishioners, and at certain moments in their subsequent history they have become quite transparently what they always were. When French refugees living in Whitechapel protested in the eighteenth century at the decline in their trade, the troops that crushed the uprising were barracked in Christ Church. That Hawksmoor's churches continue to project this illusion of state control (blamed in contemporary psycho-geographical literature for crimes resulting from the state's *failure* to prevent economic and societal breakdown!) is a perverse measure of the extent to which the architect had succeeded in fulfilling his brief. 'These are centre of power for those territories', notes Sinclair: 'sentinel, sphinx-form, slack dynamos abandoned as the culture they supported goes into retreat. The power remains latent, the frustration mounts on a current of animal magnetism, and victims are still claimed.'[26]

From the start, writers have struggled to speak of the aesthetic effects achieved in the churches without resort to the term *gothic* – whether in the literary or the architectural sense. In 1734 the Palladian critic James Ralph condemned the church buildings as 'Gothique heaps of stone, without form or order' – criticism rejected by Hawksmoor for the improper 'use of the word Gothick to signifye every thing that displeases him, as the Greeks and Roman calld every Nation Barbarous that, were not in their way of Police and Education'.[27] But long after the rehabilitation of the term with the gothic revival, contemporary writers tend to speak of the churches in much the same way as Ralph. In Moore's *From Hell*, the Ripper claims that, 'Hawksmoor cut stone to hold shadows; a gothic trait, though Hawksmoor's influences were somewhat ... older'.[28] The observation echoes the depiction of Hawksmoor's work as an Art of Shadows in Ackroyd's novel: 'It is only the Darknesse that can give trew Forme to our Work and trew Perspective to our Fabrick, for there is no Light without Darknesse and no Substance without Shaddowe.'[29] This characterisation is not without basis in fact. In the course of creating the London Underground headquarters in Westminster and the Senate House for the University of London (in the streets immediately behind St George Bloomsbury), Charles Holden reflected on the properties of his building material, Portland stone. In addition to being resilient and resonant of London's past, he noted, no other stone can at once be stained so dark by the atmosphere and yet weather so white when exposed to rain. Hawksmoor cannot have been unaware of the striking chiaroscuro effect he would achieve in setting recessed windows into walls that would shine out all the more brightly about them, white and flat. But to suggest that this art of shadows, if it be such, is equivalent to the gloom of gothic horror is misleading. In spite of sometimes cramped urban settings, Hawksmoor's churches produce spaces, inside and out, that are open, airy and light. To walk about Christ Church, Spitalfields, after a shower is to experience the polar opposite of what Moore describes in *From Hell*, when 'even on the brightest days, the surrounding streets are drowned and lost in its shadow'.[30] Christ Church shines too brilliantly to look at, the surrounding streets illuminated by the light it reflects. If Moore is right in suggesting that the tower has a 'subliminal menace', this cannot be explained by relating this structure to what is meant by *gothic* in either literature or architecture. As Kerry Downes points out, that the churches remind us of gothic structures is incidental. At Wapping, for instance, 'From the west the tower appears to burst upwards from the ground, splitting the pediment in two with a force we usually associate with the soaring lines of Gothic towers; yet the conscious origins of Hawksmoor's towers do not seem to be Gothic'. In fact, in most instances the derivation is demonstrably classical: 'he arrived at the forms of the two Stepney steeples wholly by means of Renaissance or Antique detail'.[31]

To underline this point: Hawksmoor's churches are fundamentally unlike gothic buildings. Though both share a similar upward momentum, the gothic is diffuse where Hawksmoor is concentrate. Throwing out arches, buttresses, flying buttresses, the gothic supports its giddy ascent by striving for a lightness that is achieved through dispersal of the outward thrust generated by weight of roof and spire. Hawksmoor's churches, in contrast, marshal energy not to be released. Load-bearing elements are typically emphasised, appearing too big for the weight that they support: pillars, pilasters and piers, too massy or long, project an upward force that is stressed through outsized cornices, through elements above this pedestal which seem too far set back, too light a load for the emphatic machinery beneath; basement windows push up out of the earth, headed by colossal triple keystones; roman arches punch up through string-line and cornice, puncture the pediment. These building are at once energetic and oppressive; what looks to be an unstoppable momentum skyward is held, pent up, in torsion. Tectonic forces strain within a feeling for form, an impending subterranean outburst under control.

To understand where Hawksmoor's churches are coming from, consider the first proposal he produced in response to the Commission's request for 'one general design or Forme' for the churches. His hypothetical plan for a 'Basilica After the Primitive Christians' is a sketch in pencil and sepia ink with thin blue wash to indicate sacred precincts, of a Roman palace in a graveyard complex, which attempts a reconstruction of the 'Manner of Building the Church as it was in ye fourth Century in ye purest times of Christianity'.[32] Hawksmoor was taking church architecture back to its origin, to the moment the new faith emerged from the catacombs (subterranean pagan burial grounds in which it had been compelled to shelter in the first centuries of persecution) in order to begin adapting Roman basilicas for the Christian ritual. The result is a bricolage – a cobbling together of pre-existing architectural elements, of symbols and structures developed by pagan cultures from across the ancient world. Considered in relation to Hegel's thoughts on the origins of architecture, Hawksmoor's project must be seen to be repeating that first imitation and above-ground blossoming of a buried architecture that Hegel considers no 'positive building but rather the removal of a negative'.[33] Hawksmoor had taken architecture back to the beginning – not merely to the beginning of Christian architecture but to the original reproduction above ground of that emptying that makes a space for the dead. According to Hegel, the pyramid marks the point at which architecture became a positive procedure but ceased to possess an independent meaning, was itself emptied, negated. 'In this way pyramids though astonishing in themselves are just simple crystals, shells enclosing a kernel, a departed spirit, and serve to preserve enduring body and form', writes Hegel.

> Therefore in this deceased person, acquiring presentation on his own account, the entire meaning is concentrated; but architecture, which previously had meaning independently in itself as architecture, now becomes separated from meaning and, in this cleavage, subservient to something else.[34]

Incorporating Roman altars, Etruscan urns, Egyptian obelisks, horologions, pyramids, the Mausoleum of Kos, into structures that would represent the triumph of a rational faith over pagan magic, Hawksmoor was attempting to manipulate signs that could not be relied upon to stimulate the one idea which their erection aimed at arousing, 'for they can just as easily recall all sorts of other things'.[35] Hawksmoor could not realistically hope to impose limits on the signifying potential of the resulting bricolage – a fact that might have occurred to him had he questioned the Protestant assumption that the first centuries of the Christian era were 'ye purest'. As Edward Gibbon would later demonstrate, this was the age of heresy, a time of flamboyant hybrids. Indeed, it is tempting to connect its syncretic approach to religion with that syncretic architecture that Hawksmoor emulated. 'Relate them to the four Egyptian protector-goddesses, guardians of the canopic jars', writes Sinclair. 'I associate these churches with rites of autopsy on a more than local scale.'[36] In the light of Hegel's thoughts on the beginning of architecture,

Architects of the occult

Sinclair's comparison of the pyramids set into the ground near the eastern churches to the brains removed from a mummy is most suggestive. Like Egyptian coffins, the churches are inactive engines, layers upon layers of symbol that insist on interpretation. But despite being endlessly open-ended, the brutally forceful formal properties of these churches will not concede any reading (however outré) to have been unforeseen and unintended by the architect. They are the perfect paranoia machines.

Fire maps

Hawksmoor's proposed and actual use of pyramids, sphinxes, obelisks, sacrificial altars must seem incompatible with our ideas of the eighteenth century as an age that privileged reason over traditional wisdom, and this is reflected in some of the recent fiction inspired by the architect. In Ackroyd's *Hawksmoor*, the protagonist is depicted as diametrically opposed to the rationalism embodied in that novel by Sir Christopher Wren. In the course of a visit to Stonehenge the two characters are shown talking at cross-purposes for the best part of a chapter; oblivious to the dark delight his student is displaying in the possibility that the monument might have been the scene of blood sacrifice, Wren runs about the structure taking measurements, expressing his delight at being able to say that logarithms are an entirely British invention. But the exceptional nature of Hawksmoor's work is not so clearly defined in other psycho-geographical fiction. The binary in Ackroyd is very much what one might expect in a gothic novel: forces repressed by our scientific culture return to haunt the present. But the most remarkable feature of writing by Moore and Sinclair and Home is the extent to which it breaks with this familiar gothic paradigm. St Paul's is part of the pattern in *From Hell*. The British Museum and Greenwich Observatory are marked out as significant in the survey set out in *Lud Heat*. And in the psycho-geographical bulletins of Stewart Home, the entire world heritage site at Greenwich, consisting of buildings designed by Inigo Jones, John Webb, Nicholas Hawksmoor and Sir Christopher Wren, stands accused of being a Masonic conspiracy to harness the energies of the "ley line" more generally known as the Prime Meridian, in order to conjure up the British empire and to reinforce the power of the 'Occult

Establishment'.[37] In this deliciously paranoid material, Hawksmoor is presented not as atypical but as archetypal. His acknowledged interest in Egyptian hieroglyphs, freemasonry, his proposed and actual use of magical funerary objects, is not opposed to but intrinsically a part of the movement towards neo-classicism in the culture of the period. Surprisingly, the most recent architectural historian to have written extensively on Hawksmoor might endorse this assessment. 'It may seem paradoxical that, despite the early eighteenth century's appeal to reason, this was also the period of rapid growth in freemasonry as an institution, whose attraction lay in its apparent mystery, ritual, secrecy and quest for hidden truth,' writes Vaughan Hart. 'Nevertheless, behind this cultivation of ancient mysteries and signs lay a rational approach to religion based on the non-sectarian theology of Deism.'[38] Thus, the occult history of the Masons written up and published by John Anderson is very closely modelled on the history of architecture advanced by Wren and Newton. And even the most freakish use of pagan funerary objects in Hawksmoor's projects – the Mausoleum set upon the tower of St George Bloomsbury – can be seen to have had its origin in a sketch Hawksmoor produced for the last of Wren's tracts on architecture. His interest in the Christian basilica was merely part of a more general interest, on the part of those architects working with Wren, in recovering alternative traditions of architecture that might provide the Reformed Church of England with a form of building suitable to its needs, that would reflect its break with the medieval past.

Hawksmoor's mechanisms for paranoia, installed to secure a psycho-geographical hold on non-conformist parishes of the East End, can be traced back to the creative procedures developed by the Wren office as a whole, in response to their collective failure to impose a rational plan upon the City of London. 'They had so favourable an opportunity to Rebuild London ye most August Towne in ye world', complained Hawksmoor in his letter to Dr Brooke in 1712, 'and either have Keept it to its old Dimention, or if it was reasonable to let it swell to a Larger, they ought for ye Publick good to Guided it into a Regular and commodious form, and not have sufferd it to Run into an ugly inconvenient self destroying unweildly Monster'.[39] He was referring to the Great Fire of 1666, an event that visited a devastation that was unprecedented upon the historic centre of the largest city in Europe. The Great Fire wiped out 13,200 houses, the Royal Exchange, the Custom House, the halls of the City's Companies, the Guild Hall and nearly all the City buildings, St Paul's Cathedral, and eighty-seven of the parish churches. In total the bill was reckoned at more than £10 million, and 80,000 people were made homeless.[40] The work of a thousand years had been wiped out, leaving nothing but names. The weeks that followed were to witness concerted attempts to overcome this profound erasure of the urban topography: rationalised street plans that simplified and geometrised the city, rendering it immediately graspable. The most famous, and most influential, of these fire maps was produced by Christopher Wren (King's Surveyor of Works from 1669). His plan presented a radical break with the informality of the medieval city, introducing an inventive combination of new ideas for town planning. In the west, the plan calls for an asterisk street plan over the region about Fleet Street: a piazza in the centre from which lines of straight main streets radiate out. To the east, the plan envisages the grid pattern now standard in the United States, but with much wider streets cutting through this at a diagonal from the piazza about St Paul's Cathedral. These extend to a series of other asterisk patterns, or starbursts, towards the Tower, the greatest of which contains the Royal Exchange. The plan opens up clear lines of sight within the city, many culminating in monuments to the power of the state – an official building, or a statue, or a church. But the scheme was defeated by 'the obstinate Averseness of great Part of the Citizens to alter their Old Properties, and to recede from building their Houses again on the old Ground and Foundations'.[41] If the view in the Wren family memoir *Parentalia* (1750) is an accurate representation of the Surveyor's own opinions on this subject, it would seem that Wren shared, or even inspired, the belief of his assistant Hawksmoor: 'By these Means, the Opportunity, in a great Degree, was lost, of making the new City the most magnificent, as well as commodious for Health and Trade of any upon Earth.'[42]

But citizens had good reason for distrust. London had been the heart of the English Revolution, which had been put down only a few years previously with the Restoration of the Stuart dynasty, and it was therefore perceived by courtiers such as John Evelyn as an urban space that was politically malfunctional. London is a 'City consisting of a wooden, northern, and inartificiall congestion of Houses', he wrote, before the Great Fire, in 1659, 'as deformed

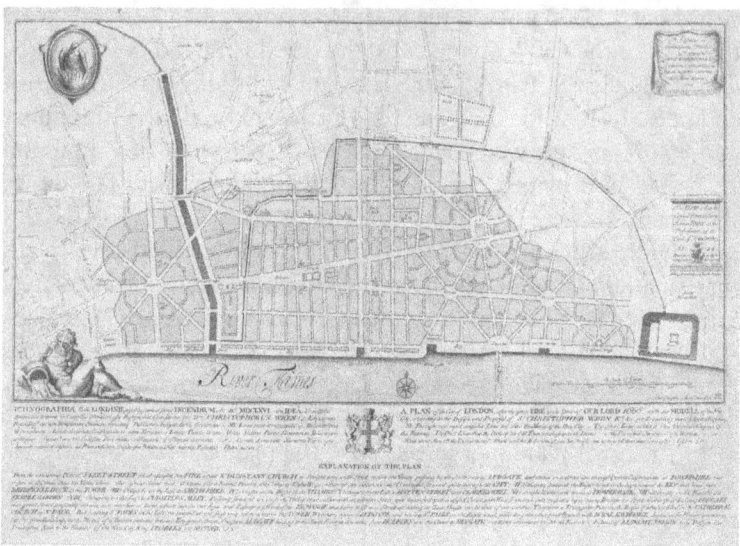

Figure 2.2 Sir Christopher Wren, *Ichnographia urbis Londinii (A Plan of the City of London, after the Great FIRE, in the Year of Our Lord 1666)*. Today Wren's original 1666 plan is lost. This version was drawn in 1744 by the engraver P. Fourdrinier, who claims to have replicated exactly a scarce 1724 original owned by the Earl of Pembroke.

as the minds & confusions of the people'.[43] The total transformation of space proposed in the plans would accordingly reshape the political principles of the populace; they would reform the bad character of the capital. Based on the models established in Paris and Rome, the fire maps created by these royalist planners were specifically geared to extending the power of the state into everyday life. The men who laid out the new Rome, for instance, called main streets *viae militares*, or military ways, and Palladio had explicitly said that 'the ways will be more convenient if they are made everywhere equal; that is to say, that there be no place in them where armies may not easily march'. Indeed, as the architectural historian Lewis Mumford insists: 'This uniform oversized street ... had a purely military basis'.[44] In opening up lines of sight in the city, these plans were not just expressing the values of a culture that equated reason with light, but were facilitating the army's movement through a space of political opposition while frustrating the guerrilla tactics that had enabled a small group of puritan radicals to wreak havoc in the city just a few years earlier; they were enabling the monarch to monitor the populace while impressing upon them his overwhelming power, through monuments to Church and state which terminated each axial route. The Monument to the Great Fire provides by far the clearest insight into how the Surveyor conceived of his project. This structure incorporates a shaft into the central pillar, with spaces into which to slot lenses along the length. There is a laboratory basement beneath, and a hatch in the ornament on the building is in fact a device known as a fixed telescope.[45] The Monument is a scientific instrument for the measurement of time and space. It is hard to imagine a clearer way to signal a total break with the messy contingency of the medieval past than this object, raised upon the spot that saw the Great Fire begin in closely packed wooden streets about a bread oven. But in the relief carved on the western panel, the powers of reason and scientific endeavour are utterly identified with an authoritarian monarch, the one king in English history to successfully abolish parliament in order to rule by divine right. Each radial street pattern or starburst on the fire map evinces the same ideological premise that underpins the masques of Ben Jonson, or the painted ceiling under which these took place in the Banqueting Hall – the conflation of reason with the totalitarian political order imposed by the power of a sun king.

Having lost this historic opportunity to reform the medieval tangle of streets within the "liberties" of London, the king's town planners were restricted to a superficial reordering of the urban environment. Royal proclamations insist that houses be built with brick instead of timber to protect against fire, that certain routes be widened and straightened, and that all the buildings should be built to a uniform pattern, the height of each building relating to its function and location.[46] The end result was something that presented the appearance of the most modern city in Europe, built of brick and Portland stone, in a uniform and rational architectural style – but which was overlaid upon the old street plan, an urban environment that was still fundamentally medieval or gothic. This disjunction is at its most pronounced in the centrepiece to the rebuilt London, St Paul's Cathedral. After a false start (proposals for a series of detached buildings – produced in order to comply with an initially low budget – that would later evolve into Trinity

College Library, Cambridge, and the hemispherical dome at St Stephen Walbrook), Wren produced a large scale model in wood of a neo-classical building that would have been the most radical cathedral structure in Western Europe. Drawing upon Bramante's unrealised plans for St Peter's Basilica in the Vatican and the subsequent work of Michelangelo, Wren's Great Model offered a definitive break with the gothic style. Where the plan of the former cathedral of St Paul's was based on a Latin cross with long aisles suitable for processions, the plan of the Great Model is based upon a Greek cross – a square with the inner corners cut off – that would permit everyone in the church to see and hear everything without internal obstruction, reflecting the reformed religion's emphasis on the spoken Word. Instead of a steeple propped up with buttresses, the Great Model called for a technologically innovative dome. And rather than an exterior broken up by flying buttresses (to hold up the wall), the Great Model presented clear-cut forms, flat surfaces that possess real volume and bulk. According to *Parentalia*, 'the *Surveyor* in private Conversation, always seem'd to set a higher Value on this *Design*, than any he had made before or since; as what was labour'd with more Study and Success'.[47] But in a sequence of events that echoes the lost opportunity to rebuild London, the Great Model was rejected by the Clergy on the basis that it was 'not enough of a Cathedral-fashion; to instance particularly, in that, the Quire was design'd Circular'.[48] Wren therefore turned his thought to creating the plan now known as the Warrant Design; apparently put together in haste from a much earlier design for repairing the existing gothic cathedral, the proposal secured the consent Wren required in order to proceed, though the Great Model represented that which 'he would have put in Execution with more Chearfulness, and Satisfaction to himself than the latter'.[49] If the final result looks rather more like the Great Model than the Warrant Design, this is because the architect had the king's permission 'to make some Variations, rather ornamental, than essential', to reconcile, 'as near as possible, the *Gothick* to a better Manner of Architecture'.[50] Examine the walls: these present the illusion of a solid block, consisting of two storeys like the Banqueting Hall of Inigo Jones, rather than the Great Model; but the upper storey is entirely façade, a blank wall to conceal the flying buttresses required by the plan, only there to bulk out the outer wall. Examine the dome: this is not a load-bearing cupola like that of St Peter's (the plan rendered that impossible) but a structure like the late-medieval octagonal lantern above Ely Cathedral. What appears to be a dome is a skin made of lead and keyed to a concealed cone of brick, which supports the stone lantern above, with a scaffold of wood. In the cathedral as built, we have a gothic structure – a Latin cross, lantern tower, flying buttresses – but with variations (rather ornamental than essential) that conceal this failure on the part of the king and king's surveyor to build a temple that would have embodied, rather than merely projecting, the tyranny of political enlightenment. In order to maintain the illusion the cathedral had been transformed into a rational space, Wren had been compelled to develop an architecture that relied upon a sort of visual magic, a *trompe de l'oeil*.

From the start, this discrepancy was to have peculiar and far-reaching consequences for the way in which Londoners have experienced their city. Take this passage from Daniel Defoe's *Colonel Jack* (1722):

> Run, Jack, says he, for our lives; and away he scours, and I after him, never resting, or scarce looking about me, till we got quite up into Fenchurch-street, through Lime-street, into Leadenhall-street, down St. Mary-Axe, to London-Wall, then through Bishopsgate-street, and down Old Bedlam into Moorfields ... So away he had me through Long-alley, and cross Hog-lane, and Holloway-lane, into the middle of the great field, which, since that, has been called the Farthing Pie-house Fields. There we would have sat down, but it was all full of water; so we went on, crossed the road at Anniseed Cleer, and went into the Field where now the Great Hospital stands.[51]

Note the listing of place names. As Cynthia Wall demonstrates in her study of the *Literary and Cultural Spaces of Restoration London* (1998), this is typical in writing from this period – symptomatic of the shock induced by the erasure of the metropolis in the Great Fire. In Defoe, city streets are still being named in order to grasp a terrain suddenly made strange. But there is more here: an effect like that of double exposure, as Jack seems to run through two cities at once, superimposing the image of a past London onto the present: 'historical past, the London known; and the passing of that past, the London destroyed'.[52] It is as though the prose is haunted by the gothic street plan that persisted beneath the modern superstructure. In presenting the illusion of a total aesthetic revolution without having truly achieved it, the rebuilding of London had produced precisely those conditions that Anthony Vidler, in a book on the architectural uncanny, considered to be ripe for uncanny sensations: 'this uncanny', wrote Freud, 'is in reality nothing new or alien, but something which is familiar and old-established in the mind and which has become alienated from it only through the process of repression ... The uncanny [is] something which ought to have remained hidden but has come to light.'[53] The fact that the eighteenth-century literature of terror acquired a gothic architecture is – at least in part – the result of a suppression at once brutal and incomplete; the neo-classical reconstruction of London made the medieval *ghost*-like, killed organic forms that had evolved over a thousand years of communal struggle but had left the grave shallow, had even formulated the aesthetic required for its return as revenant, no longer a living thing but a historical curio. Consider Wren's St Mary Aldermary, Hawksmoor's St Michael Cornhill, Vanbrugh's Castle Maze Hill, the spire planned for Westminster Abbey with the towers by Hawksmoor on the west end: these buildings offered a concession to sentiment, an antiquarian inclination that anticipated the gothic revival. Note that Ruskin shared Wren's hatred of flying buttresses; that Pugin's Palace of Westminster resembles Hawksmoor's western towers more closely than sections of Westminster Abbey built by Henry III. The Revival preferred an eighteenth-century fantasy version of gothic architecture to the real thing, the simulacrum of the medieval that had been adapted to please modern taste by the Wren School.

But there is insufficient space to discuss this here – and the purpose of this chapter is to explore the mechanisms that produce the *unheimlich*. Perhaps the most interesting implication of Vidler's architectural uncanny is that incessant reference to avant-garde technique without the originating ideological impulse, the appearance of revolution stripped of social redemption, must produce a space doubly haunted – by every ghost the architects have not successfully laid, and by every apparition they have raised rather than made real. Such a distinction (not spelled out in Vidler's book) would represent in architectural terms those crucial distinctions that Freud insists upon in his famous essay on 'The Uncanny' (1919): (1) the uncanny feeling that can be traced 'without exception to something familiar that has been repressed', and (2) the uncanny 'associated with the omnipotence of thoughts, with the prompt fulfilment of wishes, with secret injurious powers and with the return of the dead'.[54] Freud notes that the former kind of uncanny is not of frequent occurrence in real life. As most of the examples offered are taken from the realm of fiction, the implication seems to be that this uncanny is usually aroused by imaginative writing – and this is interesting given the extent to which this particular variety of uncanny has dominated the gothic genre. It is the latter sort of uncanny that is much more likely to belong to actual experience.[55] Such uncanny effects are often and easily produced, writes Freud, 'when the distinction between imagination and reality is effaced, as when something we have hitherto regarded as imaginary appears before us in reality or when a symbol takes over the full functions of the thing it symbolizes'. He suggests that this 'is the factor which contributes not a little to the uncanny effect attaching to magical practices'.[56] And Freud confesses that he would 'not be surprised to hear that psychoanalysis, which is concerned with laying bare these hidden forces, has itself become uncanny to many people for that very reason'.[57] Of course, 'we must not let our predilection for smooth solutions and lucid exposition blind us to the fact that the two classes of uncanny experience are not always sharply distinguishable'.[58] His description of the first class as one in which the frightening element is something repressed that recurs certainly recalls the epigraph to Sinclair's *Lud Heat*: 'All perils, specially malignant, are recurrent.'[59] But what is distinctive about psycho-geographical fiction is clearly to be connected to the second class: an attention to those "magical practices" that are capable of reactivating a superstitious conviction in the omnipotent psychokinetic capacities of the practitioner.

Robinsonades

Before closing I would like to note that the potential for a "gothic" literature that privileged the uncanny effects produced by magical practices was there from the start, that the theory and practice of the New Architecture provided the precondition for that reconfiguration of Early Modern prose writing that resulted in what is often believed to be the original English novel. In the late 1690s, Daniel

Defoe was actively involved in the construction business, running a tile and brick factory at Tilbury. He supplied the bricks for a number of Wren's projects in the capital, such as Greenwich Hospital, until the business failed in 1703, wiped out by a storm that left much of south England requiring roof tiles – and Defoe in no position to supply them. From Defoe's writing it is clear that he and Wren talked at length about the latter's views on architecture on at least one occasion, and that they must have talked about the dome of the cathedral, for which Defoe might have supplied, or been intending to supply, the bricks required for the concealed cone.

> Sir Christopher's design was, indeed, very unhappily baulked in several things at the beginning, as well in the conclusion of this work, which, because very few may have heard of, I shall mention in publick, *from the mouth of its author* ... namely, the covering of the dome, which Sir Christopher would have had been of copper double gilded with gold; but he was over-ruled by Party, and the city thereby deprived of the most glorious sight that the world ever saw, since the temple of Solomon.[60]

What else might the two have talked about? At the heart of the royal surveyor's architectural philosophies was a (then radical) belief that classical buildings had a rational basis in the natural world. In his unpublished tracts he writes:

> In the hot Countries, where Civility first began, they desired to exclude the Sun only, and admit all possible Air for Coolness and Health: this brought in naturally the Use of Porticoes, or Roofs for Shade, set upon Pillars ... in which we see they imitated Nature, most Trees in their Prime, that are not Sapplings, or Dotards, observe near the proportion of Dorick Pillars in the Length of their Bole, before they part into Branches.[61]

This idea anticipated the neo-classical architect Marc-Antoine Laugier's belief that architecture has its basis in nature, that its forms have their origin in the primitive hut. In his parable, man in his first state tries and fails to find suitable shelter in forest and cave; the former is no protection against rain and the latter not sufficiently ventilated. He therefore resolves to rectify, through his own work, the inattention and negligence of nature. He sets up four branches vertically in a square. He places four branches horizontally across them, and puts other branches on top of these on an incline so that the two sides meet together in a point. 'The small rustic hut that I have just described is the model on which all the great creations of architecture have been conceived', Laugier claimed, in his influential *Essai sur l'architecture* (1755). 'It is by staying close to the simplicity of this first model that one will avoid the essential defaults and that one will achieve true perfection.'[62] In the story man fills up the gaps himself, but in an allegorical frontispiece the pillars themselves provide man with shelter, having transformed into living trees. If one now considers Defoe's account of his castaway's hut, the extent to which the first English novelist is drawing on the new architectural discourse of the era must become immediately apparent:

> I built me a little kind of Bower, and surrounded it at a distance with a strong Fence, being a double Hedge as high as I could reach, well stak'd, and fill'd between with *Brushwood* ... The Circle or double Hedge that I had made was not only firm and entire, but the Stakes which I had cut out of some Trees that grew thereabouts were all shot out, and grown with long Branches, as much as a Willow-Tree usually shoots the first Year after lopping its Head ... I was surpriz'd, and yet very well pleas'd to see the young Trees grow, and I pruned them, and led them up to grow as much alike as I could. And it is scarce credible how beautiful a Figure they grew into in three Years; so that though the Hedge made a Circle of about twenty-five Yards in Diameter, yet the Trees, for such I might now call them, soon covered it, and it was a complete Shade, sufficient to lodge under all the dry Season.[63]

This famous image was enormously influential. As Marx noted in *Grundisse* (1857/58), every single eighteenth-century utopia was based on the formulation of the individual subject, not as a historic result, but as posited by nature: it must now be recognised that these 'Robinsonades' had their origins in the discourse of the New Architecture.[64] 'So I went to work', says Crusoe:

> and here I must needs observe that as Reason is the Substance and Original of the Mathematicks, so by stating and squaring every thing by Reason, and by making the most rational Judgement of things, every Man may be in time Master of every mechanick Art. I had never handled a Tool in my Life, and yet in time by Labour, Application and Contrivance, I found at last that I wanted nothing but I could have made it.[65]

But as Cynthia Wall points out, our understanding of the hut and everything that it signifies must be complicated by the way in which Crusoe continues to develop his structures on learning there are cannibals on a neighbouring island. 'As for my Wall', says Crusoe, 'made, *as before*, with long Stakes or Piles, those Piles grew all like Trees, and were by this Time grown so big, and spread so very much, that there was not the least Appearance, to any one's View, of any Habitation behind them.'[66]

> Thus in two Years Time I had a thick Grove; and in five or six Years Time I had a Wood before my Dwelling, growing so monstrously thick and strong that it was indeed perfectly impassable: and no Men, of what kind soever, could ever imagine that there was any Thing beyond it, much less a Habitation.[67]

In Wall's account this weird development is related to pressure faced by the non-conformists with whom Defoe was connected, by their need to render houses of prayer invisible to the agents of an oppressive state religion. Having studied the equally devious procedures the latter were required to adopt in this period – and having noted the extent to which Defoe's fiction-making is steeped in the discourse of the Wren School – we are in a position to conclude that the state-sponsored church-building programme will provide a much closer analogue. For it is not exactly the condition of *invisibility* that Crusoe strives so hard to achieve, but rather 'that if any People were to come on Shore there, they would not perceive any Thing like a Habitation'.[68] In fact, Crusoe would seem to be building on an idea put forward in Wren's tracts to explain how colonnades evolved. 'The first Temples were, in all Probability, in the ruder Times, only little *Cellae* to inclose the Idol', says Wren:

> but in the southern Climates, a Grove was necessary not only to shade the Devout, but, from the Darkness of the Place, to strike some Terror and Recollection in their Approachers; therefore the Trees being always an Adjunct to the *Cellae*, the *Israelites* were commanded to destroy not only the Idols, but to cut down the Groves which surrounded them.[69]

Initially planted for shade, Crusoe's trees ultimately serve precisely the same purpose as the giant portico on the front of Hawksmoor's St George Bloomsbury, or the rows of twinned pilasters running the length of the wall that pretends an upper storey at St Paul's cathedral. These *homely* structures have been rendered *unheimlich* in order to project what Marx refers to as the 'illusion' of the 'Natural Individual', a rational subject without historical contingency, omnipotent in thought, 'king of the psychological world'. Using techniques derived from nature to transform his 'Hutch' into his 'Castle', his 'Bower' into a 'Garrison', Robinson Crusoe effects a psycho-geographical manipulation of space in order to strike terror and recollection into those that approach him – and thereby secures himself an absolute power. In his final years on the island, the 'Governour' can defeat cannibals and mutinous sailors using no weapon but fear:

> We could hear them call to one another in a most lamentable Manner, telling one another, they were gotten into an inchanted Island; that either there were Inhabitants in it, and they should all be murther'd, or else there were Devils and Spirits in it, and they should be all carry'd away and devoured.[70]

Defoe's novel is not merely an expression of the natural philosophy he had derived from the New Architecture but an object lesson in the successful political application of the secondary – relatively overlooked – variety of uncanny effects that these *occult practices* make possible.

Neo-baroque

Though the phenomenon that is here explored has been occluded in the English "gothic" tradition, to such an extent that one is hard pressed to speak of it without resorting to terms that must mislead, the attention Freud bestows equally upon the uncanny we associate with the revenant and that we would relate to occult practices serves to highlight the prominence of the latter in German literature. If the earliest gothic fiction in England is clearly a legacy of the historical rupture produced by the middle-class rejection of feudalism, Catholicism and Europe (the horror resulting from fear of being subsumed by a resurrected past in the attempt to acquire that power), much of the contemporary literature of terror produced in the Holy Roman Empire concentrates on subjects that have only recently received "gothic" treatment in the UK. As noted in the introductory chapter, Friedrich Schiller's *Der Geisterseher* had represented the agents of the Inquisition (Jesuits) and the agents of Modernity (Freemasons and Illuminati) as doubles of each other, and his book gave rise to a great many imitations, such as *The Necromancer* by Carl Friedrich Kahlert (trans. 1795), *The Victim of Magical Delusion* by Cajetan Tschink (trans. 1795) and *Horrid Mysteries* by Karl Grosse (trans. 1796). As their titles suggest, these "gothic" tales focus upon the uncanny effects that might be achieved by agents of modernity manipulating occult science. They were read with interest in England, but the writers of this country were ultimately to ignore both Masons and Illuminati, in order to focus their creative paranoia on the Jesuits.[71] To see so much – and so much significant – "gothic" fiction focused on the Freemasons themselves appear suddenly in the UK from the late 1970s must suggest that a historic transition is taking place, that the coordinates of the "gothic" are being realigned to reflect a more general shift in attitudes towards the Enlightenment.

And here it would be tempting to relate this extraordinary re-evaluation of the English baroque with the emergence of the new, post-modernist, architectural aesthetic that began to appear in London at this point, and its revival of many of the architectural elements considered in this chapter: the clusters of Corinthian pilasters on Robert Venturi's extension to the National Gallery, the playful classical frieze that runs around Terry Farrel's "Battenburg" building or the proscenium arches that frame his Charing Cross Station, or his MI6 Headquarters Building. Indeed, the latter would feature in a particularly memorable scene (involving a spliff) in Sinclair's collection of essays *Lights Out for the Territory* (1997), and his fantasy novel *Downriver* (1991) would envisage the construction of a pyramid (to memorialise the then Prime Minister's consort, Denis Thatcher) between Hawksmoor's St Anne's Limehouse and a newly regenerated Canary Wharf. One might suggest that this architecture of the English baroque, ripe as it was for uncanny sensations, began to inspire the very peculiar paranoia that is considered in this chapter only *as a result* of its being appropriated, revitalised and repurposed by the post-modernist architects of Thatcherism.

The dates would seem to rule against this. Sinclair's vision of decaying dynamos of a culture now in retreat were produced before the earliest post-modernist construction schemes in the capital, and are in any case surely far more evocative of the Modernist that were then beginning their long decay, as the economic and political consensus that had produced and maintained them began to fall apart from the 1970s. If psycho-geographical literature ultimately attacks the post-modernism of Thatcherite London, I would suggest that this is because the latter is seen to continue, to quite literally build upon, to amplify, to valorise, something that was already there in its Modernist predecessor – a gap between form and function, between signifier and signified. Like English baroque, post-modernism should be understood to be an aesthetic philosophy that (proudly) lacks all integrity, being in each case a reaction against an earlier failure of transparency, an earlier attempt to ensure that form should equal function, Stuart neo-classicism in the first instance, and Le Corbusier's International Style in the second, celebrating and valorising a circumstance that the earlier aesthetic philosophy would have regarded as a serious failing and taken rigorous steps to eliminate. The next chapter will demonstrate that this lack of integrity, which is in Vidler's view a precondition for the architectural uncanny, is already present in iconic works of inter-war Modernism designed by the celebrated British architect Berthold Lubetkin.

Notes

1 Cicero, *De Oratore*, Book II, lxxxvi, 351–354, trans. E. W. Sutton and H. Rackham (Loeb Classics: London, 1942).
2 Frances Yates, *The Art of Memory* (Chicago: University of Chicago Press, 1966, 2001), 1–2.
3 From the Latin *monere*, 'to mind'.
4 Peter Ackroyd, *Hawksmoor* (London: Penguin, 1985, 1993), 205.
5 Ackroyd, *Hawksmoor*, 20.
6 E.J. Clery, 'The Genesis of "Gothic" Fiction', Jerrold E. Hogle (ed.), *The Cambridge Guide to Gothic Fiction* (Cambridge: Cambridge University Press, 2003), 21.
7 Jerrold E. Hogle, 'Introduction', Hogle (ed.), *Cambridge Guide*, 14.
8 Alan Moore and Eddie Campbell, *From Hell* (London: Knockabout, 2000), IV: 8.
9 *Ibid.*, IV: 11.
10 *Ibid.*, IV: 21.
11 *Ibid.*, VI: 35.

12 *Ibid.*, Appendix II, 16.
13 *Ibid.*, IV: 19.
14 *Ibid.*, IV: 36.
15 *Ibid.*, IV: 32.
16 *Ibid.*, II: 14.
17 Alfred Watkins, *The Old Straight Track* (London: Abacus, 1970), 25.
18 Iain Sinclair, *Lud Heat and Suicide Bridge* (London: Granta, 1998), 20.
19 *Ibid.*, 18–19.
20 *Ibid.*, 16.
21 Moore and Campbell, *From Hell*, Appendix I, 11.
22 *Ibid.*, Appendix I, 11.
23 Sinclair, *Lud Heat*, 14.
24 *Ibid.*, 13.
25 Kerry Downes, *Hawksmoor* (London: Praeger, 1970), 105.
26 Sinclair, *Lud Heat*, 15.
27 Downes, *Hawksmoor*, 160.
28 Moore and Campbell, *From Hell*, II: 14.
29 Ackroyd, Hawksmoor, 5.
30 Moore and Campbell, *From Hell*, Appendix I, 16.
31 Downes, *Hawksmoor*, 121.
32 Pierre De La Ruffiniere Du Prey, 'Hawksmoor's "Basilica After the Primitive Christians": Architecture and Theology', *Journal of the Society of Architectural Historians*, Vol. 48, No. 1 (Mar 1989), 38–52.
33 G.W.F. Hegel, *Aesthetics*, trans. T. M. Knox (Oxford: Clarendon Press, 1974), Vol. II, 649.
34 *Ibid.*, 653.
35 *Ibid.*, 636.
36 Sinclair, *Lud Heat*, 28.
37 See the bulletins of the London Psychogeographical Association reproduced in Stewart Home, *Mind Invaders* (London: Serpent's Tail, 1997).
38 Vaughan Hart, *Nicholas Hawksmoor: Rebuilding Ancient Wonders* (New Haven, CT and London: Yale University Press, 2002); 98.
39 Nicholas Hawksmoor, Letter to Dr Brooke, 1712.
40 See Cynthia Wall, *The Literary and Cultural Spaces of Restoration London* (Cambridge: Cambridge University Press, 1998).
41 Christopher Wren, Christopher Wren Junior and Stephen Wren, *Parentalia: Or, Memoirs of the Family of the Wrens ... Chiefly of Sir Christopher Wren* (London: T. Osborn and R. Dodsley, 1750), 269.
42 *Ibid.*, 269.
43 John Evelyn, *Character of England, As It Was Lately Presented in a Letter, to a Noble Man of FRANCE*, 3rd edition (London, 1659), 9.

44 Lewis Mumford, *The City in History* (New York: Harbinger, 1961), 369.
45 See Lisa Jardine, *On a Grander Scale: The Outstanding Life of Sir Christopher Wren* (New York: HarperCollins, 2002), xi–xiv and 315–321.
46 Wren, Wren and Wren, *Parentalia*, 269.
47 *Ibid.*, 282.
48 *Ibid.*, 282.
49 *Ibid.*, 282.
50 *Ibid.*, 282–283.
51 Daniel Defoe, *Colonel Jack* (1722), ed. Samuel Holt Monk (London: Oxford University Press, 1965), 43.
52 Wall, *Literary and Cultural Spaces*, 24.
53 Sigmund Freud, 'The Uncanny' (1919), James Strachey (trans.), *The Standard Edition of the Complete Psychological Works* (London: Hogarth Press, 1955), Vol. XVII, 241.
54 *Ibid.*, 247.
55 *Ibid.*, 248.
56 *Ibid.*, 244.
57 *Ibid.*, 243.
58 *Ibid.*, 249.
59 See *ibid.*, 241, and Sinclair, *Lud Heat*, 13. The epigraph is from Thomas De Quincy, *On Murder Considered As One of the Fine Arts*, an appendix to which recounts the history of the Ratcliffe Highway murders.
60 Daniel Defoe, *A Tour thro' the Whole Island of Great Britain* (1724–1727), ed. N. Furbank, W. R. Owens and A. J. Coulson (New Haven, CT: Yale University Press, 1991), Letter Five, Part II, 143.
61 'Tract I', Wren, Wren and Wren, *Paternalia*, 353.
62 Marc-Antoine Laugier, *An Essay on Architecture* (1755), trans. Wolfgang Herrmann (Santa Monica, CA: Hennessey & Ingalls, 1985), quoted in Richard A. Etlin, *Symbolic Space* (Chicago: University of Chicago Press, 1994), 92.
63 Daniel Defoe, *Robinson Crusoe* (1719), ed. J. M. Coetzee (Oxford: Oxford University Press, 1999), 103 and 107.
64 Karl Marx, *Grundisse: Foundations of the Critique of Political Economy (Rough Draft)*, trans Martin Nicolaus (London: Penguin, 1993), 83.
65 Defoe, *Robinson Crusoe* (1719), ed. Doreen Roberts and Keith Carabine (Ware, Hertfordshire: Wordsworth Classics, 1997), 69.
66 *Ibid.*, 153.
67 *Ibid.*, 163.

68 *Ibid.*, 78.
69 'Tract II', Wren, Wren and Wren, *Paternalia*, 355.
70 *Ibid.*, 266.
71 Note the changes made in Anne Radcliffe's adaptation of Schiller's novel *The Italian* (1797).

3

Gorillas in the House of Light: Inter-war Modernism as crisis management at London Zoo

The rational animal

Five shuffle past a plate-glass door. Two men in coats. A family of three: a small girl topped with a knitted hat pulled along by her father and mother. They pass through a dark space of curving metal out into the light. A guard stoops to unlatch and seal the doors shut. In the next shot, a sheer glass-front onto something that might be a laboratory, or an observatory: a ceiling in motion, rotating to flood the white space and reflective surface of the glass screen with sun. The eye can make nothing of this. Nothing is substantial, nothing is still. Some futurist fantasy of a vast and abstract mechanism for the movement of shadow and light. Both a building and a machine. But what? The roof and wall fully retract to reveal a colossal cage. Mok and Moina are kept here: the baby gorillas at London Zoo. Face pressed to the bars and chicken wire, one of the

Figure 3.1 Tecton, model for the Gorilla House, London Zoo, Regent's Park, London (1933). (RIBA Ref, No. RIBA4769.)

infants looks up to the right, the concrete wall sliding around to enclose him. In winter the House is shut – public in one half, apes in the other. In summer the cage is revolved and the glass screen pulled back, the infant gorillas occupying the complete circle while the public watches from without.

In this motion picture by László Moholy-Nagy, *The New Architecture and the London Zoo* (1936), the Gorilla House at London Zoo, by Berthold Lubetkin's firm Tecton, is hailed as the beginning of a new era, ushered in by the use of reinforced concrete.[1] Zoo enclosures were a significant milestone for the Modernist movement. For most of those working-class Londoners who flocked to see the gorilla-children in their new home, this was their first encounter with the New Architecture. Built at a time when the works of the Modernist mainstream, centred in Paris, remained for the most part on the drawing board, the Gorilla House, with subsequent enclosures by Tecton in London, Dudley and Whipsnade, was perceived to be providing a sane blueprint for the future development of the human metropolis. In fact, the project can be interpreted as a form of animal testing. As science historian Peder Anker has noted, Peter Chalmers-Mitchell, secretary of the Zoological Society, believed that if gorillas and penguins could be shown to thrive in 'the most unnatural conditions' the same would hold for the poor, who were in desperate need of being liberated from their "natural" conditions of criminal and filthy slums. 'It was thus of revolutionary importance to display thriving animals in an unnatural setting as if to prove that humans too could prosper in a new environment.'[2] Following London's widespread ruin in the course of the Blitz, this ambition would at last be realised, as the architect Lubetkin began to apply the Modernist architecture he had pioneered at London Zoo to the problem of mass housing. The kernel of that future city we now inhabit is this Le Corbusian *machine for habitation* in London Zoo – this first House of Light.

The fate of the infant gorillas therefore holds peculiar horror. After six months in their new home Mok and Moina were dead, their bodies subjected to a Persian funeral, put in a cage on a roof in the sun to be picked clean by carrion crows.[3] The tussle over where to assign blame – to poor maintenance or to poor design, to owner or to architect – must now seem an ironic foreshadowing of the argument that would rage, in subsequent decades, over Modernist mass housing in the UK. I wish to explore the possibility that the gorillas in their House of Light were the victims not of an oversight, as the architect maintained, but of a terrible mistake in the Cartesian philosophy underpinning modernist thought. I suggest that in addition to representing a turning point for Modernism, the Gorilla House occupies an important place in the crisis in humanism identified by Jacques Derrida. The gorilla can be seen to have possessed extraordinary resonance in the early twentieth century: a symbol for a crisis of faith in the Cartesian definition of the human being.

In *The Animal That Therefore I Am* (2007) Derrida set out to track the systematic relegation of the Animal in Western philosophy back to the theoretical break initiated by Descartes: the stark binary that defines the human by corralling every other species on the planet into a single concept, under a single name, "The Animal".[4] This consistent characterisation of the Animal as that which is deprived of the Logos, the right and power to respond, is the root of the misery inflicted on other animal species by humans, or on other humans unfortunate enough to have themselves been marked out as "Animal". The gorillas in the House of Light represent the culmination of this Enlightenment reduction of the Animal: the subject is held in a fearsome geometry, a lyrical celebration of humanist reason. But this extremity is also a symptom of societal unease – an anthropocentric reinstitution of the "Human" over the "Animal" that testifies to the panic generated by 'humanity's second trauma': *evolution* – the knowledge that humanity is intimately involved in everything that humanists have for so long tried to disavow as other, as "Animal".

The horror of the ape

But what did René Descartes actually say, and in what way does his theoretical formulation of the human–animal binary differ from the earlier idea, stretching right back to Aristotle, that human beings are animals distinguished from the rest by their capacity for rational thought: the rational animal? As Derrida points out, Descartes is a man in a hurry, compelled to eliminate everything that is not certain and indubitable. Here is the passage in the *Meditations* in which Descartes called time on the earlier definition:

> What, then, did I formerly think I was? I thought I was a man. But what is a man? Shall I say rational animal? No indeed: for it would be necessary next to inquire what is meant by animal, and what by rational, and, in this way, from one single question, we would fall unwittingly into an infinite number of others, more difficult and awkward than the first, and I would not wish to waste the little time and leisure remaining to me by using it to unravel subtleties of this kind.[5]

To arrive at what 'I am', it is necessary to begin by dismissing the concept of the rational animal. This frees Descartes to reach a new formulation in *Discourse on Method* – 'I think therefore I am'.[6] On first impression, this might seem to be merely reasserting the idea that humanity's defining characteristic is reason: I think – I have the capacity for rational thought. But what must follow? I am a Human Being? No. I think therefore I *am*. Something truly radical has taken place here in relation to that earlier tradition: a moment of rupture that has had profound implications for humanity's relationship to the Animal. In a startling move, the capacity for rational thought has been equated with Being itself, with the very Name of God.

Previous philosophers had insisted that the Animal lacked reason, though Aristotle, for instance, clearly believed that humans and animals shared much else. Certain animals possessed qualities nearly akin to those common to humankind in greater or less measure: 'For just as we pointed out resemblances in the physical organs, so in a number of animals we observe gentleness and fierceness, mildness or cross-temper, courage or timidity, fear or confidence, high spirits or low cunning, and with regard to intelligence, something akin to sagacity.'[7] In contrast, the new means for defining the essence of what it is to be human cut us off from animals in the world, and from everything that is animal in our own selves.

> But I, who am certain that I am, do not yet know clearly enough what I am; so that henceforth I must take great care not imprudently to take some other object for myself, and thus avoid going astray in this knowledge which I maintain to be more certain and evident than all I have had hitherto.[8]

To this end Descartes abstracted from the 'I am' his own living body, which is presented objectively as a machine or corpse: 'I considered myself, firstly, as having a face, hands, arms, and the whole machine made up of flesh and bones, such as it appears in a corpse and which I designated by the name of body'.[9] In short, he is a 'thing that thinks'.[10] And anything lacking the capacity for rational thought is nothing more than a machine, is empty of the living Name of God. The Animal is therefore, in a sense, unreal: no longer capable of a meaningful response – of saying 'I am'.

In order to illustrate this point, Descartes presents us with a famous allegory that curiously anticipates the science fiction of Philip K. Dick. Imagine a future in which humans have never seen an animal. Imagine humans have created a machine that precisely simulates the appearance, movement and sound of an irrational animal.[11] According to Descartes, one could not distinguish between real and simulated animal, because there would be no fundamental difference. But no one could make such a mistake if confronted with a clockwork man, and this is because a human being is capable of responding in intelligent fashion to any questions put to them.

> And this shows not only that animals have less reason than men, but that they have none at all; for we see that very little of it is required in order to be able to speak; and since one notices inequality among animals of the same species as well as among men, and that some are easier to train than others, it is unbelievable that the most perfect monkey or parrot of its species should not equal in this the most stupid, or at least a child with a disturbed brain, unless their souls were not of an altogether different nature from our own.[12]

The discovery of the gorilla in the middle of the nineteenth century posed a challenge to this thought experiment, presenting new possibilities that were at once profoundly unsettling to a distinction fundamental to humanist thought but also framed from the outset by imperialist procedures for asserting, extending and consolidating power and control over far-flung territories and their natural resources; the flora, the fauna and the indigenous people. The earliest gorilla specimens (a skull and other bones) were obtained by American physician and missionary Thomas Staughton Savage in Liberia and presented to the scientific community as *Troglodytes Gorilla* in *Proceedings of the Boston Society of Natural History* in 1847.[13] The first part of the name means *cave-dweller*, but the second part is derived from a mysterious word that occurs in the *Periplus of Hanno the Navigator*: a translation into Greek of a

Punic account of a colonial voyage along the coast of West Africa in the fifth century BC.[14] After cataloguing the fauna and prominent landmarks encountered (a carroch of the gods, a river of fire pouring into the sea), General Hanno speaks of a skirmish between the Carthaginians and a tribe of hairy folk:

> By flame for three days to South Horn, the bayou,
> the island of folk hairy and savage
> whom our Lixtae said were Gorillas.
> We cd. not take any man, but three of their women.
> Their men clomb up the crags,
> Rained stone, but we took three women
> who bit, scratched, wd. not follow their takers.
> Killed, flayed, brought back their pelts into Carthage.
> Went no further that voyage,
> as were at end of provisions.[15]

Neither Greek nor Punic, the word *gorilla* might be related to *gorku*, the Fulani word for *man*, the diminutive form of which is *gorel* (quite literally, *homunculus* in Latin, but who or what is the magician?) It is impossible to be sure if Hanno's *gorilla* ought to be identified with the non-human species later designated as such. In any event, this name proved an inspired choice; with its echo of a remote, mythical past, Staughton Savage's *gorilla* fired the imagination, initiating a rush for specimens on the part of museums across the world.

The first stuffed gorillas were displayed in Paris in 1852. The explorer Paul du Chaillu became the first Western man to see a living gorilla on his expedition of 1856–59 and brought the first dead specimen to England in 1861.[16] But in spite of the mounting interest provoked by these scientific discoveries, which only intensified following publication of Charles Darwin's theory of evolution in 1859, no systematic field study took place until the 1920s, when the American Museum of Natural History sent Carl Akeley to secure specimens for the collection.[17] For over seventy years the term *gorilla* would mark, no less than it had in the time of Hanno, the point at which knowledge failed, the edge of uncharted territory – a space for speculation and for doubt.

First, and perhaps most unsettling, of the new monsters to emerge from this vanishing point is the sculpture *Gorilla Dragging Away a Dead Negress* (1859) by Emmanuel Fremiet. In this colossal image there is none of the twisted eroticism that hindsight might lead us to expect in this, the first representation of that now familiar trope of the gorilla and the girl. Crushed tight by a huge, stubby hand, the woman's face and body are pressed into the flabby bulk of a female gorilla; a big hoop swings from the ear beneath an elaborate headdress; the robes are heavy, funereal; the arm let swing is not that of some sylph from the Salon but muscular, the fingers a taut claw; no poetry, no glamour; a real corpse. The gorilla's face is a blank, fixed snarl – but the eyes are sad. Surging forward, the gorilla is an unstoppable force bearing away the dead. But it is impossible to read reasons or circumstances into this sombre tableau. The piece possesses a mystery that is profoundly troubling; something terrible has taken place, something of a mythical order, not spelled out. Exhibited in the same year that saw the publication of the *Origin of Species*, it is little wonder that the Paris Salon refused to show the piece, consenting to do so only on the condition that the gorilla was screened by a curtain, or that they hastened to have the sculpture destroyed after the exhibition. The gorilla entered the art of the West freighted with humanity's second trauma, hauling off the shell of what was once thought to be the image of God.

Fremiet's next treatment of the motif greatly refined the gorilla's symbolic potential. His *Gorilla Carrying Off a Woman* of 1887 won the Paris Salon Medal of Honour, and the Republic approved a bronze reproduction edition that proved highly popular.[18] This is rather a curious reversal, since this image might appear to be more sensational than the first. Once again a gorilla is carrying away a woman, tucked tight under its biceps – but the woman is beating and pushing the monster, her breasts crushed big against the ape, her thighs behind soft and full, embodying a sensuality in shocking juxtaposition with an immense knot of bone and muscle and hair; no uncertainty, no ambiguity as to intent; an alpha male gorilla in heat; hefting a sharp-edged rock, screaming through a mouthful of fang. But in some respects this image is safer, though more explicit, rather more conventional, than that of 1859. The original was shocking because Fremiet had adopted a style that drew on his training as an illustrator at the Parisian Museum of Natural History: stiffly respectable, rigorously researched and anatomically correct, best remembered for the Terrible Lizards that roam through Crystal Palace Park – that stocky mid-Victorian naturalism

Figure 3.2 Emmanuel Fremiet, *Gorilla Dragging Away a Dead Negress* (1859). (Photograph reproduced in Philipe Faure Fremiet, *Les Maitres de l'art: Fremiet*, Paris: Plon, 1934, 118.)

which had become inextricably identified with scientific veracity. In contrast, the later *Gorilla* is in a style more in keeping with the aesthetic of the Paris Salon. The woman is now Caucasian; the scene is of no particular time or place but is set in some mythical past. The sculpture could be a modern recapitulation of the *Centauromachy* – an allegory in classical art expressing humanity's struggle to overcome the irrational or animal. The motif has been reconfigured as a conflict – the outcome of which is far from clear cut.

Fremiet's iconic revision of the gorilla and the girl is recapitulated with remarkably little elaboration in the scores of gorilla-related horror movies that were produced in the early twentieth century. Around one hundred films with gorillas were made between 1908 and 1948 and of these the vast majority were horrors. Most of the gorillas in the genre were played by men in gorilla costumes – a dedicated band of professional ape impersonators, often taking their passion for realism to alarming lengths. If no one has heard of Charlie Gemora, the Master of the Art, in part this is because this

Gorillas in the House of Light 53

Figure 3.3 Emmanuel Fremiet, *Gorilla Carrying Off a Woman* (1887). (Photograph by Gustav Ollendorf, *Salon de 1887*, ed. Ludovic Baschet, Paris: Librairie d'art, 1887, 210.)

remarkable actor would insist on having his name removed from the credits in order to maintain the realism of the production. The maker of his own gorilla suit, and the sculptor of the gigantic hand that reaches into a hotel-room to snatch Fay Wray in *King Kong* (1933), Gemora was the leading figure in a genre that testifies to the tremendous unease that surrounded these recently discovered creatures in the public mind, rehearsing the psychopathologies that the collapsing Cartesian paradigm had generated beneath the veneer of twentieth-century culture, often with surprising sensitivity and sophistication.

The motif of the gorilla and the girl, repeated *ad infinitum* in these films, owed its popularity to the fact that it successfully channelled as yet vague new fears into a familiar and therefore reassuring template: the conflict between Man and his inner Animal. This fact is nowhere clearer than in Edward D. Wood Jnr's sole contribution to the genre – his brilliantly twisted script for *Bride and the Beast* (1958), in which a couple have their wedding night disturbed by the violent bull-gorilla that the husband, Dan, keeps locked up in a dungeon (complete with flaming torches) underneath the house. The gorilla is called Spanky, and Dan is not a little disturbed to discover that his new wife (played by Charlotte Austin), who insists on sleeping in a separate bed to her husband, smoulders with a sexual intensity rarely caught on celluloid whenever in the presence of the gorilla. A jealous Dan shoots Spanky dead, and Charlotte Austin is subjected to hypnotherapy and regressed to a past life, in which she was an albino gorilla. Readers who have seen Tim Burton's wonderful biopic *Ed Wood* (1994) will have no difficulty in recognising the confession that emerges in the course of the hypnosis as an expression of the director's own unconventional sexual drives: 'Soft like kitten's fur', says Charlotte Austin, recalling her former pelt. 'Felt so good on me.'[19] Though rather more candid in this respect than most, the process of projection crystallised in this particular gorilla movie is a characteristic feature of a genre that could have been invented for the sole purpose of illustrating the psychoanalytical interpretation of animal-phobia developed earlier in the century by Sigmund Freud. In short, this is the theory that sexual desires deemed abhorrent by the father, together with hatred of the father provoked by that repression, are displaced onto an animal. 'By *wild-beasts* the dream-work usually symbolises passionate impulses' Freud explains; 'those of the dreamer, and also those of other persons of whom the dreamer is afraid; or thus, by means of a very slight displacement, the persons who experience those passions'.[20] In fact, Freud's thoughts on this topic seem eerily prescient, when one remembers that so many gorillas in these movies are treated precisely as a totem animal: 'From [the dream] it is not very far to the totemistic representation of the dreaded *father* by means of vicious animals, dogs, wild horses, etc. One might say that wild-beasts serve to represent the *libido*, feared by the ego, and combated by repression.'[21]

The *conflict between Man and his inner Animal*: this is clearly how many engaging with the trope of the gorilla at the time themselves explained the motif. Consider Aldous Huxley's satirical representation of the American film industry in *Ape and Essence* (1948). Huxley picks up on the recurring imagery of the ape in films produced in this era, and incorporates this into a meta-fictional film script discovered by an exploratory expedition sent to a Hollywood destroyed by nuclear war. In the following passage the Freudian-Darwinian understanding of the horror of the ape outlined above is presented as self-evident:

> Surely it's obvious.
> Doesn't every schoolboy know it?
> Ends are ape-chosen; only the means are man's ...
> Church and State,
> Greed and Hate: –
> Two Baboon-Persons in one Supreme Gorilla.[22]

But there is a problem with this psychoanalytical approach. The Animal itself is entirely eliminated from the equation. The specific horror of the ape is neutralised in the moment of its expression. In becoming a sign for the "bestial" – the term which most accurately describes the horror of what you see in these movies – the gorilla has become a symbol of something from which beasts are exempt by definition. As Derrida has observed, 'One cannot speak ... of the *bêtise* or bestiality of an animal. It would be an anthropomorphic projection of something that remains the preserve of man.'[23] In presenting the gorilla as a symbol of the inner Animal, moviemakers and writers were re-enacting the disavowal of something intrinsically human. The gorilla is reduced to an empty sign, interchangeable with any other animal species in a structure of meaning that is the product of that sign-making power thought proper to humankind. These motion pictures ultimately reassert the problematic Cartesian formulation of the Human subject and the Animal object.

But is the gorilla interchangeable with any other species? It is true that every creature imaginable has at some point or another been rendered an object of horror by the film industry: there have been birds, there have been sharks, there have even been killer shrews. In any number of gorilla horror movies, from Bela Lugosi's *Murders in the Rue Morgue* (1932) to Acquanetta's *Captive Wild Women* (1943), the horror of the ape can be seen to derive not merely from its role as a symbol, one among many, for the depredations of the subconscious mind, but from the fact that the gorilla was perceived to be the embodiment of the challenge that the great apes posed to the thought experiment set out in the *Discourse on Method*. Descartes asserted that the machine or animal would always be recognised as such by us because the animal-machine could not respond, and because an intelligent response could not be simulated. But could the Logos be aped?

In *The Descent of Man* (1871), Charles Darwin had remarked that: 'It is not the mere power of articulation that distinguishes man from other animals, for as everyone knows, parrots can talk; but it is his large power of connecting definite sounds with definite ideas.'[24] But having clearly signalled his engagement in this way with Cartesian thought, Darwin then observed that this is an Art and therefore achieved through imitation: 'As bearing on the subject of imitation, the strong tendency in our nearest allies, the monkeys, in microcephalous idiots, and in the barbarous races of mankind, to imitate whatever they hear deserves notice.'[25] If those dull, stupid men mentioned by Descartes could be conflated in this way with mere monkeys and said to be entirely capable of the mimicry that permitted language, what might happen when explorers eventually discovered the "perfect ape"?[26] Could we count on our ability to tell the simulation or aping of a response by this sophisticated animal-machine from the real thing?

One should bear in mind just how little was known concerning gorillas in this period. No one yet knew what feats these beasts were capable of – and for the vast majority of people in the 1930s and 1940s, the gorilla was, of course, a man in a costume called Charlie Gemora! It is possible that the gorilla horror movies of the period played no small part in exacerbating the anxieties that sustained them, presenting their uninformed audiences with preternaturally intelligent gorilla-men.

The nature of this anxiety emerges particularly clearly in what must be the original ape-related horror story and primary prototype for the genre considered above, *The Murders in the Rue Morgue* (1841) by Edgar Allan Poe. The unsettling effect of the story stems in large part from the fact that the sleuth Dupin refers to the deaths in the Rue Morgue as 'murders' after he has utterly eliminated the possibility that the perpetrator could be human: 'In the manner of thrusting the corpse up the chimney, you will admit that there was something excessively outré – something altogether irreconcilable with our common notions of human action, even when we suppose the actors the most depraved of men.'[27] The narrator confesses to feeling 'a creeping of the flesh' on hearing Dupin's summary of the case; and one can understand why, when one appreciates that a murder that represents a 'horror absolutely alien from humanity' necessarily involves a paradox.[28] For as Will Smith observes in *I, Robot* (2004), only a human can be guilty of homicide – a restatement of the familiar Cartesian conflation of the human being with the capacity for rational judgement. It is significant that when the narrator speculates 'A madman ... has done this deed – some raving maniac, escaped from a neighbouring *Maison de Santé*', Dupin concedes that the 'idea is not irrelevant'.[29] Presumably the idea is not irrelevant because a madman would not have been tried for a murder in any court. In solving the 'murders' in the Rue Morgue, Dupin discovers that *no murder took place* – and so no one is charged for this offence at the end – because the perpetrator is an ape. Not a gorilla – the mystery was published six years before the scientific discovery of that species – but a 'large fulvous Ourang-Outang of the East Indian Islands'.[30] The violent deaths were not murder but the result of the mechanical imitation believed to be proper to an ape – aping a man shaving – followed by violent reaction to a sudden fright. Poe presented the reader with the perfect *simulation* of a crime by an animal lacking capacity for rational thought: the most intelligent men on the Parisian police force were shown to have failed that test on which Descartes had grounded his case for setting human beings apart from animal-machines; they were shown to be incapable of distinguishing the illusion of the Logos from the real thing. Nor, one should point out, is the effect of Dupin's intervention exactly to restore these imperilled boundaries. In his famous preface, Poe explains that the purpose of the narrative is to provide a commentary on his proposition that there is a hitherto unrecognised distinction between ingenuity and analysis.

The consecutive or combining power, by which ingenuity is usually manifested, and to which the phrenologists (I believe erroneously) have assigned a separate organ, supposing it a primitive faculty, has been so frequently seen in those whose intellect bordered otherwise upon idiocy, as to have attracted general observations among writers on morals.[31]

Against the ingenuity of a retentive memory and of playing by the book, Poe sets up the analysis that he characterises as the very soul and essence of method; 'it is in matters beyond the limits of mere rule that the skill of the analyst is evinced'.[32] The narrative presents a very clear difference between the acumen of Dupin and the mere cunning of the Prefect of Police. But it is hard to say how one can distinguish the cunning exhibited by the Parisian police from the cunning exhibited – to rather more effect! – by the Ourang-Outang. In each case, cunning is based on a retentive memory and the capacity for repeating certain procedures in a mechanical, unreflective way. Perhaps the most terrifying element in this landmark horror story is a variation on the familiar Cartesian distinction between response and reaction that puts most of humanity beyond the pale, with little or nothing to distinguish the "ingenuity" of which they boast from the "cunning" of the merely animal.

The full implications of this impending ontological crisis are set out in Pierre Boulle's novel *La Planète des Singes* (1963). The film adaptation, *Planet of the Apes* (1968), significantly revised the plot of Boulle's novel in order to present a timely satire on the "bestiality" of mankind, merely reconfirming the Cartesian Human–Animal binary in the act of inverting it. The book is very different. Everything horrific in the novel stems from the fact that for the most part, everyday life is pure "reaction" rather than "response" – and can therefore be aped. It is in this traditional belief that it is the capacity for imitation that is characteristic of the ape that the specific anxieties that became attached to the new anthropoid apes, and the unfortunate gorilla in particular, are to be found. In these passages from *La Planète des Singes* we have fully realised the horror of the ape:

> What is it that characterises a civilisation? Is it the exceptional genius? No, it is everyday life ... Is it possible that creatures devoid of intelligence could have perpetuated it by a simple process of imitation? ... This should be able to be achieved by monkeys, who are

essentially imitators, provided of course they are able to make use of language ... At the level of administration, the quality of aping seemed even easier to admit. To continue our system, the gorillas would merely have to imitate certain attitudes and deliver a few harangues, all based on the same model.[33]

The Gorilla House

Charlie Gemora would have instantly recognised the compositional elements in the Gorilla House at London Zoo. The 'intrinsic human ceremony' enacted by a porch ushering the public into a dark theatre.[34] And that sliding panel – like the false walls that conceal Spanky's dungeon or that of Bela Lugosi in *The Ape-Man* (1943), or like the curtains that screen King Kong, or Fremiet's first *Gorilla*. Everything in the approach to the building worked towards a particular theatrical effect. The big reveal of a horror intended to figure the spectator's own primitive drives – suddenly there and held in a spotlight. If the Gorilla House presents certain strong similarities to the Cabinet of Dr Caligari, the laboratory of the Mad Scientist, this is perhaps no coincidence. For there is evidence to suggest that Lubetkin may have been inspired in his design by the same sources. 'There are two possible methods of approach to the problem of zoo design', explained Lubetkin:

> [T]he first, which we may call the 'naturalistic' method, is typified in the Hamburg and Paris zoos, where an attempt is made, as far as possible, to reproduce the natural habitat of each animal; the second approach, which, for want of a better word, we may call the 'geometric', consists of designing architectural settings for the animals in such a way as to present them dramatically to the public, in an atmosphere comparable to that of a circus.[35]

Lubetkin was committed to ensuring his enclosures drew upon traditional spaces of popular entertainment. His Elephant Paddock at Whipsnade Zoo emulates a big top, for instance. The famous Penguin Pool at London Zoo resembles a lido. And, perhaps most troubling, his pit for the polar bears at Dudley Zoo can only have been modelled on the Elizabethan bear-pit – a vertical tube in which bears were set upon by dogs for the amusement of the public. In the light of this commitment it seems at least highly probable that

Lubetkin's first structure for London Zoo should be based upon the platform for the popular exhibition of the gorilla referenced by so much cinema of the period: that is to say, the freak show at a circus or fairground.

This was not lost on contemporary critics. An American critic, for instance, argued that the modernist projects at London Zoo had the 'flavor of a circus or a country carnival' for the 'pure pleasure and amusement of their owner' – with the result being that 'the educational or scientific value of an English zoo is nearly zero'.[36] In a recent article surveying the legacy of Bauhaus ideas in the UK, science historian Peder Anker cites this passage and explains that this interpretation of the project (that is to say, the architect's own understanding of his zoo buildings) can only obscure the very real scientific objectives that the management at London Zoo hoped to achieve through commissioning these new buildings. 'Though they welcomed entertainment that could generate general interest in biology (and money from entrance fees), they were not willing to pursue amusement at the expense of their scientific integrity', insists Anker. 'It was the promotion of public health and not amusement which prompted the Zoo keepers to build modernist architecture.' His subsequent focus on the discourse of the *healthy environment*, shared by zookeepers, newspapers and architects alike, is entirely correct, and the article as a whole extremely illuminating. But I would like to suggest that Lubetkin's conception of nature as a circus for human entertainment was not incompatible with at least one key scientific and educational objective of the London Zoological Society's research anatomist, Solly Zuckerman, who played a major role in securing the commission for Tecton.

For much of his life, Zuckerman saw himself as engaged in unrelenting struggle against the cardinal error of inferring that the 'comparison of animal and human social life will enable us to discover some of the basic instincts and impulses upon which the whole edifice of human society is reared'. It is true that Zuckerman believed the life of primates to be a crude picture of a social level from which our earliest human ancestors emerged: 'But', Zuckerman immediately goes on to say, 'only that'.[37] Contrary to Anker's assertion, Zuckerman's landmark thesis on primate behaviour, *The Social Life of Monkeys and Apes* (1932), does not present this material as a model for explaining deeper sexual and social instincts in humans.

'Indeed much could be said for divorcing the study of man's behaviour from that of other animals in relation to the subject matter of sociological discussion.'[38] It is explained that:

> When the impetus given to biological inquiry by Darwin's exposition of the evolutionary hypothesis made them prominent subjects for discussion, both these aspects of mammalian behaviour were at first considered together, and there accumulated a wealth of literature to fill the Cartesian gulf separating man from the beasts, and proving the continuity of mind and society through the world of living organisms.[39]

Thus Kropotkin's *Mutual Aid* (1919) examined organised social groups in the animal kingdom to prove that progress is best fostered by the practice of mutual cooperation and support.[40] E. Westermarck's *The History of Human Marriage* (1921) provided an anecdotal account of the 'family group' of the gorilla, in order to establish a natural basis for the human institution of marriage.[41] And Yerkes and Yerkes took certain facts about a New World monkey to indicate 'a species of communism' as being 'of the utmost importance to mankind'.[42] Zuckerman casts a caustic eye on that 'somewhat surprising discovery of politico-economic systems at a biological level in which work and production, in the economic sense, can hardly be thought of as existing'.[43] He proceeds to point out that the mating habits of even closely aligned species like spotted deer and red deer can differ enormously: 'it is even more misleading to attempt to infer the mating habits of the first men from those of the gorilla or any other sub-human primate'.[44] *The Social Life of Monkeys and Apes* would take a very different approach; it signalled this intent on the very first page, which opens by quoting Hoppius, a naturalist of the eighteenth century, who advised posterity that 'it would lead not a little to Philosophy, if one were to spend a day' with apes, 'exploring how far human wit exceeds theirs, what distance lies between Brutish and rational discrimination'.[45] The book that follows is very much in keeping with these "Cartesian principles", providing an epoch-making account of the atrocities that took place on Monkey Hill between 1925 and 1930. 'It is in their demonstration of the ways in which human social behaviour has renounced its biological background that studies of Old World apes and monkeys have greatest significance', Zuckerman later explained in his article 'The Biological Background of Human Social Behaviour' (1937), 'Such studies do not indicate fundamental limiting factors in primate social expressions, but they show the full extent to which human behaviour has altered in the course of human evolution'.[46] The sexual violence inflicted on the living and the dead on Monkey Hill should most certainly not be read, it is implied, in order to gain an insight into what we are as a species – and one suspects that the often gruesome details in Zuckerman's account were intended precisely to forestall any such effort. 'Those who study the social behaviour of apes', he continued in his characteristically dry fashion, 'in the belief that they are significantly helping in the provision of data that will allow of the better ordering of human society would appear to be somewhat mistaken,'[47] If his study of the sexual power struggles among baboons at London Zoo was intended to serve this end, there is a terrible irony in the fact that Zuckerman's account was so often received in the opposite spirit by his readers. This is registered in the postscript to the belated second edition of *The Social Life of Monkeys and Apes* (1981), in which Zuckerman attacked the ongoing misuse of information about the social lives of primates to provide a natural foundation for theories about humankind's political problems:

> The proposition that the aggressive 'instincts' we have inherited from our primitive forebears have something to do with the control of overpopulation or possible nuclear war, is no more sophisticated or useful a message than was the view of Sir Arthur Keith, that renowned British physical anthropologist of the early half of our century, that 'war is Nature's pruning fork' – a conclusion which he was able to reach without the benefit of the writings of latter-day primatologists.[48]

This is not to say that Zuckerman denied that the ferocious sexual drives displayed on Monkey Hill held some place in the unconscious of the human psyche. In fact, in 'The Biological Background to Human Social Behaviour' he readily identifies with the theory, developed by Freud in *Totem and Taboo*, that 'The price of our emergence as man would seem to have been the overt renunciation of a dominant primate impulse in the field of sex'.[49] There can be no doubt that Anker is correct to suggest that Zuckerman believed 'Visitors at the Zoo observing the gorillas would thus also observe and reflect upon their own primitive desires'.[50] But it should be recognised that this belief must have been enormously complicated by that scientist's lifelong battle against those who made easy analogical comparisons with the ways of monkeys and apes in order to shore up their own theories on human society. Instead of ignoring the elements in the Gorilla House that reference the circus freak show, on the basis that this format is incompatible with serious scientific objectives, we should recognise this aspect of the design as the fulfilment of a specific educational requirement. The structure would permit the public to witness 'a crude picture of that social level from which emerged our earliest human ancestors' but, since 'we have little or nothing to gain from watching the behaviour of animals' in seeking 'a solution to our own social and political problems', this engagement with the ape could only be presented as catharsis:[51] a recognition of our functional affinities with the animal-machine in order to induce a yet more rigorous repression of that shared past – a repression that would re-enforce, since in Zuckerman's philosophy it originally constituted, the essence of our human identity. '[It is] idle to suppose that because man is a primate, and sub-human primates lead their lives blindly according to scales of dominance and submission, human beings must therefore resign themselves to an eternity of conflict over material things', he insisted, on reviewing his horrific survey of subhuman social behaviour. 'The price of our continued existence may well be further repressions of dominant impulses, and further developments of the operative behaviour whose beginnings can be vaguely seen in our transition from a simian to a human level of existence.'[52]

The estrangement that "pulp" elements in the design of the Gorilla House effected therefore served an important purpose. Like much of the cinema of the period, Lubetkin's theatre offered scope for a popular ritual of regression: the primitive drives that threatened civilised society were not permitted to fester in darkness, but were rendered safe by being brought to light. Lubetkin's Gorilla House rigorously asserted throughout the viewing experience the traditional Cartesian gulf between Human subject and Animal object, preventing that process of "anthropomorphising" that Solly Zuckerman feared and wished to guard against.

In Bertold Lubetkin, the London Zoological Society had found exactly the right architect to respond to Zuckerman's concerns over how the lives of the great apes might be interpreted by an uninformed public. As architectural historian John Allan has observed, the theatrical approach is 'readily traced back to Lubetkin's philosophic commitment to the rationalist ideal'.[53] Allan notes that the architect chose to place a Corinthian capital (unearthed in the course of excavation; part of the Nashe project in this district during the Regency) next to the entrance like a talisman, or an embryonic caryatid. 'For Lubetkin, even a gorilla house was not merely a machine for gorillas to live in: it was a declaration of human values.'[54] (And, one might add, the imperial dominance with which humanism had been so closely associated.) The architect's own daughter describes this commitment rather more bluntly: 'He believed that human reason was an irresistible force; that science would unlock every secret, cure every ill, and that human beings, by virtue of their rationality, were superior to all other forms of life.' Her father is said to have clung to these credenda 'fiercely and proclaimed them with a passion which was anything but rational'.[55] In her account of a childhood on the Gloucestershire farm that Lubetkin took over after retiring from the capital, Louise Kehoe relates how these beliefs propelled the builder of zoos into pioneering new industrial methods of farming, including one contraption that he called a "cattle crush" – which apparently did just what the name implied.

> Factory farming had not then been invented, but he discovered it for himself, turning his architectural skills to the task of designing slat-floored prisons in which pigs and cows could be immobilized and forcibly, repeatedly mated to ensure the best yield of offspring with the least fallow time.[56]

Kehoe is quick to add that Lubetkin was not unsympathetic to his animals: he could be kind and took great pleasure in watching their antics. But his philosophy bound him to the idea that the Animal is a machine, while only the Human can be said to have mind. His zoo buildings aggressively insisted on this fact in an era when this tenet central to the Cartesian tradition seemed to have been threatened by Darwinism and the discovery of the great apes. As Kehoe obverses, 'by juxtaposing the cool, mathematical precision of pure geometric shapes – cylinders, spirals, ellipses, cast in thin sections of white reinforced concrete – with the lumbering gait and awkward, unrefined behaviour of the captive tenants, he made clowns and performers of them in spite of themselves'.[57] The animal is held in patterns from Euclidean geometry, mapped on a Cartesian grid, that testify to the imperial power of the rational mind. 'The animals became living monuments to rationalism, imprisoned not so much by bars or cages, but by their intellectual inferiority to humankind, whose will had wrought the seamless, soaring concrete canopies that sheltered them.'[58]

In many of the zoo buildings this tendency is not nearly as pronounced as Kehoe suggests, and Lubetkin has been justly hailed for developing a new form of civic architecture that permitted unprecedented interactions between man and beast. But, as Louis MacNeice recognised on viewing the structure shortly after its completion, there *was* something excessive in the Gorilla House's formal emphasis on circulation and control:

> Beyond the Elephant House is one of the very newest and grandest of the Zoo buildings, the circular gorilla House of white concrete ... by Messers Tecton. This is all gadgets, central heating, coddling and slickness, and like all this firm's designs, is, aesthetically, a trifle frigid. We must of course always plump for the animal's health and comfort rather than for our own probably sentimental, certainly irrelevant, delight in a more homely and cowshed atmosphere, but all the same we may remember that Alfred, the Bristol gorilla ... has lived in perfect health for years in much more primitive quarters without any of this air-conditioning or up-to-the-minute setting. And we may remember that Americans, with all their science-in-the-home and centrally heated houses, beat the world when it comes to catching colds.[59]

Ostensibly there to protect the gorillas from airborne infection and a northern climate to which they were not adapted, the obtrusive nature of the systems for air-conditioning, running water, sliding dust screen, revolving sunroom, are said to represent an unwarranted thoroughness of treatment. In point of fact, these elements seem to have been lifted from the design for a tuberculosis clinic that in the end was never built.[60] When the care taken over the formal integration of measures for the flow of human traffic through the building is also taken into account, it becomes evident that these systems were not in place merely for the sake of the gorillas, but were part of a wider preoccupation on the part of the architect with the aesthetics of circulation and control. 'In the new house the audience is encouraged to keep moving: porches, entrances and public spaces are designed to give directions to the visitor and to propel him forward', runs a contemporary report in the journal *Architectural Designs and Construction* (June 1933). 'The old game of discovering family likenesses at the Zoo is, therefore, discouraged.'[61] This attention to the structure's formal emphasis on movement is also evident in the film on the Modernist architecture at London and Whipsnade by Lazlo Maholy-Nagy, referred to earlier in this chapter, in which a series of simple animations highlight the kinetic properties of the Gorilla House and Penguin Pool. Significantly, the treatment of the two gorillas in this motion picture differs considerably from that accorded the other zoo animals; while giraffes and penguins are captured rushing through their new enclosures, in shots that convey an exhilarating sensation of freedom and speed, the gorillas alone do not move but cling and stare as the building itself moves about them. The freedom of movement celebrated in this section of the film is not proper to the gorillas but a property of the machine they inhabit; while the other structures suggest movement, only the Gorilla House is a moving object; while the rest seem to inspire a delight in movement on the part of the animals, the Gorilla House reduces the apes it contains to passive spectators.

The architect's preoccupation with the systematic regulation of circulation is a striking manifestation of a concept that has been a characteristic element in European thought since the Enlightenment, and that has been the fundamental basis for Anglo-Saxon modes of imperial activity: the metaphor of circulation. As David Trotter has shown in his book on this subject, over the course of the eighteenth and nineteenth centuries this concept, initially derived from medicine, became an all-encompassing metaphor that politicians, economists, urban planners, philosophers and philanthropists applied to an extraordinary range of different problems, enabling them to formulate and instal those systems that our technological, highly populated and urbanised civilisation now depends upon.[62] 'The formula is as simple as can be', remarks Wolfgang Schivelbusch: 'whatever was part of circulation was regarded as healthy, progressive, constructive; all that was detached from circulation, on the other hand, appeared diseased, medieval, subversive, threatening'.[63] It should come as no surprise that we should find Zuckerman struggling for this word in the 1930s when he came to define the essence of *culture*, that which sets us apart from the rest of the animal world: 'By virtue of the tools we construct, we organize our lives to a large extent according to means of production and exchange', he claimed.[64] And Zuckerman expressed this idea more stridently in later years, having talked with Lévi-Strauss: 'I believe Lévi-Strauss to be right when he makes the point that "humanisation" implies a synthesis of a number of cultural elements (among which *exchange* is critical) which, as it were, became combined in a flash' (my italics).[65] No less than the Corinthian capital set up at the entrance, Lubetkin's formal emphasis on circulation is an emphatic expression not merely of the logic underpinning British imperial but also "Human" values, as formulated in the Enlightenment. The animal that might have successfully aped our human capacity to respond is held immobile in the midst of systems for the circulation of light, water, air, heat and the crowd, powerless within a cultural paradigm that had become the entelechy of that Logos proper to the Human. No longer free to say 'I am' but bound within a fearsome structure of thought, the inmates are given space only to play at being what we think of as gorilla: in this instance, as has been suggested, the embodiment of a peculiarly human quality, a culturally specific notion of the bestiality of the Id. Mok and Moina were in one sense dead on arrival; they could only ever have been experienced as human artefacts, in this House of Light.

The House of Light

Before closing this chapter, I would like to indicate that the formal procedures employed in the Tecton Gorilla House are by no means unique but might well reflect a more general tendency in that phase of theory and practice to which the term *Modernist* is applied. To demonstrate this effectively would require more space than is available here. But an examination of an extract from a monumental work of literary Modernism may serve to show that the aggressive procedures set out in this chapter can cast light on analogous structures in material by Modernist writers and artists, thereby contributing to the groundbreaking work currently being conducted on the Modernist Animal by Carrie Rohman and Carey Wolfe.[66] Published a year after the completion of the Gorilla House at London Zoo, the passage of poetry at the start of this chapter, the translation of the Punic *Periplus of Hanno the Navigator*, is in fact a component in *The Cantos* of Ezra Pound, one of the largest fragments in that monster mosaic inspired by the glittering canopy of the Galla Placidia, Ravenna: the circle of gold in the gloom that gathers the light against it. Hanno's gorillas are one luminous detail in Pound's epic poem. They too have been enclosed in a House of Light. Having studied the role that these apes were compelled to perform in a contemporaneous Modernist structure, we are now in a position to contend that, though overlooked by previous commentators on Canto XL, the gorillas represent a discourse central to a full understanding of the themes developed in that text.

Critics have noted that the financial conspiracies, war profiteering and institutionalised swindling that occupy the poet's attention in the first part of the canto are counterpointed by Hanno's *Periplus*; that is to say, 'a journey not by fixed charts or stars, but by intuition and reason; not by plotting a course ahead on paper, but by looking directly at what is in front of you and acting accordingly'. Or as Pound himself puts it in Canto LIX: 'periplum, not as land looks on a map / but as sea bord seen by men sailing'.[67] In contrast to the destructive activities of the war profiteers, we are presented with the exemplary account of an ancient voyage of discovery that represents a valuable contribution to human knowledge. An equivalent to Pound's project in fact, the *Periplus* is a recurring motif in *The Cantos*.[68]

But there is mystery and speculation surrounding Hanno's account, of which Ezra Pound cannot have been unaware. As B. H. Warmington noted in 1964, a whole literature of scholarship had grown up round the report: he explains that 'From everything we know about Carthaginian practice, the resolute determination to keep all knowledge of and access to the western markets from the Greeks, it is incredible that they would have allowed the publication of an accurate description of the voyage for all to read'.[69] The interest of Hanno's *Periplus* resides not so much in what has been recorded as in what has been omitted – that which the Carthaginians were looking for in Senegal (*Sene Khole*: river of gold). 'The very purpose of the voyage, the consolidation of the route to the gold market, is not even mentioned.'[70] The significance of this omission is signalled in Pound's translation by a capital mid-sentence, at the point the Carthaginian ships mysteriously turn back on themselves, presumably to deposit their newly acquired cargo, before proceeding into the unknown: 'Next is a river wide, full of water / crocodiles, river horses, Thence we turned back to Cyrne / for 12 days coasted the shore / Aethiops fled at our coming / Our Lixtae cd. not understand them.'[71] The possibility so unlikely in the first half of the canto has been realised in the second. 'If a nation will master its money', the poet sighed, and in this object lesson from the past, Pound shows how this was once achieved. The *Periplus* is an emblem of a Latin motto cited at the start of *Eleven New Cantos* (1934) – '*Tempus loquendi / Tempus tacendi*'.[72] The report is a public secret that enables the state to maintain absolute control over the medium of exchange and the circulation of wealth.

Privateers have been forestalled by a political expedient on the part of the Prince. Given the extent to which the gorilla in this period represented precisely that blurring of ontological categories that Pound execrated elsewhere in *The Cantos*, their violent treatment must represent a triumph over that error. Throughout that poem, 'obstructors of knowledge, / obstructors of distribution' are associated with types of animal, and the evil of usury, 'corrupter of all things', cutting loose the signifier from the signified, is represented as Satan-Geryon, or Neschek – that is, as irredeemably hybrid.[73] In Pound's vision the achievement of earthly harmony is inextricably bound up with the extirpation of the bestial: 'The fourth; the dimension of stillness' requires one to exercise 'the power over wild beasts'.[74] The first recorded encounter with the gorilla is therefore re-enacted to serve a definite purpose. The species that was the embodiment of that lack of 'clear demarcation', hated by Pound, is emptied of being:[75] 'Killed, flayed, brought back their pelts to Carthage.'[76] According to Roman historian Pliny, the Prince 'placed the skins of two of these females in the temple of Juno, which were to be seen until the capture of Carthage'.[77] Like Mok and Moina, the gorillas in Pound's Canto are put on public display, a necessary sacrifice to that regulation of circulation that constitutes the basis for the imperialism celebrated and signified by the House of Light. An image of this radiant temple, to which these artefacts are dedicated, concludes Canto XL.

> To the high air, to the stratosphere, to the imperial
> calm, to the empyrean, to the baily of the four towers
> the NOUS, the ineffable crystal:
> Karxedonion Basileos
>   hung this with his map in their temple.[78]

The Mad Scientist

What has emerged from this investigation on the Modernist Animal? I would suggest that the animosity we have identified here is the result of a significant fault-line in early twentieth-century thought: an extraordinarily aggressive rearguard action, on the part of a certain group of Modernists, against a rival group. Briefly, we might say that the former tend to self-define as classicist, and (mis-?)represent their opponents as Romantic. The classicists comprise Hegelian phenomenologists, Marxist dialectical-materialists and Stirnerian existentialists (for instance, Ezra Pound, Berthold Lubetkin, Wyndham Lewis), and the so-called Romantics are what we would usually call the radical empiricist or psychological Modernists (for instance, Gertrude Stein, Marcel Proust, Virginia Woolf) inspired by Arthur Schopenhauer, Friedrich Nietzsche, William James, Henri Bergson and Sigmund Freud. This is surely familiar terrain. But we have approached it from a new starting point and are in a position to speculate that this intensely polarised culture may be related to T. S. Eliot's notion that European culture had suffered from a 'dissociation of sensibility' he believed to have set in some point during the early seventeenth century – that is to say, from the time that René Descartes separated the Human soul from the Animal body. Eliot's (notoriously vague) formulations concerning this have come in for a great deal of ill-tempered critical ridicule over the years, but, I would suggest, we would now be very well advised to re-evaluate Eliot's thoughts on this historical 'dissociation' of body and mind in light of what we have discovered in the course of this chapter. Indeed, I would go so far as to suggest that Modernism (a label now sorely in need of a definition) might fruitfully be defined as that very division – or rather, as the history of the various attempts made to overcome that division – to effect a synthesis of these two estranged traditions. That is to say, Modernism might eventually be understood not as a corpus of writing or a movement, nor as a network, but rather as the synthetic phase within a centuries-old dialectical process, as thinkers and practitioners began to converge upon two (rival) syntheses: the dialectical materialism of Karl Marx, and the psychoanalytical theories of Sigmund Freud.

But to outline these points fully will require another book, and these ideas relate to our present purpose only in so far as they permit us to trace the roots of the post-modern demonisation of mid-twentieth-century Modernist Promethean ambitions. The present chapter has shown how a Marxist (Berthold Lubetkin) developed a series of formal procedures to see off the perceived threat posed by proponents of the evolutionary theory of Darwin and psychoanalytical theories of Freud, and can be seen to fulfil (with their references to gorilla horror movies and the trope of the Mad Scientist) Freud's own speculation that the psychoanalyst might, himself, eventually come to be regarded as possessing uncanny powers: 'like a sort of mephistophelian Dr. Caligari', writes Wyndham Lewis, in *Time and Western Man* (1928), his monumental diatribe against radical empiricist philosophy in twentieth-century culture, 'that old magician, Sigmund Freud'.[79]

Having considered the formal expression of such animosity in the "classical" Modernist architecture of the inter-war period, in the following chapter we will show how this mode of Modernism was itself demonised by an author committed to the "Romantic" tradition of modern Western philosophy. Deeply immersed in the Indo-European philology developed by Orientalists William Jones and F. R. W. Schlegel (which directly influenced Schopenhauer, Nietzsche and the radical empiricists who would follow), J. R. R. Tolkien might appear an unlikely combatant in the great culture war that defines Modernist creativity. And yet it is Tolkien who produces what is surely far and away the most unforgettable and subversive expression of that horror of the Enlightenment that we are considering here: the familiar all-seeing eye upon a pyramid perversely reimagined as an evil eye upon a dark tower – motivated by the threat posed to his own philological convictions by the new Marxist linguistic doctrine then being developed in the USSR.

Notes

1 László Moholy-Nagy (dir.), *The New Architecture and London Zoo* (Museum of Modern Art Film Library, 1936).
2 Peder Anker, 'The Bauhaus of Nature', *Modernism/Modernity*, Vol. 12, No. 2 (2005), 239.

3 Berthold Lubetkin, Notes for 'Samizdat', 40, RIBA, Lubetkin's Papers, Box 1, LuB/25/4.
4 Jacques Derrida, *The Animal That Therefore I Am*, ed. Marie-Louise Mallet, trans. David Wills (New York: Fordham University Press, 2008), 32.
5 René Descartes, *Discourse on Method and Other Writings*, trans. F. E. Sutcliffe (London: Penguin, 1968), 103–104.
6 *Ibid.*, 53.
7 Aristotle, *History of Animals*, VIII.i, in *The Complete Works of Aristotle: The Revised Oxford Translation*, Vol. 1,ed. Jonathan Barnes (Princeton, NJ, Princeton University Press, 1995), 921.
8 Descartes, *Discourse*, 103.
9 *Ibid.*, 104.
10 *Ibid.*, 106.
11 *Ibid.*, 73–75.
12 *Ibid.*, 75.
13 Thomas S. Savage, 'Notice of the External Characters and Habits of Troglodytes Gorilla, a New Species of Orang from the Gaboon River' and Jeffries Wyman, 'Osteology of the Same', *Boston Journal of Natural History*, Vol. 5, No. 4 (Dec 1847), 417–443.
14 See M. T. Ashley Montagu, "Knowledge of the Ape in Antiquity", *Isis*, Vol. 32, No. 1 (1940), 87–102.
15 Ezra Pound, translation of the *Periplus of Hanno of Carthage*, in *Eleven New Cantos* (1934), *The Cantos* (London: Faber, 1987), 200–201.
16 Paul du Chaillu, *Explorations and Adventures in Equatorial Africa: With Accounts of the Manners and Customs of the People, and of the Chase of the Gorilla, the Crocodile, Leopard, Elephant, Hippopotamus, and Other Animals* (London: J. Murray, 1861).
17 An expedition later recounted by mystery writer Mary Bradley in *On the Gorilla Trail* (New York: Appleton, 1922).
18 For a discussion of the evolution of this motif in Fremiet's work, see Ted Gott's comprehensive survey of the gorilla in Western art, 'It Is Lovely To Be a Gorilla, Sometimes: The Art and Influence of Emmanuel Fremiet, Gorilla Sculptor', Joseph Burke Lecture 2006, David R. Marshall (ed.), *Art, Site and Spectacle: Studies in Early Modern Visual Culture* (Melbourne: Fine Arts Network, 2007).
19 Adrian Weiss (dir.), *The Bride and the Beast* (Allied Artists Pictures, 1958).
20 Sigmund Freud, *The Interpretation of Dreams* (1913), trans. A. A. Brill (London: Wordsworth Classics, 1997), 270.
21 *Ibid.*, 270. See also *On Murder, Mourning and Melancholia* (1913), ed. Maud Ellman, trans. Shauen Whiteside (London: Penguin, 2005), 127–132.

22 Aldous Huxley, *Ape and Essence* (1948), ed. David Bradshaw (London: Vintage, 1994), 32–33.
23 Derrida, *The Animal*, 41.
24 Charles Darwin, *The Descent of Man* (1871), ed. James Moore and Adrian Desmond (London: Penguin, 2004) 107.
25 *Ibid.*, 109.
26 Descartes, *Discourse*, 75.
27 Edgar Allen Poe, 'The Murders in the Rue Morgue' (1841), Graham Clarke (ed.), *Tales of Mystery and Imagination* (London: Everyman, 1993), 435.
28 *Ibid.*, 436.
29 *Ibid.*, 436.
30 *Ibid.*, 437.
31 *Ibid.*, 121.
32 *Ibid.*, 120.
33 Pierre Boulle, *Planet of the Apes* (1963), ed. Brian Aldiss, trans. Xan Fielding (London: Penguin, 2001), 136–139.
34 Lubetkin, in conversation in 1974, quoted in John Allan, *Berthold Lubetkin: Architecture and the Tradition of Progress* (London: RIBA Publications, 1992), 208.
35 Berthold Lubetkin, unpublished transcript, 'Dudley Zoo'. Unpublished transcript, c. 1938. RIBA, Lubetkin's Papers, Box 1, LuB/25/4.
36 F. A. Gutheim, 'Building for Beasts', *Magazine of Art*, Vol. 29 (Oct 1936), 455–463.
37 *Ibid.*, 26.
38 *Ibid.*, 172.
39 *Ibid.*, 9.
40 *Ibid.*, 10.
41 *Ibid.*, 13.
42 *Ibid.*, 14.
43 *Ibid.*, 14.
44 *Ibid.*, 25.
45 *Ibid.*, 1.
46 S. Zuckerman, 'The Biological Background of Human Social Behaviour' (1937), *The Social Life of Monkeys and Apes* (London: Routledge and Kegan Paul, 1981), 433.
47 *Ibid.*, 433–434.
48 Zuckerman, 'Postscript' (1981), *Social Life*, 400.
49 Zuckerman, 'Biological Background', 434.
50 Anker, 'The Bauhaus of Nature', 239.
51 Zuckerman, *Social Life*, 315, 400.
52 Zuckerman, 'Biological Background', 433–434.
53 Allan, *Berthold Lubetkin*, 201.

54 Ibid., 208.
55 Louise Kehoe, *In This Dark House* (New York: Schocken Books, 1995), 40–41.
56 Ibid., 42.
57 Ibid., 41.
58 Ibid., 41.
59 Louis MacNeice, *Zoo* (London: Michael Joseph, 1938), 50.
60 Allan, *Berthold Lubetkin*, 208.
61 Anon., *Architectural Designs and Construction* (June 1933), 316–318.
62 David Trotter, *Circulation: Defoe, Dickens, and the Economics of the Novel* (Basingstoke, Hampshire: Macmillan, 1988), 67.
63 Wolfgang Schivelbusch, *The Railway Journey: The Industrialization of Time and Space in the Nineteenth Century* (Leamington Spa, Warwickshire: Berg Publishers, 1986), 195.
64 Zuckerman, 'Biological Background', 434.
65 Zuckerman, 'Postscript', 397.
66 For some of the best work currently being undertaken on this topic see Carrie Rohman, *Stalking the Subject: Modernism and the Animal* (New York: Columbia University Press, 2008), and Carey Wolfe (ed.), *Zoontologies* (Minneapolis: University of Minnesota Press, 2003).
67 Pound, *The Cantos*, 324.
68 The book opens with this motif: see Canto I, 'And then went down to the ship ...'.
69 B. H. Warmington, *Carthage* (London: Penguin, 1964), 79.
70 Ibid., 79.
71 Pound, *The Cantos*, 200.
72 Ibid., 198, 153.
73 Ibid., 425, 812.
74 Ibid., 245.
75 Ibid., 229.
76 Ibid., 201.
77 Pliny, *The Natural History*, trans. John Bostock and H. T. Riley (London: Taylor and Francis, 1855), VI: 6, 200.
78 Pound, *The Cantos*, 201.
79 Wyndham Lewis, *Time and Western Man* (1927), ed. Paul Edwards (Santa Rosa, CA: Black Sparrow Press, 1993), 301 and 101.

4

Orc-talk: Spectres of Marx in Tolkien's Middle-Earth

A frightful hobgoblin

A spectre begins by coming back; a frightful hobgoblin appears apropos of nothing. Familiar to most English readers through the Samuel Moore translation of 1888, the famous spectre one remembers haunting the opening line of *The Communist Manifesto* (1848) is a late arrival in England, too late for the first English version produced by the Chartist writer Helen Macfarlane and published by the journal *Red Republican* in 1850. *Das Gespenst des Kommunismus*, the thing expected, will not appear. Instead: 'A frightful Hobgoblin stalks throughout Europe'. And this might or might not be the "spirit" that follows: 'We are haunted by a ghost, the ghost of Communism. All the Powers of the Past have joined in a holy crusade to lay this ghost to rest.'[1]

Derided ever since as a comically inadequate rendering of the German original, Macfarlane's frightful hobgoblin should not be so simply dismissed. As David Black's remarkable and richly rewarding investigation into the writer's life and work has established, Macfarlane's knowledge and understanding of German philosophy was equalled only at that time in the United Kingdom by the novelist George Eliot, and no subsequent English translator has been better placed to gain insights into the composition of the *Manifesto* than Macfarlane, who befriended Karl Marx and Friedrich Engels shortly after the beginning of their exile following the counter-revolutions of 1848. In a letter to Engels, written in February 1851, Marx described Macfarlane as 'a rare bird' – 'the only collaborator on [the *Red Republican*] who had original ideas'.[2]

Her decision to translate *Das Gespenst* as a hobgoblin therefore merits attention, not least because it maintains a distinction between the spectre (*Gespenst*) and the spirit (*Geist*). As Jacques Derrida once noted, the spectre and spirit are *not* the same thing, though the spectre is *of the spirit* and participates in it even as it follows and reiterates it: a ghostly double.[3] 'The difference between the two is precisely what tends to disappear in the ghost effect, just as the concept of such a difference or the argumentative movement that puts it to work in the rhetoric tends to vanish.'[4] In the course of sharpening this difference, Derrida observes that 'what distinguishes the spectre or the *revenant* from the *spirit*, including the spirit in the sense of the ghost in general, is doubtless a supernatural and paradoxical phenomenality, the furtive and ungraspable visibility of the invisible, or an invisibility of a visible X'.[5] That is to say, a spectre is produced by an incarnation of spirit: 'Once ideas or thoughts (*Gedanke*) are detached from their substratum, one engenders [the spectre] by *giving them a body*. Not by returning to the living body from which ideas and thoughts have been torn loose, but by incarnating the latter in *another artificial body, a prosthetic body*.'[6] And in the chapters that follow, Derrida suggests that the commodity fetish that appears in *Das Kapital* would be the given, or rather lent, borrowed body.[7]

> The wood comes alive and is peopled with spirits: credulity, occultism, obscurantism, lack of maturity before Enlightenment, childish or primitive humanity ... But, inversely, the spirit, soul, or life that animates it remains caught in the opaque and heavy thingness of the *hulē*, in the inert thickness of its ligneous body, autonomy no more than the mask of automatism.
>
> ... The automaton mimes the living. The Thing is neither dead nor alive, it is dead and alive at the same time. It survives. At once cunning, inventive, and machine-like, igneous and unpredictable, this war machine is a theatrical machine, a *mekhanē*. What one has just seen cross the stage is an apparition, a quasi-divinity – fallen from the sky or come out of the earth.[8]

Here, Derrida could be describing the goblins that have proliferated in the West in the modern era. From the hobgoblins that haunt the early printing press and the renaissance theatre to the Orcs that now thrive in paperbacks, tabletop role-playing games (RPGs), video games and blockbuster cinematic franchises, these creatures from folklore have drawn increasing and uncanny vitality from each generation of mass media entertainment technology, acquiring at last, with the most recent advances in CGI, bodies entirely spectral. No longer needing even the silicon prosthetics required for "practical" Orcs, Azog the Defiler, a lead antagonist in Peter Jackson's *Hobbit* trilogy, is a digital image created by the VFX company Weta Digital using real-time facial- and motion-capture and muscle-simulation software, rotoscoped over live action elements obtained on Red Epic cameras at a resolution of 5K and 48 f.s. via a diversity map and integrated using 3D: white, brutal and beautiful, this phantasmal war machine is a theatrical wonder that compels one to recall the spectacular inventiveness of 'the wizard who evoked the powers of darkness, but could neither master them, nor yet get rid of them when they had come at his bidding'.[9]

Like *Das Gespenst*, the hobgoblin is an apparition that seems to embody even as it refuses merely to represent the spirit of our modern history: and this tension is peculiarly apparent in the writing of the man responsible for its development into the orc. 'There is no "symbolism" or conscious allegory in my story', insisted J. R. R. Tolkien. 'To ask if the Orcs "are" Communists is to me as sensible as asking if Communists are Orcs'.[10] But with increasing interest in his work and widening knowledge of the author's political opinions, this extremely reductive reading was to become increasingly prevalent. Humphrey Carpenter's biography (1977), for instance, revealed that Tolkien 'was suspicious not so much of German intentions as of those of Soviet Russia', and that he had 'a loathing of being on any side that includes Russia'. In his diary, Tolkien is said to have written, 'One fancies that Russia is probably ultimately far more responsible for the present crisis and choice of moment than Hitler'.[11] And the publication of his letters revealed that the author had held a pro-Fascist position on the Spanish Civil War: 'Nothing is a greater tribute to Red propaganda than the fact that [C. S. Lewis] (who knows they are in all other subjects liars and traducers) believes all that is said against Franco, and nothing that is said for him.'[12] All this has served only to compound the misapprehension that Tolkien was so keen to repudiate – and that his own translators appear to have shared. The introduction to the first Swedish edition of *The Lord of the Rings* explained that: 'Here [in Mordor] rules the personification of satanic might Sauron (read perhaps ... as Stalin)' – a reading that infuriated Tolkien. 'There is no "perhaps" about it', he raged. 'I utterly repudiate any such "reading", which angers me. The situation was conceived long before the Russian revolution. Such allegory is entirely foreign to my thought.'[13] And in his foreword to the second edition, Tolkien felt compelled to point out that the War of the Ring resembled the Second World War in neither its process nor its conclusion. 'I think that many confuse "applicability" with "allegory",' he suggests. 'An author cannot of course remain unaffected by his experience, but the ways in which a story-germ uses the soil of experience are extremely complex, and attempts to define the process are at best guesses from evidence that is inadequate and ambiguous.' In order to be quite clear, Tolkien explains that 'I cordially dislike allegory in all its manifestations [and] I much prefer history, true or feigned, with its varied applicability to the thought and experience of readers'.[14]

But if Tolkien is in earnest in what he says about history, this can only invite further questions concerning the nature of the connection that seems to persist between his race of goblins and the Zeitgeist. The 'undisguised ghost story' Marx is attacking in *The German Ideology* and subverting in *The Communist Manifesto* is the History of Spirit, is the very concept of World History. And Tolkien's work (produced in an era in which wars were waged over the nature and significance of that concept) is being presented to us (apparently in all seriousness) as a hypothetical model of historical process extending over some twenty thousand years.

I contend that if we really are to approach these texts in the spirit intended, that must require our raising a spectre which the author himself could not quite lay to rest. Bearing in mind the admonition against allegory – remembering that it is not merely Tolkien but Derrida too who cautions against mistaking the ghost for Platonic symbol – in this third chapter I shall explore the circumstances whereby the goblins of tradition mutate in Tolkien's writing into the Orcs of the twenty-first-century mass media. In so doing, I hope to establish new perspectives on Marx's impure history of spirit (*die unreine Geistergeschicte*) – that is to say, the history of demonic possessions, which will break with prevailing views in the considerable body of scholarship that has built up in relation to the Derridean *revenant*.

The goblin tradition

In a letter to Naomi Mitchison written on 25 April 1954, Tolkien makes a curious point of insisting that 'Orcs are not based on direct experience' while conceding that 'they owe ... a good deal to the goblin tradition (*goblin* is used as a translation in *The Hobbit*, where *orc* only occurs once, I think), especially as it appears in George MacDonald, except for the soft feet which I never believed in.'[15] Since that is the case, it would be well for us to begin by considering, briefly, MacDonald and the goblin tradition.

In 1735 the chemist Georg Brandt had named the first metal to be discovered since prehistory *cobalt*, "the goblin metal", following the peculiar usage of *Kobold* by miners in Bohemia to refer to a 'species of gnomes, who haunted the dark and solitary places, and were often seen in the mines, where they seemed to imitate the labours of the miners, and sometimes took pleasure in frustrating their objects and rendering their toil unfruitful'.[16] Subsequently, associations acquired by the German Kobold began to modify conceptions of the English hobgoblin: and it is this version of the goblin we encounter in *The Princess and the Goblin* (1872) by Victorian children's author George MacDonald, 'a strange race of beings, called by some gnomes, by some kobolds, by some goblins', which live in subterranean caverns in the mountains above a mining community.[17] According to a legend current in the country, these goblins at one time lived above ground, and were much like other people. But having taken refuge in dark wet places far away from the sun they have in the course of many generations undergone a profound and terrible physical transformation. 'And as they grew misshapen in body they had grown in knowledge and cleverness, and now were able to do things no mortal could see the possibility of.'[18] Published twenty years before *The Time Machine* (1895), MacDonald's goblins could easily be the inspiration for the Morlocks (a race of beings often taken to be the lower classes in a cautionary tale exploring the implications of industrial revolution). Knowing the iconic role that working-class mining communities would subsequently play in the social history of the United Kingdom, one might be tempted to conclude that we have in this text a clear instance of what Tolkien was so keen to deny – that is, goblins functioning as a symbol for a demonised working class. Given the importance of MacDonald's goblins to Tolkien's Orcs, this would be a significant lead. But (like the Morlocks) these goblins are not what they might seem.

In a previous book I have shown that the Morlocks and the Eloi were conceived as an allegory not of industrial class division, but rather of the consequences that must follow from the slow divorce of the arts and the sciences – C. P. Snow's "two cultures" – as the middle classes drifted apart along railway lines into sprawling suburban communities. The 'different legendary theories' as to why the Goblins go underground, though various, indicate clearly that, whatever the reason might be, it is likely a bourgeois liberal rather than a working-class socialist revolt: 'the king had laid what they thought too severe taxes upon them, or had required observances of them they did not like, or had begun to treat them with more severity, in some way or other, and impose stricter laws'.[19] The goblins are in fact the *middle class* conspicuously absent from this story (of a Royal household and mining community). And such a reading would be consistent with the other great portrayal of goblins in this era: purveyors of luxuries (with aggressive marketing practices!) the goblin merchant men in Christina Rossetti's *Goblin Market* (1862) have more in common with the managers of the department store in Emile Zola's *Au Bonheur des Dames* (1883) than with, say, the Hellcats of Wodgate in Benjamin Disraeli's *Sybil* (1845). 'One hauls a basket, / One bears a plate, / One lugs a golden dish / Of many pounds weight.'[20] Whatever their original, the goblins that appear in the Victorian fictions which directly influenced Tolkien are *not* rooted in any demonisation of the working classes; indeed, 'Who knows upon what soil they fed / Their hungry thirsty roots?'[21]

Drawing heavily upon MacDonald in his own children's story, *The Hobbit* (1937), Tolkien's goblins are equally hard to relate to the conceptions of the industrial labouring class we inherit from Disraeli and Marx. On the one hand, his goblins possess great metallurgical expertise. 'Hammers, axes, swords, daggers, pickaxes, tongs, and instruments of torture, they make very well', writes Tolkien. 'It is not unlikely they invented some of the machines that have since troubled the world, especially the ingenious devices for killing large numbers of people at once, for wheels and engines and explosions always delighted them.'[22] On the other hand, they 'get other people to make to their design [these clever things], prisoners and slaves that have to work till they die for want of air and light'.[23]

In fact, it is said the goblins create wheels and engines precisely because they prefer 'not working with their own hands more than they could help'.[24] It would seem goblins exploit labour rather than provide it! For different reasons, his Orcs are equally difficult to read through the prism of class: while the two Orc soldiers who take a moment to share the latest war news, in a scene at the end of *The Two Towers* (1954), might conceivably be delivering their lines in the working-class London accent they acquire in the film adaptation, the latter is hard to reconcile with what is said by Orcs elsewhere in the trilogy.

> 'My dear tender little fools,' hissed Grisnákh, 'everything you have, and everything you know, will be got out of you in due time: everything! You'll wish there was more that you could tell to satisfy the Questioner, indeed you will: quite soon. We shan't hurry the enquiry. Oh dear no! What do you think you've been kept alive for? My dear little fellows, please believe me when I say that it was not out of kindness: that's not even one of Uglúk's faults.'[25]

Lines that one can imagine being spoken by the bully in *Thomas Brown's School Days* (1957), these are surely not the result of mere inconsistency or of slipshod execution. In a letter to a radio broadcaster looking to adapt his trilogy, Tolkien himself rejected the suggestion that Orcs should be associated with a class accent, noting that 'it would probably be better to avoid certain, actual or conventional, features of modern "vulgar" English in representing Orcs – such as the dropping of aitches'. Observing that people confuse "accent" with impressions of different intonation, articulation and tempo, Tolkien suggests that those adapting his text for the radio or film 'will, I suppose, have to use such means to make Orcs sound nasty!'[26] In short, it proves to be impossible to relate either the goblins or the Orcs to a recognisable class – and this in turn rules out the sort of straightforward political readings that Tolkien rejected.[27] Though the redistributive policy pursued by goblin-men in the Shire, for instance, must appear to hold out a tantalising parallel, one cannot but admit that Tolkien was probably right to dismiss this as a false analogy. What the author says elsewhere, in relation to the alien *Pfifltriggi*, in C. S. Lewis's sci-fi *Out of the Silent Planet* (1938), is also applicable to goblins and Orcs in his own work: 'In conclusion I may say that in designating the *Pfifltriggi* as the "workers" your reader ... is misled by current notions that are not applicable.'[28]

If there be any doubt on this score, this must be settled when one remembers that the context in which this writer formed his impressions of industry conforms not in the slightest to the more familiar, hierarchical manufactories of Lancashire and Yorkshire upon which the Marxist theory of class struggle (together with more loosely held notions regarding the make-up of the social classes in the United Kingdom) is, for the most part, based. 'The more the factory system has taken possession of a branch of industry, the more the working men employed in it participate in the labour movement; the sharper the opposition between working men and capitalists, the clearer the proletarian consciousness in the working men', explained Frederick Engels, in his study of *The Conditions of the Working Classes in England* (1845).[29] But, as he himself observed, the factory system had never entirely taken root in Birmingham, where traces of a much older industrial system survive to this day in the Jewellery Quarter.

> The disposition of the work has retained at Birmingham, as in most places where metals are wrought, something of the old handicraft character; the small employers are still to be found, who work with their apprentices in the shop at home, or when they need steam-power, in great factory buildings which are divided into little shops, each feted to a small employer, and supplied with a shaft moved by the engine, and furnishing motive power for the machinery.[30]

Terming this unusual arrangement 'Democratic Industry', Engels suggests an important consequence of this is that 'these small employers are neither genuine proletarians, since they live in part upon the work of their apprentices, nor genuine bourgeois, since their principal means of support is their own work'.[31] In fact, Birmingham iron workers are said to be occupying 'an unhappy middle ground between proletarian Chartism and shopkeepers' Radicalism'; and, Engels believes, this 'peculiar midway position' is to blame for their having so rarely joined wholly and unreservedly in the English labour movements: 'Birmingham is politically radical, but not a Chartist town'.[32] Indeed, Birmingham developed its own idiosyncratic and profoundly influential response to the social challenge of industrial revolution in liberal unionism, a political philosophy that permitted the apparent paradox whereby (as socialist Sydney Webb had complained):

> The Individualist City Councillor will walk along the municipal pavement, lit by municipal gas and cleansed by municipal brooms with municipal water, and seeing by the municipal clock in the municipal market, that he is too early to meet his children coming from the municipal school hard by the county lunatic asylum and municipal hospital, will use the national telegraph system to tell them not to walk through the municipal park but to come by the municipal tramway, to meet him in the municipal reading room, by the municipal art gallery, museum and library, where he intends to consult some of the national publications in order to prepare his next speech in the municipal town-hall, in favour of the nationalisation of canals and the increase of the government control over the railway system.[33]

He will do all this and more, and yet say, 'Socialism, sir, ... don't waste the time of a practical man by your fantastic absurdities! Self-help, sir, individual self-help, that's what's made our city what it is.'[34]

Given this context, one should neither expect the spectres of industry lurking in Tolkien's writing to conform to the pattern of a general theory of class developed in Manchester, nor be much surprised to discover the clear Marxist distinction between bourgeois liberal industrial revolution and the coming proletariat social revolution so thoroughly collapsed. For the history of Birmingham embodies a perspective more specific and more expansive. Add to this Tolkien's being raised by a priest within the religious community established in the city by Cardinal J. H. Newman and one really does begin to see how the great stadial history described by Marx might blur to a vanity of small differences in a quarrel between rival Protestant sects. 'It is not easy for us to tell the difference between two mortals', said the Elf. 'To sheep other sheep no doubt appear different.'[35] From the lofty vantage point of Newman's Oratory, the Observatory built by the Enlightenment "Lunar Men" and the Waterworks Building produced by Chamberlain's municipal socialism might be twin towers, iterations of a single idea. And so, while Tolkien does not lend himself to a reading through Marx, he might just assist us in a reading of Marx, offering us a fresh perspective on the mystery right at the heart of the theory of capital: the precise nature of the connection Derrida identified between the spectre of communism and the anthropological concept of the fetish.

Veritable Orcs

In Tolkien's very earliest treatment of the Orcs, in the body of writing that later formed the basis for *The Silmarillion*, this species had been bred by the Powers of Evil, golem-like, from the slime of the Earth. But by the time he came to write *The Lord of the Rings*, Tolkien (a devout Catholic) had come to regard this explanation as theologically unacceptable, and so in a letter written to author Naomi Mitchison, for instance, he claimed that 'Orcs are nowhere clearly stated to be of any particular origin. But since they are servants of the Dark Power, and later of Sauron, neither of whom could or would produce living things, they must be "corruptions".'[36] In fact, it would seem that Tolkien had come to believe that Orcs were derived from Men. But this would have caused insurmountable chronological difficulties within his cycle of legends relating to the First Age. So, for many years, Tolkien continued to maintain that the Orcs might have been Elves – taken and corrupted by the Dark Power (and this, you will remember, is the explanation offered by Christopher Lee in the first of the film adaptations). But he could never quite bring himself to believe that so horrible a metamorphosis could befall his beloved Elves – and rather than accept this he would eventually embark upon a comprehensive and ultimately doomed reworking of the earlier material in order to establish that Orcs were corrupted from Men. In the notes on this very late material, published in his monumental *History of Middle-Earth*, Christopher Tolkien concludes this was his father's final view on the question:

> Orcs were bred from Men, and 'if the conception in mind of the Orcs may go far back into the night of Morgoth's thought' it was Sauron who, during the ages of Melkor's captivity in Aman, brought into being the black armies that were available to his Master when he returned.[37]

The idea can be traced back to the period when Tolkien was writing what would become *The Return of the King*, when the characters discover mysterious statues of 'Púkel-men' in the mountains near Rohan. The Anglo-Saxon form of *Puck*, a term considered interchangeable with *hobgoblin* in the Early Modern period, these 'Púkel-men' are subsequently revealed to be the creations of the aboriginal inhabitants of this region: a people called the 'Drúedain' (an Elvish term meaning "Wild Men"). Tolkien remarks that:

> To the eyes of Elves and other Men they were unlovely in looks: they were stumpy (some four foot high) but very broad, with heavy buttocks and short thick legs; their wide faces had deep-set eyes with heavy brows, and flat noses, and grew no hair below their eyebrows, except in a few men (who were proud of the distinction) a small tail of black hair in the midst of the chin. Their features were usually impassive, the most mobile being their wide mouths; and the movement of their wary eyes could not be observed save from close at hand, for they were so black that the pupils could not be distinguished, but in anger they glowed red. Their voices were deep and guttural, but their laughter was a surprise: it was rich and rolling.[38]

The Wild Men are said to refer to themselves as 'Drûg-hu', and the suffix, meaning *folk*, might suggest that Tolkien conceived of this race of men, from the outset, as in some way related to the Orcs: *-hu* certainly bears more than a passing resemblance to its equivalent in the Black Speech, *-hai*. In later writing, Tolkien would express this connection more forthrightly, though no less tentatively:

> To the unfriendly who, not knowing them well, declared that Morgoth must have bred the Orcs from such a stock the Eldar answered: 'Doubtless Morgoth, since he can make no living thing, bred Orcs from various kinds of Men, but the Drúedain must have escaped his Shadow; for their laughter and the laughter of Orcs are as different as is the light of Aman from the darkness of Angband'. But some thought, nevertheless, that there had been a remote kinship, which accounted for their special enmity. Orcs and Drûgs each regarded the other as renegades.[39]

Our interest in this arcane point consists in the Púkel-men the Drûgs are credited with fashioning. As noted above, their name derives from the Proto-Indo-European root that lives on in the words *Puck*, *spectre* and *spook*, the domestic hearth god that would appear to be the basis for the later accretions that come to be referred to as goblins, and so the Púkel-men offer us a unique insight into Tolkien's own thoughts on the meaning of these creatures. In an essay published in *Unfinished Tales*, the Drûgs are said to delight in carving figures, to which the most skilled among them could give vivid semblance of life. 'Sometimes these images were strange and fantastic, or even fearful: among the grim jests to which they put their skill was the making of Orc-figures which they set at the borders of the land, shaped as if fleeing from it, shrieking in terror.'[40] They were also said to make images of themselves: the Púkel-men that appear in *Return of the King*. 'These they called "watch-stones" of which the most notable were set near the Crossings of Teiglin, each representing a Drúadan, larger than the life, squatting heavily upon a dead Orc.'[41] According to Tolkien, 'the Orcs feared them and believed them to be filled with the malice of the *Oghor-hai* [the term in the Black Speech for *Drûg-hu*] and able to hold communication with them'.[42] In a style recalling the anthropological reports produced by Finnish philosopher and sociologist Edvard Westermarck, Tolkien then embeds two short stories (that he claims to be merely reproducing) in the body of his essay, by way of illustrating the extent to which a Púkel-man is believed to be imbued with the spirit of its creator, through the uncanny and magical power of the Drûg-hu. The second of these stories, entitled 'The Faithful Stone', tells how a watch-stone produced by a Drûg known as Aghan to protect his friend Barach is found, the morning after an Orc-Raid, moved from its original position, sitting on a dead Orc; its legs are blackened by fire, and when Aghan returns it is revealed that he too, while away, has suffered injuries to his legs and feet. 'Alas!' Aghan is reported to say: 'If some power passes from you to a thing that you have made, then you must take a share in its hurts.'[43] The story could have appeared in one of those accounts Hegel draws on in his *History of Religion* in order to illustrate the principles of sorcery or shamanism practised in Siberia! If the exact nature of the relationship between the Orcs and these fetish-making sorcerers remains rather mysterious (are the Uruk-hai derived from the Drûg-hu themselves or are they malware-infected Púkel-men?) the conclusion that anthropological studies play some key role in Tolkien's reinvention of the goblin tradition is hard to discount.

Incidentally, this association with sorcery might go some way towards explaining Tolkien's preference for *Orc* over *goblin*.[44] As Christopher Tolkien has observed, the former term first became prevalent during the phase of writing and rewriting that took place between 1942 and 1944, which subsequently became the second part of *The Fellowship of the Ring* (1954). 'My father first wrote here: "veritable Orcs".'[45] But the term had been used previously: on two occasions in *The Hobbit* (1937) to refer to larger varieties of goblin,[46] and in the very early stories that Tolkien began to produce during the First World War, which would eventually be published posthumously as *The Silmarillion* (1977). Orc is Anglo-Saxon in origin ('the word is as far as I am concerned actually derived from Old English *orc* "demon"') and is presented as such in the frame narrative that Tolkien had initially envisaged for his mythology, wherein an Anglo-Saxon mariner called Aelfwine had travelled into the West to learn lore from the Elves. But, having discarded this original frame narrative, Tolkien had retroactively developed an etymology for the word in his Elvish language Sindarin, and would later claim to use the Old English word only for its phonetic suitability:

> Orc is the form of the name that other races had for this foul people as it was in the language of Rohan. In Sindarin it was *orch*. Related, no doubt, was the word *uruk* of the Black Speech, though this was applied as a rule only to the great soldier-Orcs that at this time issued from Mordor and Isengard.[47]

The etymology of the Anglo-Saxon word is obscure: and though Tolkien clearly had ideas on this point, he refused to speculate in writing further than to say that he did not think it to be derived, as is often suggested, from the Latin *Orcus* [Hades]: 'I doubt this, though the matter is too involved to set out here.'[48]

Having traced the Orkish connection with Shamanic magical practices in some detail, we are now in a position to expand upon this frustrating ellipsis; to speculate that Tolkien might have believed the word to be connected to Old English *Earg*, or to its cognates in other Germanic languages, Old Frisian *Etch* (West Frisian *Erg*), Middle Low German *Arch* (Dutch *Erg*), High German *Arg* (German *Arg*) and Nordic *Argr* (Icelandic *Argur*). Meaning "cowardly" or "evil", these words have strong but ill-defined associations with the sorcery and sexual transformations of shamanic magic (*Seid*). From Proto-Germanic **argaz*, Tolkien would have known that the word derived ultimately from Proto-Indo-European **h¹orĝh* "testicles", and possesses more distant cognates, in Latin *orchis*, Greek *órkheis*, Armenian *orjikc*, Irish *uirge*, Avestan *ərəzi*, Iranian *uirge*, Lithuanian *eržilas*, and Russian *jórzat*, meaning respectively "testicles", "penis", "stallion" and "copulate".[49] Though this must remain a surmise, the coincidence of sound and sense is remarkable enough to merit attention, while the unsavoury pedigree goes a long way to explaining Tolkien's (uncharacteristic!) reticence concerning the etymology.[50]

If this point appears to be of merely antiquarian interest, consider the following passages from another letter written to Naomi Mitchison:

> The Enemy, or those who have become like him, go in for "machinery" – with destructive and evil effects – because "magicians", who have become chiefly concerned to use *magia* for their own power, who would do so [do so]. The basic motive for *magia* – quite apart from any philosophic consideration of how it would work – is immediacy: speed, reduction of labour, and reduction also to a minimum (or vanishing point) of the gap between the idea or desire and the result or effect.[51]

In a passage that (no doubt unconsciously) echoes the famous passages from *The Communist Manifesto* quoted earlier in this chapter, Tolkien reflects that, 'to have command of abundant slave-labour or machinery (often only the same thing concealed)' resembles 'the *magia*' in other respects too: 'it may be as quick or quick enough to push mountains over, wreck forests, or build pyramids by such means'.[52] And in a note on *The Faithful Stone*, Tolkien would later reflect that tales such as this, 'that speak of [the Drûg-hu] transferring part of their "powers" to their artefacts, remind one in miniature of Sauron's transference of power to the foundations of the Barad-dûr and to the Ruling Ring'.[53] It would appear that the necromancers in *The Hobbit* and *The Communist Manifesto* have rather more in common than the reputation of each author might have reasonably led one to expect. Marx and Tolkien can be seen to have drawn on the anthropological conception of the fetish – in order to create mythologies that have each, in their own way, proven adequate to modernity, giving shape and significance to what T. S. Eliot once called that 'immense panorama of futility and anarchy which is contemporary history'.[54] And, as Tolkien was, we have argued, peculiarly ill placed to distinguish capitalist from socialist revolution, so we find fetish objects confused with goblins or spectres: an idea that surely clarifies what remains obscure in Marx, where the spectre of communism is like the enchanted fetish object that is the commodity precisely because both are brought into being by the magic of Capital – the proletariat being the very greatest of the wonders conjured into existence by that 'wizard who evoked the powers of darkness but could neither master them, nor yet get rid of them when they had come at his bidding'.[55]

Excepting the animus, rather than enthusiasm, with which Tolkien describes the phenomenon, there really is little here with which an orthodox Marxist would choose to disagree. And this raises further questions. For how are we to account for what must appear to be a satirical reiteration of Marxist theory in the writing of an author who insisted that political allegory of this kind was entirely foreign to his way of thought? I would like to suggest that there is good reason for taking Tolkien at his word, for believing these curious parallels to have their origin not in politics but in what the author himself declared his chief source of inspiration: philology. Developed chiefly in Germany over the course of the eighteenth and nineteenth centuries, philology had been the paradigm within which critics and philosophers had lived and breathed till the First World War; and while Marx had been among the first to attack philology, in *Scorpion and Felix* (1837),[56] Tolkien had continued to define himself as a philologist, and to defend his field from its detractors, long after it had lost its grip upon the European imagination, under the twin pressures of communist revolution in the East and anti-German prejudice in the West.[57] '[P]hilology itself, conceived as a purely German invention is in some quarters treated as though it were one of the things that the late war was fought to end, a thing whose absence does credit to an Englishman,' complained Tolkien in *The Year's Work in English Studies* in 1924, where he argues that it is, in fact, an 'essential piece of apparatus ... as universal as is the use of language'.[58] In the final section of this chapter I will show that the Orcs, or rather the language that they speak, present a direct response to Marxist subversion of the philological tradition, and that it is in this goblin or spectre that we can trace the clearest link to the spirit that seems to haunt Tolkien's Middle-Earth.

The Black Speech

Tolkien once observed that the primary fact to be grasped concerning his writing is that it is all of a piece and *fundamentally linguistic* in inspiration. 'The invention of languages is the foundation. The "stories" were made rather to provide a world for the languages than the reverse.' Explaining that 'To me a name comes first and the story follows', Tolkien claimed that, 'It is to me, anyway, largely an essay in "linguistic aesthetic", as I sometimes say to people who ask me "what is it all about?"'[59] The evolution of the Orc, from the goblin tradition, between 1942 and 1944, would certainly seem to bear this out, as this sudden transition can be seen to coincide with the development of personal and place names, Grishnákh, Uglúk, Lugbúrz and Uruk-Hai, in a language apparently peculiar to the Orcs that is called the Black Speech. In order to understand where the Orcs are coming from we must establish what this speech is, and how and why Tolkien came to construct it in this fashion.

Alone among the tongues that populate Tolkien's legendarium, the Black Speech is presented as precisely that which it is: a "conlang", a constructed or artificial language. 'The Orcs had a language of their own, devised for them by the Dark Lord of old', writes Tolkien, in his initial notes on this language, 'but it was so full of harsh and hideous sounds and vile words that other mouths found it difficult to compass, and few indeed were willing to make the attempt'.[60] As Tolkien and conlang specialist Helge Fauskanger observes, in his essay 'Orkish and the Black Speech: A Base Language for Base Purposes', there is apparently nothing inherent in the language itself that might justify this poor appraisal: 'The Black Speech possesses the plosives b, g, d, p, t, k, the spirants th, gh (and possibly f and kh, attested in Orc-names only), the lateral l, the vibrant r, the nasals m, n, and the sibilants s, z, sh', observes Fauskanger. 'The vowels are a, i, o, u; the vowel o is said by Tolkien to be rare'.[61] Yet the tongue has a profound impact upon its hearers on the one occasion it is spoken by Gandalf: 'his voice ... suddenly became menacing, powerful, harsh as stone', writes Tolkien. 'A shadow seemed to pass over the high sun, and the porch for a moment grew dark.'[62] Clearly the innate power ascribed to the language extends well beyond mere Elvish prejudice, and this might reflect its affinities with the speech of the Valarin: the gods who represent the Natural Powers of Tolkien's universe. As con-linguist Anthony Appleyard points out, at least one word in Sauron's Black Speech, *nazg*, "ring", would seem to be borrowed from the Valarin *Mâchananaškad*, "Ring of Doom"; as a Maia, the Dark Lord would know Valarin, and curiously the divine language is said to be equally unpleasant in much the same way: 'the effect of Valarin upon Elvish ears was not pleasing', remarks fictional philologist Pengolodh.

> The tongues and voices of the Valar are great and stern ... and yet also swift and subtle in movement, making sounds that we find hard to counterfeit; and their words are mostly long and rapid, like the glitter of swords, like the rush of leaves in a great wind or the fall of stones in the mountains.[63]

In fact, Tolkien can be seen to have said as much in his very earliest recorded thoughts concerning the language of the Orcs, dating from before 1938: '*Orquian*, the language of the Orcs, the soldiers and creatures of Morgoth, was partly itself of Valian origin, for it was derived from the Vala Morgoth', he writes. 'But the speech which he taught he perverted wilfully to evil, as he did all things, and the language of the Orcs was hideous and foul and utterly unlike the languages of the Quendi [i.e. the Elves].'[64]

Indeed, Tolkien eventually came to consider the spirit of inchoate evil infecting this tongue to be fundamentally incompatible with language itself:

> goblins had languages of their own, as hideous as all things that they made or used, and since some remnant of good will, and true thought and perception, is required to keep even a base language alive and useful even for base purposes, their tongues were endlessly diversified in form as they were deadly monotonous in purport, fluent only in the expression of abuse, hatred and fear.[65]

The result is that this conlang is peculiarly self-defeating: so fissiparous and heterogenous it can no longer fulfil its basic communicative function. 'It is said that the Black Speech was devised by Sauron in the Dark Years and that he had desired to make it the language of all those that served him, but he failed in that purpose.'[66] In fact, Tolkien concluded, Orcs could hardly be said to have "had" this language at all, and so, in the final version of this note, the Orcs lose their connection to what had been their own language entirely:

> It is said they had no language of their own, but took what they could of other tongues and perverted it to their own liking; yet made only brutal jargons, scarcely sufficient even for their own needs, unless it were for curses and abuse. And these creatures, being filled with malice, hating even their own kind, quickly developed as many

barbarous dialects as there were groups or settlements of their race, so that their Orkish speech was of little use to them in intercourse with different tribes.[67]

The corpus of texts in the Black Speech is extremely limited, making an informed critique of this language problematic. In addition to isolated words such as *ghâsh* "fire", *snaga* "slave" and *sharku* "old man", there is the inscription on the One Ring in the ancient Black Speech, and the curse of the Mordor-Orc in the more debased form used by the soldiers of the Dark Tower.[68] The latter reads 'Uglúk u bagronk sha pushdug Saruman-glob bûb-hosh skai!' – variously translated by Tolkien as: 'Uglúk to the dung pit with the stinking Saruman-filth – pig-guts gah!' and 'Uglúk to the cesspool, sha! the dungfilth; the great Saruman-fool, skai!' The inscription on the ring, appearing first in an Elvish script (Tengwar), is later transcribed in the Latin script as:

Ash nazg durbatulûk, ash nazg gimbatul,
ash nazg thrakatulûk agh burzum-ishi krimpatul.

Tolkien then presents the following as a translation; though in truth the version in English can be seen, in the published drafts, to have *preceded* the development of the Black Speech: 'One Ring to rule them all, One Ring to find them. / One Ring to bring them all and in the Darkness bind them.' Following Helge Fauskanger's analysis, we can conclude that *Nazg* is "ring", as we have elsewhere *Nazgûl* "Ring-wraith(s)". *Ash* is the number one, and *agh* would be the conjunction "and". *Burzum* is "darkness", incorporating the same element *búrz/burz* – "dark" as in *Lugbúrz* "Tower-dark". 'Hence, the *-um* of *burzum* must be an abstract suffix like "-ness" in the corresponding English word "darkness".'[69] Separated from *burzum* by a hyphen in the transcription, but with no equivalent to this in the Tengwar on the Ring, the additional suffix *-ishi* "in the" might be considered either a post-position or a locative ending. Fauskanger further speculates that, 'In the word *durbatulûk* "to rule them all" the morphemes may be tentatively segmented *durb-at-ul-ûk*.'[70] Likewise *gimb-at-ul* "find-to-them", *thrak-at-ul-ûk* "bring-to-them-all", and *krimp-at-ul* "bind-to-them". The Black Speech employs a suffix *-ul* to express "them" and also a suffix to express "all": *-ûk*. Verbs with the ending *-at* are translated with infinitives – *durbat, gimbat, thrakat, krimpat* = "to rule", "to find", "to bring", "to bind": and so, Fauskanger concludes, 'we may speak of verbs ending in -*at* as infinitives, though it may also be a specialised "intentive" form indicating purpose [a suggestive point to which I will return shortly]: the Ring was made in order to rule, find, bring and bind the other Rings of Power'.[71]

Tolkien himself professed to remain puzzled – 'and indeed sometimes irritated' – by many of the guesses at the "sources" of the nomenclature, the theories and fancies concerning hidden meanings.[72] In an angry letter to one such misguided reader, Tolkien complained such theories too often displayed little understanding of the process a philologist might be expected to pursue in creating an artificial language. 'Investigators, indeed, seem mostly confused in mind between (a) the meaning of names *within*, and appropriate to, my story and belonging to a fictional "historic" construction, and (b) the origins or sources in my mind, *exterior* to the story, of the forms of these names.'[73] Citing two cases which might have involved unconscious "borrowing", Tolkien refers the reader to (1) *Erech*, the place where Isildur set the covenant-stone, and (2) *nazg*, the word for "ring" in the Black Speech. According to Tolkien it is probable, but by no means certain, that these names were "echoes". 'Since naturally, as one interested in antiquity and notably in the history of languages and "writing", I knew and had read a good deal about Mesopotamia, I must have known *Erech* the name of that most ancient city', remarks Tolkien; and, though congruences (of form + sense) do occur in real languages that are quite unrelated, 'it remains remarkable that *nasc* is the word for "ring" in Gaelic (Irish: in Scottish usually written *nasg*)'.[74] But while conceding that certain names in his legendarium might have an origin in some word lodged in his linguistic memory, Tolkien is emphatic that the "source", if any, provided solely the sound sequence (or suggestions for its stimulus), and that its original purport is totally irrelevant. 'It is therefore idle to compare chance-similarities between names made from "Elvish tongues" and words in exterior "real" languages', concludes Tolkien, 'especially if this is supposed to have any bearing on the meaning or ideas in my story'.[75]

Most readers would probably reject Tolkien's assertion that no meaning should or could be deduced from the unconscious components in an author's writings. But he is surely correct to warn his readers against inferring too much from what might amount to no more than circumstantial similarities to signifiers in natural languages, and it would be well for us to proceed with this admonition in mind, particularly in the present case, where we are dealing with such a limited corpus. Let us rather approach this issue, as Tolkien suggests, in the spirit in which a philologist might go about it, focusing not on homophones but on the morphology and syntax of the language. Even our preliminary examination of the Ring inscription has shown these to be peculiar, and if they possess systematic parallels with a particular natural language, it will be fair to assume that these analogies are not the result of mere circumstance or unconscious association. And here, I suggest, the extremely circumscribed nature of the corpus might actually give us good grounds for expecting such a parallel, for what Tolkien says concerning "echoes" in constructed language can hardly apply to the Black Speech, which was conceived in haste and swiftly put out of mind. In contrast to the Elvish languages Tolkien loved so much, which have their inception in the years immediately prior to the First World War, the Orquian tongue was first considered as a possibility only in 1937. And while Quenya and Sindarin ultimately acquire entire dictionaries and grammars, Tolkien composed only a 'few scraps' in the Black Speech, relatively swiftly, between 1942 and 1944.[76] Indeed, he would eventually come to entertain a near-superstitious horror of the language – refusing, for instance, to drink from a steel goblet, sent to him by a fan, which had been 'engraved with the terrible words seen on the Ring'.[77] In such circumstances, one can reasonably expect to find that the internal logic that brought about such vast changes in the Elvish languages over time, and that render their comparison with natural languages fraught with difficulty, is *not* in play here with the Black Speech: an unholy abortion, it is a relatively (and surprisingly) simple matter, in this instance, to identify Tolkien's primary sources.

In a letter to Fauskanger, reproduced in his essay 'Orkish and the Black Speech: A Base Language for Base Purposes', the historian Alexandre Nemirovsky points out that the main points of grammar, evident in the Ring inscription alone, narrow the range of possible sources quite considerably: 'cases are expressed by post-logs (*ishi*), only the Nominative case has a zero ending (*nazg*), and ... the personal pronoun naming the object of a transitive action is included in the verbal form only'. In fact, verbal suffixes can even come after it in such a case (root + *ul* "them" + *ûk* "completely, to the very end"). In other words, what we are looking at is an agglutinative ergative language – something of a rarity even now, and all the more so in the early 1940s (long before the great contemporary achievement of R. M. W. Dixon, the world's leading authority on ergativity), when Tolkien could have drawn upon research relating to only around thirty to forty such languages. Ergativity had achieved recognition only some fourteen years earlier, following the publication of Adolf Dirr's review of the Caucasian languages *Einfüring in das Studium de kaukasichen Sprachen* (1928). In fashioning an agglutinative ergative language, Tolkien was engaging with the very latest research in his field – and the information upon which he based it must therefore derive from the Caucasus mountains, the Basque region, Mesopotamia or Tibet. 'Now my main hypothesis is that this Black Speech was designed by Tolkien after some acquaintance with Hurrian-Urartian language(s)', writes Nemirovsky. 'For now I want to emphasize that Hurrian ... is an agglutinative ergative language, where personal pronouns are included in the verbal forms.'[78] Indeed, the Assyriologist E. A. Speiser thought the bound forms one of Hurrian's most remarkable characteristics – as in the Black Speech, these elements are placed invariably after the supporting root, being joined to it directly or through the mediation of suffixes: 'a technique that is agglutinative to an appreciable degree'.[79] And Hurrian possesses the syntactic dichotomy which enables a given transitive verb to figure as active or passive, as in Caucasian languages (i.e. ergativity), but differs from these in that it treats passively all finite forms. 'Intransitives reflect the same differentiation of aspects', explains Speiser, in his 'Studies in Hurrian Grammar' (1939), 'but their syntax is necessarily uniform in that the subject is in the "nominative" throughout'.[80] And (as Nemirovsky points out) this presents the most striking parallel with the Ring inscription, in which one sees a "them" formant with the absence of any formant expressing the agent: 'jussive forms in Hurrian never include the pronoun expressing the agent/subject of a transitive action, but often include the pronoun, expressing its object', explains Nemirovsky; and while 'In Hurrian all cases except the Nominative are expressed with various flexions, Nominative is expressed with zero flexion – again just as in the Black Speech',[81] In these circumstances, the fact that so many Orkish words are seen to present parallels in Hurrian must seem more significant than it might do otherwise. Nemirovsky sets out a long list of potential sources for the words on the Ring inscription – and if most of the parallels for the nouns and verbs fail to impress (Tolkien himself insists that *Nazg* was suggested by the Irish, while *gimb* could as easily come from Carroll's 'Jabberwocky'), the suffixes present an uncanny correspondence in sound and the syntactical relations expressed.

at – formant of jussive / intended future in verbal forms / *ed* – formant of future in verbs.
-*ul* – "them" as object of action in transitive verbal forms / -*lla*, -*l* – "them" as object of action in transitive verbal forms.
-*ûk* – "completely" as a morpheme in a verbal form / -*ok* – formant with a meaning "fully, truthfully, really" in a verbal form.[82]

To this we might now add -*hai*, which is, in both the Black Speech and Hurrian, a formant pertaining to a person in the plural; 'the ending -*hi/he* appears in ethnic terms like *Hurru-he* [Hurrians], *Kuššu-hai* [Kassites], and very likely *Cardu-chi* [Kurds]'.[83] We know that Tolkien had read a good deal about Mesopotamia, and Nemirovsky is surely correct when he argues that the author could hardly have been unaware of (or uninterested in) the scholarly controversies surrounding Hurrian or of E. A. Speiser's landmark publications, *Mesopotamian Origins* (1930), *Introduction to Hurrian* (1940) and *Hurrians and Subarians* (1948). With striking parallels to the morphology and syntactical structures of the Black Speech, a mysterious history and the topical interest it possessed in the interwar period, Hurrian appears to be the most likely prototype for the language of the Orcs and the Dark Lord.

Nemirovsky's argument is compelling but rather raises the question: what did Tolkien have against Hurrian? Here I suggest Speiser's curious means of referring to the Hurrian-Urartian languages might constitute an important clue. Observing that 'Sem and Ham have been in the harness for a long time', Speiser remarks that 'the third brother might also be of service', proposing the Biblical Japhet be used as a convenient 'catch-all' for languages of the ancient Near East 'which are not placed already with the Hamites, Semites, Indo-Europeans, or with any other well defined groups such as the Altaic, Dravidian, and the like'. Though Speiser could not be clearer when he insists that 'The name need not be committed geographically, linguistically, or in any other way', explaining that 'its sense would be primarily negative', his use of this term was, he himself complains, perceived to be an endorsement of the hugely controversial theory from which it is derived: the "Japhetic theory" of the Georgian philologist Nikolai Yakovlevich Marr. Emerging from research into *Der japhetitsche Kaukasus und das dritte ethnische Element im Bildungsprozess der mittelländ-ischen Kultur* (1923), Marr's New Linguistic Doctrine (*novoe uchenie o yazyke*) was at once a culmination of and a profound threat to the philology that had, to this point, underpinned the creation of languages in Tolkien's work. Ideologically consistent with Marxist philosophy, the New Linguistic Doctrine had attained the status of an orthodoxy in the USSR prior to 1950. And so the Hurrian component identified in Black Speech is not without meaning but involves Tolkien in what must surely be the most politically fraught episode in the history of linguistics. A hotly contested topic in the 1940s, Hurrian, as the first prehistoric "Japhetic" language, had the power to make or break the new linguistic orthodoxy emerging in the USSR.

Marr had begun his career in Tsarist Russia as a traditional philologist. Working with the comparative historical method, he had tried to establish that Caucasian languages were a family descending from a single prototype, like Indo-European or Semitic: his original Japhetic theory. But, in doing so, Marr had discovered, like a great many linguists since, that the vast majority of languages simply will not conform to the branching-tree pattern which works so perfectly with Indo-European. And so, in terminology coloured by the Revolution, Marr had rejected Western philology for its Eurocentricism. 'Indo-European linguistics, exploiting the *procédés* of natural science, adapted the philosophy of a society based on religion and substituted linguistic for the religious divisions of mankind, isolated the circle of Indo-European languages, and devoted itself to the exclusive and separate study of the Indo-European peoples', wrote Marr. 'As an ethnological science interested in linguistic origins Western philology "expired" in 1880 and became merely a workshop for the elaboration of the comparative historical method.'[84] Instead, Marr proposed a new version of his Japhetic theory informed by the Hegelian-Marxist dialectic, to present a militant opposition to the "Aryan" linguistic dogma of peninsular Europe: Japhetic languages spoken by the third ethnic element in the Near East are thought no longer to be based (as Marr had first suggested) on a uniform archetype (*protoglossa*), but to be derived from the transformation of linguistic types as the result of miscegenation.[85] That is to say, Japhetic is not a language family but a linguistic area, in which the process of diffusion described by Hugo Schuchardt and Johannes Schmidt in their wave model of language had produced affinities without homogeneity over the course of a period of thousands of years. And in a move that anticipates by some seventy years certain key ideas in the punctuated-equilibrium model of R. M. W. Dixon in *The Rise and Fall of Languages* (1997), Marr speculates that this situation (*equilibrium*) had been disrupted (*punctuated*) by world-historical events – such as the development of metallurgy, for instance, to which Marr attributed the rapid formulation and fracturing of the Indo-European (or in his terminology, *Prometheid*) peoples and languages.[86] Drawing on his research into Caucasian languages, Marr concluded that the Indo-European invaders had imposed (with varying degrees of success) ruling-class languages on a Japhetic substratum, but that the language-building process (*glossogeny*) which produced the initial Japhetic equilibrium was again proceeding through the same three stages as before: 'The amorphous-synthetic [i.e. isolative] period was the period of the herd, the agglutinative – of the clan (*rod*), [and] the flexional of the individual (*litso*).'[87] As in *The New Science* (1725) of Giambattista Vico, from which Marr's theory would seem to have been derived, the history of class conflict and language proceed together, in one dialectical process, through three stages; (1) the age of gods, (2) the age of heroes and (3) the age of men, and, corresponding to these, (1) a hieroglyphic language, using holy signs, (2) a symbolic language, using heroic signs and (3) an epistolary language, using signs agreed on by the people.[88] The process seems to be cyclical. So, after the isolating phase initiated by Indo-European imperialisms, the world must expect the resulting pidgins to coalesce in a new world language: an idea inspired by Vico's *ricorso*, which curiously anticipates Dixon's "language-clock". 'As languages change over time, they tend – very roughly – to move round in a typological circle: isolating to agglutinating, to fusional, back to isolating, and so on.'[89] The result is that we must expect the 'future unified world language' predicted by Japhetic theory to resemble Georgian rather more than any current international language in so far as it must be agglutinative[90] – an idea that would have chimed neatly with enthusiasm in the early USSR (subsequently crushed by Stalin) for Esperanto.[91] That Tolkien was aware of Marr's work, albeit through intermediaries, is evident in his attaching his adverbial case-marking *-at* to his verbal-noun (or *Masdar*, a fusion of a verb with its direct object) in order to indicate futurity or purpose. A grammatical category unique to Old Georgian and Abkhaz, the adverbial case *-ad* had been identified by Marr in his *Grammar of the Old Georgian* (1925), a book that remains a go-to authority on this subject.[92] Incidentally, Georgian may also be the source for the suffix *-ishi* (for which there seems to be no parallel in Hurrian), the postposition *-ši* = "in, into". Perhaps Tolkien was drawing upon the extraordinary research resources available at Oxford, which held the most important archive pertaining to Kartvelian studies outside Georgia (the Wardrop Collection). He could not, in any case, have failed to miss the controversy relating to Marr's Japhetic theory as this unfolded in the language journals of the period. Following F. Braun's translation of Marr (1923), a brief appraisal in W. E. D. Allen's *History of the Georgian People* (1932), and W. K. Matthews' sympathetic overview in *The Slavonic and East European Review* (1948), the New Linguistics received a flurry of attention in scholarly articles by Laurat (1951), Miller (1951), Ellis and Davies (1951), Thomas (1957) and Porzig (1957). In this new context Tolkien's Black Speech can be shown to constitute part of a belated Western response to a theory that embodied the linguistic energy of the Transcaucasus; an expression of the same revolutionary fervour that inspired Velimir Khlebnikov and Aleksei Kruchenykh to write their Futurist opera *Victory Over the Sun* (1913) in what they termed *Zaum*: 'a universal poetic language, born organically, and not artificially, like Esperanto'.[93] Together with the Bellysbabble Joyce developed for *Finnegans Wake* (with its agglutinating recombinations as language passes through 'our wholemole millwheeling vicociclometer') or the Newspeak invented for *1984* by George Orwell (with its agglutinating prefixes), Tolkien's Black Speech emerges as an imaginative engagement with what was then an issue of burning topicality: a unique moment in the history of linguistics, when a theory relating to obscure languages assumed a pivotal position in an epochal war of competing ideologies.[94] Might this be the reason that Tolkien suggests those desiring an 'accurate transcription' of the Black Speech look to the avant-garde? 'I have tried to play fair linguistically', Tolkien explains, 'and it is meant to have a meaning not be a mere casual group of nasty noises, though an accurate transcription would even nowadays only be printable in the higher and artistically more advanced form of literature'. And he adds that: 'According to my taste such things are best left to Orcs, ancient and modern'.[95]

Forgotten now, this moment in the history of Russian linguistics was fleeting, as first futurism, then Esperanto, and finally Marrism attracted the suspicion and hostility of the Stalinist dictatorship. That English literature's next great fictional language, the Nadsat or teen-speak invented by Anthony Burgess for *A Clockwork Orange* (1962), should consist for the most part of words with Slavic roots, is not meaningless but accurately reflects the sea-change in Soviet linguistic policy that followed Josef Stalin's denunciation of Marrist theory in his paper 'Marxism and Lingustics' (1950). And linguists in the West (furious with Marr for undermining the status of their subject as a science) would repeat the calumnies levelled at Marrist theory by Stalin, and by the new wave of Georgian linguists led by Arnold Čikobava. In closing this section, I want to speculate that this very opprobrium might well have prompted a more sympathetic engagement on Tolkien's part towards Japhetic theory, and that the latter might even have had a transformative impact upon his later ideas concerning language. I have said that there is some connection between the races of Men and Orcs in the later work, and I believe it is significant that when Tolkien finally began to develop "Mannish" languages, in the years immediately following his experiment with the Black Speech, it was to mixed languages and creoles that he turned for inspiration. In *The Notion Club Papers* (1945), his fictional philologist Alwin Arundel Lowdham reports that Adûnaic, the language of Atlantis, is derived partly from the Elvish Sindarin and partly from the Dwarvish Khuzdul: 'The majority of the word-bases of Adûnaic were *triconsonantal* ... and in this point Adûnaic shows affinity with Khazadian [Dwarvish] rather than Nimrian [Elvish]', writes Lowdham, 'but it is precisely at the points where Adûnaic most differs from Avallonian that it approaches nearest to Khazadian'.[96] The contrast with Tolkien's early invented languages, Quenya and Sindarin, or Dwarvish Khuzdul, could not be more pronounced. While the first two (based respectively on Finnish and Welsh) possess a common prototype and exhibit in pristine fashion sound changes and branching-tree patterns predicted by the comparative historical method, Adûnaic is messy, contingent; too complex for the clean schemata of traditional Indo-European philology, this is the product not of a single family but of miscegenation in a linguistic area. The speech of Men in Atlantis is the creation of Time – where the language of the Elves is conceived to be Art. If this remarkable transition in Tolkien's development of constructed languages has attracted little attention, it might be because Adûnaic is the least visible of the languages spoken in Middle-Earth, having been "translated" (again, retroactively) out of existence. In a draft note, Tolkien explains that:

> it is assumed that the Common Speech of the time was English, and that if any language of Men appears which is related to the Common Speech, though not the same, it will be represented by languages of our world that are related to English: as for example the archaic language of Rohan is represented by ancient English, or the related tongues of the far North (as in Dale) by names of a Norse character.[97]

The word translated as *Shire* is thus the Adûnaic *Sūza-t*.[98] Though ideas relating to mixed language and linguistic areas have their inception in earlier work by Schmidt and Schuchardt, it is to Marr's school that these owed whatever topicality they had at that particular moment in time. It is thus fascinating to see Tolkien engaging with such ideas in his last experiment with invented languages, and to speculate that he might have followed 'Japhetic horses … further to perished Atlantis, to the deep-lying foundation of Mediterranean culture'.[99]

The shame totem

In much of the writing that has engaged seriously with Macfarlane's hobgoblin, its rustic character is chiefly emphasised, as scholars seek to root *Das Gespenst des Kommunismus* within the vigorous earth of the peasant imaginary. David Black notes that, in translating the *Communist Manifesto*, Macfarlane tries to give *Ein Gespenst* a double meaning: 'It is not just the ghostly apparition that haunts the castles of Shakespeare's *Macbeth* and *Hamlet*, foretelling doom and retribution for the incumbent. It is also the scary sprite that country folks tell their children lurks in the woods, in order to discourage them from wandering off on their own.'[100] Here Black is building upon Peter Linebaugh's essay on 'Karl Marx, the Theft of Wood, and Working Class Composition' (1976), which suggested that communism manifests itself in the *Manifesto* in the discourse of the agrarian commons. Following the etymology proposed by the *OED*, Linebaugh explains that *Hob* was the name of a country labourer, *goblin* a mischievous sprite, 'The substrate of the language [thus] revealing the imprint of the clouted shoon in the sixteenth century who fought to have all things in common'.[101] Taking all this into account, Manuel Yang concludes that hobgoblins 'belong to the historical imaginary ... of peasant communing', and suggests that Macfarlane's translation underscores the extent to which the spectre, though a 'philosophically mediated, reified form, divorced from the earthly spirits that directly haunt the peasant imagination,' has its 'Hegelian origin' in the 'commons' nonetheless, 'as Marx recognized'.[102] (In fact, the name of Shakespeare's hobgoblin *Puck*, from the Old English *pūca* "goblin"/"demon", shares a common root, in the distant past, with both *spectre* and *spook* – the Proto-Indo-European **(s)pāug(')-*, meaning "brilliance, spectre".) Citing Henderson and Cowan's *Scottish Fairy Belief* (2001), Yang sums up the prevailing view when he suggests that Macfarlane's hobgoblin might be the embodiment of demotic curses, 'customary laws that were intended to protect traditional popular rights from the cupidity of self-interest, the central tenet of bourgeois rationality, whose bloody acts of exorcism took the form of enclosures, privatisation, imperialism ... *Misfortune, illness, or even death might result from tampering with fairy property.*'[103] Thus, the hobgoblin (or Puck) in Shakespeare's *Midsummer Night's Dream* (1600) is said to be 'feared in field and town'.[104]

> Either I mistake your shape and making quite,
> Or else you are that shrewd and knavish sprite
> Call'd Robin Goodfellow: are not you he
> That frights the maidens of the villagery;
> Skim milk, and sometimes labour in the quern
> And bootless make the breathless housewife churn;
> And sometime make the drink to bear no barm;

Mislead night-wanderers, laughing at their harm?
Those that Hobgoblin call you and sweet Puck,
You do their work, and they shall have good luck.[105]

But the rustic quality of this famous passage should not mislead us. The plethora of possible names for this creature (perhaps euphemisms or taboo deformations) must indicate that this is no straightforward expression of a primal communism but rather the result of a long, complicated prehistory. *Hob* (and its variants *lob* and *cob*) are of uncertain origin, being fiercely disputed by early antiquarians (see, for instance, the entry on *hobgoblin* in Samuel Johnson's *Dictionary* of 1755). But the one etymology we can be sure about – that of *goblin* – is of undisputed Anglo-French extraction. (Normand: *gobelin*, apparently informed by Medieval Latin *cabalus* or *gobalus*, and this in turn by Ancient Greek κόβαλος [kobalos] "impudent rogue" or "arrant knave"). Far from revealing the imprint of the 'clouted shoon' who fought to have all things in common, the word *hobgoblin* is scarred by the boot-print of the heavily armed invader, referring not merely to a *spook* but rather to that spook as described from the outside by an insecure and foreign elite.

In a radio broadcast Louise Yeoman suggested that Helen Macfarlane might have had Jeremy Bentham's 'The Hobgoblin Argument, or, No Innovation', in his *Book of Fallacies* (1824), in mind when she translated the *Manifesto*: 'The hobgoblin, the eventual appearance of which is denounced by this argument', explains Bentham, 'is *anarchy* which tremendous spectre has for its forerunner *innovation*'.[106] Having traced the ways in which the goblins and Orcs in Tolkien's writing embody anxieties arising from innovation in fields as diverse as linguistics and industry, I want to suggest that fear is indeed the key way in which the wooden table possessed by capital (the commodity fetish) and the spectre of communism are connected to one another, as Derrida suggested. The fact is that the famous table described by Marx is *not* that to which it refers: a commodity fetish cannot be the possession *because* it is being described by Marx. Like 'the nursery-tale of the spectre of communism' (*den Märchen vom Gespenst*), the commodity fetish bears a not quite definable relation to its subject because it is that subject as seen from outside, by hostile eyes; it is conjured into being by the Enemy. The possessed table really ought in fact to be grouped within a special subset of that general category it is meant to represent: not a *commodity fetish* as that term is now generally understood, but a "shame totem", of the sort produced by the Tlingit people on the north-west coast of North America. These are (despite the misleading name) not totems, nor remotely connected to totems, but a form of satirical art that represents in order to render ridiculous the image of some power despised or feared. Witness the Lincoln Pole, produced in a spirit of resentment following United States interference. If money represents the commodity fetish in its most perfectly realised form, the North Korean super-dollar might be the equivalent shame totem: a product that circulates among all the other commodities brought into being by the primitive magic that Marx described but which is not the result of faith, of credit, but rather of pure negation; unfaithful, discrediting – a black propaganda or Dark Art.[107]

Termed by the French Situationists *détournement*, such techniques were integral to post-modernist attacks on the mid-century Modernism which represented (I argue) a synthesis of Freud and Marx, and of the two philosophical traditions from which these two rival theories had emerged. Before turning to this subject in the next chapter, I would like to point out that the sole example of Orkish art that we encounter in Tolkien's oeuvre is actually a spectacular *détournement* of a man-made statue – a stone colossus endowed with mysterious power that must recall, for all its relative sophistication, the primitive Púkel-men, from which Orcs had first been corrupted. 'The brief glow fell upon a huge sitting figure, still and solemn as the great stone kings of Argonath', writes Tolkien. 'Its head was gone, and in its place was set, in mockery, a round, rough-hewn stone, rudely painted, by savage hands, in the likeness of a grinning face with a large red eye in the midst of its forehead.' Then a startling detail: 'Upon its knees and mighty chair, and all about the pedestal, were idle scrawls mixed with the foul symbols that the maggot-folk of Mordor used' – a goblin alphabet like that which Tolkien had first envisaged in *Father Christmas Letters* (1920–1943): a cipher of tiny black figures that could equally have been inspired by a wartime signalling handbook or by the images on a Sami shaman's drum – 'strange marks, signs and scribbles, some of which have a nasty look, and (I am sure) have something to do with black magic'.[108]

Notes

1 Karl Marx and Friedrich Engels, 'Manifesto of the German Communist Party', *Red Republican*, 9, 16, 23 and 30 November 1850, ed. David Black, trans. Helen Macfarlane (London: Unkant, 2014), 119.
2 Marx, Letter to Engels, 23 February 1851, *Marx and Engels Collected Works*, Vol. 38 (London: Lawrence and Wishart, 1982), 291.
3 Jacques Derrida, *Specters of Marx: The State of the Debt, the Work of Mourning, and the New International*, trans. Peggy Kamuf (London: Routledge Classics, 2006), 5.
4 *Ibid.*, 157.
5 *Ibid.*, 6.
6 *Ibid.*, 158.
7 *Ibid.*, 158.
8 *Ibid.*, 191–193.
9 See Marx and Engels, 'Manifesto', Black and Macfarlane, *Red Republican*, 124.
10 J. R. R. Tolkien, Letter 203: To Herbert Schiro, 17 November 1957, *The Letters of J. R. R. Tolkien*, ed. Humphrey Carpenter (London: HarperCollins, 2006), 262.
11 Humphrey Carpenter, *J. R. R. Tolkien: A Biography* (Boston: Houghton Mifflin Harcourt, 2000), 193.
12 Tolkien, Letter 83: To Christopher Tolkien, 6 October 1944; *Letters*, 96.
13 Tolkien, Letter 229: To Allen & Unwin; 24 January 1961; *Letters*, 307.
14 J. R. R. Tolkien, 'Foreword to the Second Edition' (1966), *The Lord of the Rings* (London: HarperCollins, 1995), xvi–xvii.
15 Tolkien, Letter 144: To Naomi Mitchison, 25 April 1954; *Letters*, 178.
16 Sir Walter Scott, *Letters on Demonology and Witchcraft* (London: John Murray, 1830), 121.
17 George MacDonald, *The Princess and the Goblin* (Edinburgh: Strahan and Co., 1872), 2.
18 *Ibid.*, 2.
19 *Ibid.*, 2.
20 Christina Rossetti, *Goblin Market and Other Poems* (London: Macmillan, 1862).
21 *Ibid.*
22 J. R. R. Tolkien, *The Hobbit* (London: Unwin Hyman: London, 1989), 69.
23 *Ibid.*, 69.
24 *Ibid.*, 69.
25 Tolkien, *LOTR*, 445.

26 Tolkien, Letter 193: To Terence Tiller, 2 November 1956; *Letters*, 253.
27 A similar point might be made about the attempt to read Tolkien's Orcs through the prism of race, most notably in Dimitra Fimi's *Tolkien, Race and Cultural History* (2008). The decisive nature of the break with the Victorian "goblin tradition" that Tolkien is drawing upon in *The Hobbit* and *The Fellowship of the Ring* is perhaps nowhere clearer than in the following (deeply unpleasant) passage from a letter written in the late fifties, in which Tolkien rejects a cover-design produced by an artist who had (it would seem) taken inspiration from Arthur Rackham's famous illustrations to Christina Rossetti's *Goblin Market*. 'Why does Z put beaks and feathers on Orcs!?' he asks. 'The Orcs are definitely stated to be corruptions of the "human" form seen in Elves and Men. They are (or were) squat, broad, flat-nosed, sallow-skinned, with wide mouths and slant eyes: in fact degraded and repulsive versions of the (to Europeans) least lovely Mongol-types' (Tolkien 1958; 270). This would appear to be pretty clear-cut evidence that Tolkien had succumbed to the "scientific" racism that characterised the era in which he was writing, in no way mitigated by his half-hearted appeal to cultural relativism. But given Tolkien's interests, it is probable that this later concept of the Orcs had its inception in his reading of Jordanes's description of the Huns in *De origine actibusque Getarum*, where the Huns are described as 'a stunted, foul and puny tribe, scarcely human,' with 'no language save one which bore but slight resemblance to human speech,' together with 'a sort of shapeless lump, not a head, with pin-holes rather than eyes', and with faces 'furrowed by the sword' so that 'they grow old beardless' (Jordanes XXIV: 127-9). The peculiar form of the head remarked upon here is thought to be have been produced by artificial skull-deformation, a process whereby malleable skull-bones of newborn infants are compressed and sculpted into shapes rarely found in nature by wooden boards. Together with the facial scarification, this physical characteristic is the result of a cultural practice rather than a racial characteristic, extreme forms of body-modification that probably retain their power to shock those unfamiliar with such procedures even today. This is not to say that race, as we currently understand the term, does not play a part in Tolkien's work, but merely to observe that, as with class, the relationship is far from being as straightforward as many assume.
28 Tolkien, Letter 26: To Stanley Unwin, 4 March 1938; *Letters*, 34.
29 Friedrich Engels, *The Condition of the Working Class in England* (1845), ed. Victor Kiernan and Tristram Hunt (London: Penguin, 2009), 245.

30 *Ibid.*, 211.
31 *Ibid.*, 211.
32 *Ibid.*, 245.
33 Sydney Webb, *Socialism in England* (Harmondsworth: Penguin, 1974), 116–117.
34 *Ibid.*, 116–117.
35 Tolkien, *LOTR*, 230–231.
36 Tolkien, Letter 144: To Naomi Mitchison, 25 April 1954; *Letters*, 178.
37 J. R. R. Tolkien, 'Myths Transformed' (c. 1958), *Morgoth's Ring*, ed. Christopher Tolkien (London: HarperCollins, 2002), 421.
38 J. R. R. Tolkien, 'The Drúedain', *Unfinished Tales*, ed. Christopher Tolkien (London: HarperCollins, 2010), 362.
39 *Ibid.*, 368.
40 *Ibid.*, 363.
41 *Ibid.*, 363.
42 *Ibid.*, 363.
43 *Ibid.*, 366.
44 'Your preference of goblins to orcs involves a large question and a matter of taste, and perhaps historical pedantry on my part. Personally I prefer Orcs (since these creatures are not "goblins", not even the goblins of George MacDonald, which they do to some extent resemble).' Tolkien, Letter 151: To Hugh Brogan, 18 September 1954; *Letters*, 185.
45 Christopher Tolkien: 'it may be noted incidentally that "orcs", rather than "goblins" becomes pervasive in this text'. In the original version of a chapter that appears in the second part of *The Fellowship of the Ring*: 'Gandalf says there are goblins – of very evil kind, larger than usual, real orcs'. In the final version at this point Gandalf says, "There are Orcs, very many of them. And some are large and evil: black Uruks of Mordor". See J. R. R. Tolkien, *The Treason of Isengard*, ed. Christopher Tolkien (London: HarperCollins, 2002), 199–200, 205.
46 'Orc is not an English word. It occurs in one or two places but it is usually translated goblin (or hobgoblin for the larger kinds). Orc is the hobbits' form of the name given at the time to these creatures, and it is not connected at all with our orc, ork, applied to sea-animals of dolphin-kind.' Tolkien, *The Hobbit*, 11.
47 Tolkien, *LOTR*, 1105.
48 Tolkien, Letter to Gene Wolfe, 7 November 1966. Reproduced by Douglas A. Henderson in J. R. R. Tolkien, *The Annotated Hobbit: Revised and Expanded Edition*, ed. Douglas A. Henderson (Boston: Houghton Mifflin Harcourt, 2002), 146–147.

49 Henning Anderson, Reconstructing Prehistorical Dialects: Initial Vowels in Slavic and Baltic, *PS E-SE, 7.25: Proto-Baltic ERŽ-IL-A-'Stallion'* (Berlin: Mouton de Gruyter, 1996), 141.
50 See Preben M. Sørenson, *The Unmanly Man: Concepts of Sexual Defamation in Early Northern Society* (Odense: Odense University Press, 1983), 17. Also, David F. Greenberg, *The Construction of Homosexuality* (Chicago: University of Chicago Press 1988); 249.
51 Tolkien, Letter 155: To Naomi Mitchison, c. 1954; *Letters*, 200.
52 *Ibid.*, 200.
53 Tolkien, *Unfinished Tales*, 370.
54 T. S. Eliot, '*Ulysses*, Order, and Myth' (1923), Frank Kermode (ed.), *Selected Prose* (London: Faber, 1975), 177.
55 Marx and Engels, 'Manifesto', Black and Macfarlane, *Red Republican*, 124.
56 Marx, 'Chapter 21: Philological Broodings', *Scorpion and Felix: A Humoristic Novel*, published in *Book of Verse* (1837).
57 'Samuel Hynes has noted that the war ushered in a censorious campaign against German intellectual and artistic influences. By chance, this affected every area of secular culture and learning that Tolkien expounded.' John Garth, *Tolkien and the Great War: The Threshold of Middle-Earth* (Boston: Houghton Mifflin Harcourt, 2003), 289.
58 See J. R. R. Tolkien, 'Philology: General Works', *The Year's Work in English Studies*, Vol. V (London: Oxford University Press, 1924): 26–65.
59 Tolkien, Letter 165: To Houghton Mifflin Co., 30 June 1955; *Letters*, 219.
60 J. R. R. Tolkien, *The Peoples of Middle-Earth*, ed. Christopher Tolkien (London: HarperCollins, 2002), 35.
61 Helge K. Fauskanger, 'Orkish and the Black Speech: a Base Language for Base Purposes', Available online at the Ardalambion website: http://folk.uib.no/hnohf/orkish.htm (accessed 7 December 2023).
62 Tolkien, *LOTR*, 248.
63 J. R. R. Tolkien, *The War of the Jewels*, ed. Christopher Tolkien (London: HarperCollins, 2002), 398.
64 J. R. R. Tolkien, 'The Lhammas', *The Lost Road and Other Writings*, ed. Christopher Tolkien (London: HarperCollins, 2002), 178.
65 Tolkien, *The Peoples of Middle-Earth*, 21.
66 Tolkien, *LOTR*, 1105.
67 *Ibid.*, 1105.
68 *Ibid.*, 1105.
69 Fauskanger, 'Orkish and the Black Speech'.
70 *Ibid.*
71 *Ibid.*

72 Tolkien, Letter 297: To 'Mr Rang', Draft, August 1967; *Letters*, 384–385.
73 *Ibid.*, 384–385.
74 *Ibid.*, 384–385.
75 *Ibid.*, 380.
76 Tolkien, Letter 144: To Naomi Mitchison, 25 April 1954; *Letters*, 175.
77 Tolkien, Letter 343: To Sterling Lanier, 21 November 1972; *Letters*, 422.
78 *Ibid.*, 422.
79 Ephraim Avigdor Speiser, 'Introduction to Hurrian', *The Annual of the American Schools of Oriental Research*, Vol. 20 (1940), 95.
80 Ephraim Avigdor Speiser, 'Studies in Hurrian Grammar', *Journal of the American Oriental Society*, Vol. 59, No. 3 (Sept 1939), 319.
81 Nemirovsky, Letter to Fauskanger, available at the Ardalambion website: https://folk.uib.no/hnohf/orkish.htm (accessed 7 December 2023).
82 *Ibid.*
83 Ephraim Avigdor Speiser, *Mesopotamian Origins: The Basic Population of the Near East* (Philadelphia: University of Pennsylvania Press, 1930), 141.
84 W. K. Matthews, 'The Japhetic Theory', *The Slavic and East European Review*, Vol. 27, No. 68 (1948), 180.
85 *Ibid.*, 180.
86 *Ibid.*, 185.
87 *Ibid.*, 180.
88 Giambattista Vico, *The New Science* (1744), trans. David Marsh (London: Penguin, 2013), 44.
89 R. M. W. Dixon, *The Rise and Fall of Languages* (Cambridge: Cambridge University Press, 1997), 42.
90 Nikolai Yakovlevich Marr, 'Predislovie k Jafetičeskomu Sborniku, t. V' (1927), *Izbrannye raboty, Tom. 1: Ètapy razvitija jafetičeskoj teorija* (Leningrad: Izdat: GAIMK, 1933).
91 See N. Stepanov, 'Esperanto kaj Esperanto-Movado en Sovetunio' ('Esperanto and the Esperanto Movement in the Soviet Union'), in *Esperanto USA*, 4 (1991).
92 See, for instance, Brian G. Hewitt, *Typology of Subordination in Georgian and Abkhaz* (Berlin: De Gruyter Mouton, 1987).
93 Aleksei Kruchenykh, 'Declaration of Transrational Language', Anna Lawton and Herbert Eagle (trans.), *Words in Revolution: Russian Futurist Manifestoes 1912–1928* (Washington, DC: New Academia Publishing, 2005), 182.
94 James Joyce, *Finnegans Wake* (London: Faber and Faber, 1939), 614.

95 J. R. R. Tolkien, 'Words, Phrases and Passages in Various Tongues in *The Lord of the Rings*', Christopher Gilson (ed.), *Parma Eldalemberon*, 17 (Los Angeles: Mythopoetic Society, 2007), 11–12.
96 J. R. R. Tolkien, 'The Notion Club Papers: Lowdham's Report on the Adunaic Language', *Sauron Defeated*, ed. Christopher Tolkien (London: HarperCollins, 2002), 414–415.
97 Tolkien, *The Peoples of Middle Earth*, 45.
98 *Ibid.*, 45.
99 Marr, 'Predislovie k Jafetičeskomu Sborniku, t. V'. Trans. Kevin Tuite, 'The Rise and Fall and Revival of the Ibero-Caucasian Hypothesis', *Historiographia Linguistica*, Vol. 35, No. 1 (2007), 16.
100 David Black, *Helen Macfarlane: A Feminist, Revolutionary Journalist and Philosopher in Mid-19th Century England* (Lanham, MD: Lexington Books, 2004), 94.
101 Peter Linebaugh, 'Karl Marx, the Theft of Wood, and Working Class Composition', *Crime and Social Justice*, Vol. 6 (Autumn–Winter 1976).
102 Manuel Yang, Yoshimoto Taka'aki: Communal Illusion, and the Japanese New Left (Toledo: University of Toledo, 2005), xxiii.
103 *Ibid.*, xxiii.
104 Shakespeare, *A Midsummer Night's Dream*, Act III, Scene 2.
105 *Ibid.*, Act II, Scene 1.
106 Black, *Helen Macfarlane*, xxiii–xxiv.
107 Although what is said here concerning the "commodity fetish" might equally be extended to the concept of the "fetish" itself. As William Pietz has shown in his essay on the 'Problem of the Fetish', the colonial history of that concept indicates that it was elaborated to demonise the supposedly arbitrary attachment of West Africans to material objects. He writes that 'The fetish [originated] in conjunction with the emergent articulation of the ideology of the commodity form that defined itself within and against the social values and religious ideologies of two radically different types of non-capitalist society, as they encountered each other in an ongoing cross-cultural situation.' I believe the findings of this essay must support those of Pietz: 'a study of the history of the idea of the fetish may be guided by identifying those themes: that persist throughout the various discourses and disciplines that have appropriated the term.' William Pietz, 'The Problem of the Fetish', *RES: Anthropology and Aesthetics*, Vol. 9 (Spring 1985), 5–17.
108 J. R. R. Tolkien, *Letters from Father Christmas*, ed. Baillie Tolkien (London: HarperCollins, 2015), 86.

5

Pandora's box: The insidious appeal of the Brutalist dystopia

Post-mortem

An offer with an open hand. The fingers and thumb are five towers. 'The massive scale of the glass and concrete architecture, and its striking position on a bend in the river, sharply separated the development project from the run-down areas around it, decaying nineteenth-century terraced housing and empty factories already zoned for reclamation.'[1] Like the gleaming spaceship that was Lubetkin's Health Centre in Clerkenwell, J. G. Ballard suggests that this fictional 'development project', in his novel *High-Rise* (1975),

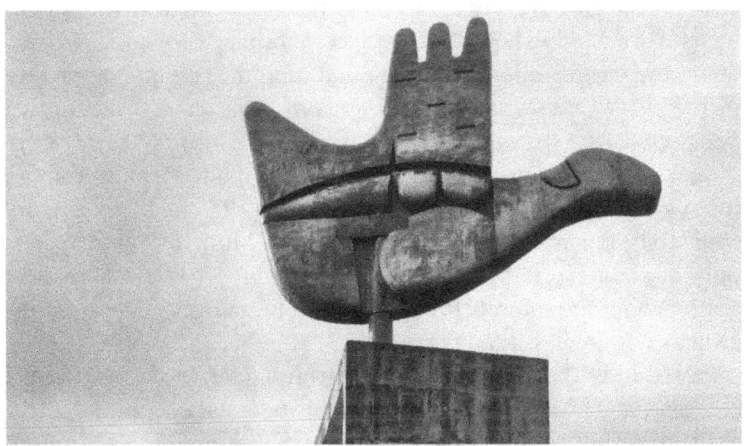

Figure 5.1 Le Corbusier's Open Hand. (From Shaun Fynn, *Chandigarh Revealed: Le Corbusier's City Today*, Hudson, NY: Princeton Architectural Press/Mapin Publishing, 2017.)

might almost belong to another world entirely, a different time and space. 'The high-rises seemed almost to challenge the sun itself – Anthony Royal and the architects who had designed the complex could not have foreseen the drama of confrontation each morning between these concrete slabs and the rising sun.'[2] Later, as he sits on his balcony eating the dog, Ballard's protagonist, Dr Robert Laing, reflects on the unusual events that had taken place within this huge apartment building over the previous three months. 'Now that everything had returned to normal, he was surprised that there had been no obvious beginning, no point beyond which their lives had moved into a clearly more sinister dimension.'[3] This macabre scene could serve as a satirical representation of the post-mortem that has been conducted on Late Modernism in the years since.

But this is a term that requires definition, as a *Late* Modernism that refers to the post-war years will probably seem rather *too* tardy to those readers accustomed to the familiar literary perspective on Modernism. Though no one can have failed to recognise the distinctive urban fabric that emerged in these years as anything but a manifestation of that movement (i.e. Brutalism, Le Corbusier's International Style), there remains a prevailing assumption that Modernism is a phenomenon that was at its height in the 1920s, with the great phase of experiment ending sometime between 1939 and 1945 – that is to say, the years that saw the deaths of W. B. Yeats, Ford Madox Ford, James Joyce, Virginia Woof and Gertrude Stein, the incarceration of Ezra Pound, and the resounding finality of the closing verses in T. S. Eliot's *Four Quartets* (1944). In this perspective, the writing of Samuel Beckett constitutes a last, lonely outlier of Modernism, or even the first *post*-modernism. Certainly, the suggestion that the period from 1950 to 1975 might eventually come to be regarded as a golden age of Late Modernist activity, not only in architecture but across the arts, must strike those readers approaching the subject through English literature or literary criticism as nothing less than perverse.

Yet this is the case: only in the third quarter of the twentieth century, 1950–1975, had Modernists at last begun to effect their profound transformation of the UK: in architecture, music, art, even literature, *this* is the era that witnessed the high-water mark of Modernist experiment, a moment when all the sketches produced in an inter-war period stymied by reactionary romantic nationalism came at last to fruition. This was the era of reconstruction in which Modernists such as Basil Spence, Ernö Goldfinger, Berthold Lubetkin, Hugh Casson, Leslie Martin, Richard Seifert, Frederick Gibberd and John Madin designed Coventry Cathedral, Trellick Tower, Bevin Court, Royal Festival Hall, Royal National Theatre, Centre Point, Liverpool Roman Catholic Cathedral and Birmingham Central Library. Elsewhere in the world, Le Corbusier, Mies van der Rohe and Oscar Niemeyer finally realised colossal projects such as the Unité d'Habitation in Marseilles, the Seagram Building and UN headquarters building, and cities at Chandigarh and Brasília. Moshe Safdie and Richard Buckminster Fuller were commissioned to develop the radical Habitat 67 and Biosphere at Expo Montreal. And perhaps the crowning achievements came towards the end of this era, during the 1970s, with the completion of the World Trade Center by Minoru Yamasaki, Stade Olympique by Roger Taillibert, the Beehive Parliament by Basil Spence and Sydney Opera House by Jørn Utzon. This belated triumph in architecture can, moreover, be seen to have had a ripple effect throughout the arts as patrons commissioned music, sculpture, painting, even theatre that would furnish the new spaces they were then bringing into being. Edgard Varese's *Poème électronique* played in Le Corbusier's Pavilion at the 1958 Brussels World Fair, and his experiments with tape loops and synthesised sound, together with those of John Cage and Steve Reich, was to inform popular music by Delia Derbyshire at the BBC Radiophonic Workshop, John Lennon and David Bowie. In New York, European emigrés like Marcel Duchamp and Salvador Dalí reinvigorated the international art scene; established Modernist sculptors Henry Moore and Barbara Hepworth enjoyed unprecedented popularity in this era; Jackson Pollock's "Drip Period" ran from 1947 to 1958; while Mark Rothko laboured on his murals for the restaurant in the Seagram Building from 1958 to 1960. Even literature received a fillip: platforms for theatrical experiment, together with major university and civic libraries and even a National Poetry Library in the Royal Festival Hall. This was the period that saw the publication of long poems and retrospective compilations that shored up the reputations of Modernist poets such as H. D., William Carlos Williams, Ezra Pound, Marianne Moore and Basil Bunting, and that saw a new generation including poets such as Charles Olson, Robert Creely, Denise Levertov, J. H.

Prynne, Tom Raworth and Denise Riley take up the baton. One might add rather more to this list were one to expand the field to include French and Latin American literature. But this perfunctory survey will serve at least to make the point.

Literary perspectives on Modernist periodicity are out of sync with the evidence, perhaps intentionally so: the result of a long series of polemical interventions that have repeatedly declared this intense phase of innovation over, to assert that our culture is *post-modernist*, precisely because that was not the case.[4] I omit here, for reasons of space, the role played by the British Movement poets, and A. Alvarez's 'negative feedback-loop', since these relate chiefly to the achievements of an earlier, more familiar "High" Modernism. Instead, I will focus on reactions to what is perhaps the most salient, and certainly the most hotly contested, product of the Late Modernist era: Brutalist architecture. As Frederic Jameson observed, in his landmark study *Post-Modernism or The Cultural Logic of Late Capitalism* (1991), discourse that we consider to be post-modernist can be seen to have had its inception in reactions against that particular mode of Modernist architecture. 'More decisively than in other arts or media, post-modernist positions in architecture have been inseparable from an implacable critique of architectural High Modernism and of Frank Lloyd Wright or the so-called international style (Le Corbusier, Mies, etc.).'[5] Only subsequently did theorists identify comparable shifts in art, literature, music, with the result that criticism has tended to occlude rather than clarify – confusing expressions of a post-modernist sensibility produced *before* the collapse of the mid-century Modernist gestalt and those produced *after*, thereby flattening out distinct phases in the movement towards post-modernity. The disappearance of Late Modernism as a distinct subject of inquiry is, I would suggest, in no small part a consequence of this post-modernist muddle. But if we follow Jameson, making the field of architectural criticism our baseline, we can readily discern the following four phases of post-modernist critique:

I. Late Modernist cultural criticism of the technological metropolis, exemplified by geographers Henri Lefebvre and Lewis Mumford, and by the Situationist International, written at a time when Late Modernism was at its height and (apparently) perfectly successful: the criticism being that such schemes were too *functional*, that form did, indeed, equal function, just as the architects had hoped; students, workers and other users are called on to resist the crushing functionalism of the space, to realise a space for play or leisure, for *Homo Ludens*.

II. "Post-"modernist manifestos, exemplified by Robert Venturi's *Learning from Las Vegas* (1972), which cited the Long Island Duck (1932) as evidence that Modernists are mistaken in believing that form *should* signify function, noting that a box with a billboard (embodying the post-structuralist separation of signifier and signified) might actually be *more* functional than something ostentatiously functionalist, in that it can be the more readily repurposed; *functionalism is not necessarily functional*.

III. Anti-Modernist interventions, emerging after the collapse of the economic consensus that had sustained Late Modernist activity, exemplified by HRH King Charles III's campaign against the architect Richard Roger's plan for an extension to the National Gallery ('a carbuncle on the face of a much-loved friend'), a commission that would, as a direct result, be given over to Venturi: form *does* equal function – and if the expression of that function is thought (by King Charles III) to be ugly, this aesthetic failure indicates that the building might be actively *dysfunctional*. Late Modernist architecture is now criticised for generating crime, squalor and graffiti: in a surprising twist, *functionalist form now equals malfunction*.

IV. Anti-anti-Modernist critical reactions that provide a refreshing counter-blast to the prevailing narrative, exemplified by Owen Hatherley, who suggests that if Brutalist buildings *are* dysfunctional this is because they were rendered so by decades of sabotage and neglect on the part of building contractors and politicians never truly committed to the Late Modernist project: the criticism here is that such buildings are an aesthetic expression (the appropriate form) of a function that society simply no longer supports – social justice – and that *functionalism would be, should be, could be, functional, if only this situation were remedied*.

Of the four perspectives, the Anti-Modernist will be the most familiar to general readers, since this has been for a great many years now by far the most prevalent in the public discourse concerning Brutalist buildings, but also perhaps the most unfamiliar, as it is never articulated fully, its logic open to scrutiny, in the way that it is here, where it might now appear untenable in its irrationality, its paranoia, its sheer perversity. And I want to suggest this perspective is worth examining, not merely because it has taken hold to the extent it has (though this would render any such investigation worthwhile), nor because it *is* so often permitted to go unexamined, but, rather, for precisely the reason that it *will not* stand scrutiny: the insane idea that Late Modernist buildings might be actively malign presences in the urban environment, incubators of the violence, vandalism and disorder that have periodically erupted in British cities since the mid-seventies. For this is precisely the conclusion that Ballard's psychotic physician Dr Robert Laing will eventually arrive at – gazing out from his balcony – while ruminating over a leg of hot dog:

> By its very efficiency, the high-rise took over the task of maintaining the social structure that supported them all. For the first time it removed the need to repress every kind of anti-social behaviour, and left them free to explore any deviant or wayward impulses ... Secure within the shell of the high-rise like passengers on board an automatically piloted airliner, they were free to behave in any way they wished, explore the darkest corners they could find. In many ways, the high-rise was a model of all that technology had done to make possible the expression of a truly 'free' psychopathology.[6]

Laing concludes that this is the 'ultimate goal of the high-rise'.[7] Far from being acts of rebellion against the oppressive functionalism of a Brutalist building, the expressions of mindless violence turn out to be part of a plan that the architect himself had not apprehended. 'Part of its appeal lay all too clearly in the fact that this was an environment built, not for man, but for man's absence.'[8] The building is not, in fact, dysfunctional at all but *perfectly functional*, and therein lies the peculiar horror of this story. 'Even the run-down nature of the high-rise was a model of the world into which the future was carrying them, a landscape beyond technology where everything was either derelict, or, more ambiguously, recombined in unexpected but more meaningful ways.'[9] In a twist on the haunted house story, we have a Brutalist building that is haunted not by the past but by a 'future that has already happened'.[10] Clearly, what we are looking at here is a manifestation of the *unheimlich*, and a variety of Promethean horror. Laing comes to feel that there is something in the feeling that the Brutalist building is a 'kind of huge animate presence, brooding over them and keeping a magisterial eye on the events taking place'.[11]

It would seem, then, that a significant portion of public discourse surrounding Brutalist buildings is motivated by *uncanny* sensations, and this would certainly account for the extraordinary ferocity and irrationality that has characterised the public debate, both *for* and *against* their demolition, with King Charles III and Owen Hatherley appearing to share, I would suggest, a near-superstitious faith in the power of these buildings for good or for evil. This chapter will attempt to make sense of this: speculating on underlying causes for the uncanny feelings that attach themselves to Late Modernism, then examining how its prevailing architectural aesthetic, and its paradigmatic economic model, might have served to activate this psychological complex. We will investigate 'an intriguing medley of geometrics – less a habitable architecture ... than the unconscious diagram of a mysterious psychic event'.[12]

The geometry of fear

The city is said to have resembled a cluster of electrical gadgets. 'There were polished metal domes that shone in the sunlight, all sorts of tall, square shaped buildings and what I described to myself as electric pylon masts and radar scanners dotted liberally around the domes and buildings.'[13] New to such sights, this visitor from 1960s London professes himself enchanted by the magnificence of the place: 'Whoever had designed it and whatever its purpose, there was an exact and beautiful symmetry about the construction and the lay-out.'[14] Struggling to describe a building that is merely a rod sticking upwards for about thirty feet, others that are square, box-like affairs, and several round ones as big as gasometers, the traveller, at length, explains:

> I call them buildings for want of a better description – but really the whole design was as if someone had commissioned Frank Lloyd Wright to build a city and then someone else had come along and pushed thousands and thousands of tons of ashy soil around it, leaving only roofs and other protuberances, then laid a metal floor over the soil and pressed downwards.[15]

But this Modernist city is neither Chandigarh nor Niemeyer's Brasília. This is Dalek City on Planet Skaro – and the quintessential expression, therefore, of public unease relating to the contemporary Modernist renewal of the UK.

For non-British readers I suppose I should explain, before proceeding any further, that the inhabitants of this city are the mutant survivors of a nuclear conflict that appear in the long-running BBC television-series *Doctor Who*. Persisting in mobile life-support units, powered like bumper cars at a fairground by an electrical charge run through the metal floors, Daleks are post-human squid-like creatures in a uniform metal shell like an upended cone, the base patterned with hemispheres and with three different rods on the front: these resembling nothing so much as a gearstick, an egg-whisk and plunger. In spite of their physical limitations (and apparently suffering the extinction of their species in their first story), the creatures have somehow contrived to transcend their original context. 'Daleks are the only great popular myth, endlessly reinvented and reinterpreted by other writers, to have been created specifically for television', observes Alwyn Turner, in a biography of their creator, the writer Terry Nation. 'Like any great myth, they have outlived and outgrown their creator, entering the popular consciousness to become instantly recognisable by name alone, even to those who have never knowingly watched *Doctor Who*.'[16] In addition to carving out a galactic empire within the series, the Daleks have featured in major motion pictures starring Peter Cushing, pop songs, comedy sketches, political speeches and merchandising. Long before George Lucas, Terry Nation and the BBC had discovered the astonishing profits to be made from spin-off products. 'The Dalekmania craze that swept Britain at the end of 1964 saw over a hundred thousand copies of a single toy sold that Christmas', observes Turner; 'although the fever inevitably abated, a decade later there were still over a hundred Dalek products on the market'. This peculiarly British obsession with Dalek-related merchandise never faded entirely, even in the wilderness years that followed cancellation of *Doctor Who* in 1989; and following a successful revival of the series by Russell T. Davies, spin-off merchandise (including die-cast toys, voice-changing helmets, inflatable Dalek suits) have repeatedly topped the list of "must-have" Christmas gifts in the UK.

Davies has professed himself baffled as to why Daleks should possess this enduring terrific appeal: 'It's a bit like asking "why is the dark scary?" I don't know. It just is.'[17] Unsurprisingly, the apparently insurmountable obstacle presented by stairs, and terrain generally, has been a source of much humour at the expense of these would-be conquerors of the universe since the late 1970s, and one senses the heroic effort required from recent screenwriters who have tried to explain away this perceived deficiency. What would appear to have been missed is that the terror these creatures provoke is so closely bound up with their inherent absurdity. A Dalek is terrifying, not *in spite* of the fact that it cannot climb stairs, but *because* it truly believes it should never have to do so, and is likely to act on this belief.[18] Like Le Corbusier, the Dalek refuses 'The Pack-Donkey's Way', preferring instead to impose its own order on the planet, 'flattening the hills and filling up the valleys', in order to achieve the state of *'nihilism'* that is, 'properly speaking', precisely what Le Corbusier thought the architect's job 'should be', in *The City of To-Morrow and Its Planning* (1929).[19] Like the great white shark, the Dalek is a predatory organism hyper-adapted to a specific environment, and it is never more terrifying than when encountered in its own element: the Modernist city. The enduring impact this species has had on the British imagination is in large part down to the unforgettable menace it possesses in that original context – the significance of which has been long overlooked.

In the novelisation produced by *Doctor Who* script editor David Whitaker (quoted at the beginning of this essay) the Dalek city is said to resemble a commission by Frank Lloyd Wright – and there might be something in this idea: a minute inspection of the model that appears momentarily in the series does seem to be drawing upon plans produced by that architect late in his career when he became preoccupied with the curving forms he had first developed for the Johnson Wax Building (1939). Thus, one building in the foreground resembles the distinctive shape of the Annunciation Greek Orthodox Church in Wauwatosa, Wisconsin (1956–1962) and the Golden Rondelle Pavilion at the New York World Fair (1964). But perhaps the most striking, and by far the most suggestive, similarities are to be found in Wright's widely publicised, but unrealised, plan for a cluster of spherical kiosks in a "grand bazaar" about an enormous central stupa in Greater Baghdad (1958). In each cityscape there is the same highly unusual latticed dome, within a network of elevated freeway, with what appears to be a tapering television antenna protruding from the top. Although the city on Skaro is clearly part of the wider phenomenon of Googie architecture (a strain of mid-century Modernism that sought to express, through sweeping curvilinear forms, the dynamism and glamour of the Space Age), this reference to the central element in Wright's Modernist proposal for Greater Baghdad serves to situate the Dalek city within the mainstream of the science fiction dystopia. As with the New Tower of Babel in Fritz Lang's *Metropolis* (1927), the storytellers are using architectural design as a shorthand to express contemporary anxieties about totalitarianism, through imagery deriving from much earlier, deeply embedded, Western fears and prejudices relating to the Orient. Here such anxieties acquire a contemporary, or even a prescient, edge – the rising wealth of Hashemite Iraq resulting directly from the fact that it was providing the petroleum that sustained the perpetual industrial growth required by Keynesian consumer economies. Living in bunkers deep underground, menaced by the threat of nuclear conflict, the Daleks are – like the entire post-war economic order – living on borrowed time.

Rolling at speed along the elevated freeways that loop about the towers of their metropolis (in vehicles reputedly cobbled together from parts mass-produced for the Morris Minor), the Daleks inhabit an urban space that is designed (like Le Corbusier's City for 3,000,000 or Oscar Niemeyer's Brasília) for a time when *walking* has been consigned to the past. In a revealing speculation on the psychological impetus behind his most successful creation, Nation remembered that:

> The one recurring dream I have is that I'm driving a car very quickly and the windscreen is a bit murky. The sun comes onto it and it becomes totally opaque. I'm still hurtling forward at incredible speed and there's nothing I can see or do and I can't stop the car.[20]

'Our present civilisation is a gigantic motor car moving along a one-way road at an ever-accelerating speed', insists cultural historian Lewis Mumford in his denunciation of post-war urbanism, *The City in History* (1961):

> Unfortunately as now constructed the car lacks both steering wheel and brakes, and the only form of control the driver exercises consists

in making the car go faster, through his fascination with the machine itself and his commitment to achieving the highest speed possible, he has quite forgotten the purpose of the journey.[21]

It would appear the Daleks owe their inception to the very metaphor that inspired J. G. Ballard to write *Atrocity Exhibition* (1970) and *Crash* (1973). If these monsters are, chiefly, stereotypical iterations of tropes derived from early totalitarian dystopias, their *automobilism* is very much of that moment, and it puts them into some interesting company.

According to Mumford, 'A large portion of the painting and sculpture of the past generation symbolically anticipates the catastrophic end products of this death-oriented culture'.[22] Mumford cites the archaic pinhead figures of Henry Moore but might equally have been thinking of that sculptor's helmet-head busts, or the odd menagerie that appeared in the British section at the XXVI Venice Biennale in 1952, the peculiar, spiky organisms created by sculptors Lynn Chadwick, William Turnbull, Reg Butler and Eduardo Paolozzi that the art critic Herbert Read immediately hailed as an iconography of despair and defiance: 'Here are images of flight, of ragged claws "scuttling across the floors of silent seas", of excoriated flesh, frustrated sex, the geometry of fear'.[23] Mumford suggests Late Modernist productions are reversions to the beginning of creative art detected by Sigmund Freud in the infant's bowel movement: 'Faced with an electronic monopoly of man's highest powers, the human can come back only at the most primitive level.'[24] Holding putrid biological matter in a jagged mechanical shell (an armature which has delighted generations of British children) and liable to sudden and explosive infantile temper tantrums, the Daleks surely constitute a popular expression of the energies animating this Late Modernist phase in the history of British art.'[25]

In Mumford's diatribe, the metropolis, in its final stage of development, becomes a collective contrivance for making this irrational system work; for giving those who are in reality its victims the illusion of power, wealth and felicity. 'But in actual fact their lives are constantly in peril, their wealth is tasteless and ephemeral, their leisure is sensationally monotonous, and their pathetic felicity is tainted by constant, well-justified anticipations of violence and sudden death.'[26] (These lines could equally well be applied to the mutant survivors on Skaro. In each case, the metropolitan denizen 'lives, not in the real world, but in a shadow world projected round him each moment by means of paper and celluloid and adroitly manipulated lights'[27] – literally so in the case of the Daleks, who live within the notoriously wobbly sets put together on a shoestring budget by the BBC – 'In short, a world of professional illusionists and their credulous victims.') 'In the end', declares Mumford, 'every aspect of life must be brought under control: controlled weather, controlled movement, controlled association, controlled production, controlled prices, controlled fantasy, controlled ideas.'[28] In fact, the Daleks are the first cyborgs to appear in fiction after the coining of that term four years previously by Manfred E. Clynes and Nathan S. Kline, and they come freighted with the now familiar moral perspective on the dehumanising effects of information technology initiated by Norbert Wiener in *Cybernetics* (1948).[29] It is not my intention to reiterate this moral discourse here; nor to repeat the key problems with its underlying assumptions set out in Donna Haraway's *Cyborg Manifesto* (1983). Instead, what I would like to do is to interrogate the aesthetic appeal that Mumford suggests the technological metropolis might possess for its credulous victims – the 'power, wealth and felicity' promised by 'professional illusionists'.[30]

> Motors in all directions, going at all speeds [wrote Le Corbusier, recalling the moment of inception for his New Architecture]. I was overwhelmed, an enthusiastic rapture filled me. Not the rapture of the shining coachwork under the gleaming lights, but the rapture of power. The simple and ingenuous pleasure of being in the centre of so much power, so much speed. We are a part of it. We are part of that race whose dawn is just awakening. We have confidence in this new society, which will in the end arrive at a magnificent expression of its power. We believe in it.[31]

Too many post-modernist philosophers of space would appear to have taken Le Corbusier at his word, when he assures his readers that his project 'is no dangerous futurism, a sort of literary dynamite flung violently at the spectator'.[32] Needless to say, this necessarily produces serious distortions in critical readings of J. G. Ballard in particular – when his writing is credited with *perversion* or a *reversion* (to the car crash that launched futurism) rather than an *extrapolation* of everything already there. I maintain that between the moral discourse of cyberneticians on one hand,

and the insurrectionary zeal of Situationists on the other, we are so disenchanted, so thoroughly convinced of the disempowering consequences of the Late Modernist city, that we are apt to forget its profound (and profoundly disturbing) psychological appeal. Britain's new national hospitals, motorways, airports, state comprehensives, nuclear weapons and provincial universities, all housed in their gleaming Brutalist shells, were a Promethean gift that promised to make universal those godlike powers acquired for humanity during the second industrial revolution:

> Motor power places gigantic forces at [man's] disposal, which, like his muscles, he can employ in any direction; thanks to ships and aircraft neither water nor air can hinder his movements; by means of spectacles he corrects defects in the lens of his own eye; by means of the telescope he sees into the far distance; and by means of the microscope he overcomes the limits of visibility set by the structure of his retina ... These things that, by his science and technology man has brought about on this earth, on which he first appeared as a feeble animal organism and on which each individual of his species must make its entry ('oh inch of nature!') as a helpless suckling – these things do not only sound like a fairy-tale, they are an actual fulfilment of every – or of almost every fairy-tale wish.[33]

But if one believes, as Freud does, that the gods were originally an embodiment of this frustrated infantile wish (and an example of "doubling" the self as a preservation against extinction), I believe we are a long way towards understanding the psychological issues that complicate perceptions of the Late Modernist city. 'For the "double" was originally an insurance against destruction to the ego, an "energetic denial of the power of death", as [Otto] Rank says; and probably the "immortal" soul was the first "double" of the body', explains Freud. 'Nowadays we no longer believe in them, we have surmounted such ways of thought; but we do not feel quite sure of our new set of beliefs, and the old ones still exist in us ready to seize upon any confirmation.'[34] But according to Freud, man *has* come very close indeed to the attainment of his infantile ideal; he has almost become a god himself: 'Man is, as it were, a prosthetic God', he writes. 'When he puts on all his auxillary organs he is truly magnificent; but those organs have not grown on to him and they still give him much trouble at times.'[35] I would suggest that we are now in a position to understand why man might be so very uneasy concerning his godlike prosthetics: 'Such ideas [concerning the omnipotence of thoughts] have sprung from the soil of unbounded self-love, from the primary narcissism which holds sway in the mind of the child as in that of primitive man; and when this stage has been left behind the double takes on a different aspect', concludes Freud. 'From having once been an assurance of immortality', our External Soul [or *Horcrux*, if one can forgive the inevitable reference here to J. K. Rowling] becomes the ghastly harbinger of death.'[36]

'This is what it means', writes poet Philip Larkin, contemplating the 'clean-sliced cliff' of the *Hull Royal Infirmary* (1963) – a Brutalist hospital designed by F. R. S. Yorke, Eugene Rosenberg and Cyril Mardell to embody the spirit of the National Health Service:

> a struggle to transcend
> The thought of dying, for unless its powers
> Outbuild cathedrals nothing contravenes
> The coming dark, though crowds each evening try
> With wasteful, weak, propitiatory flowers.[37]

Motivated by 'the same desire [that] spurred on the ancient Egyptians to the art of making of the dead into some lasting material', Late Modernist infrastructures might be said to effect the disintegration and distribution of the "natural" being among spectacular prosthetics; to realise a cybernetic organism, a new iteration of humanity, radically augmented by information technologies (poetry and art); the culmination, in fact, of that movement described by W. B. Yeats in his "Sailing to Byzantium":

> Once out of Nature I shall never take
> My bodily form of any natural thing
> But such a form as Grecian goldsmiths make
> Of hammered gold and gold enamelling[38]

And this, surely, is why Late Modernism has provoked that peculiar combination of fear and fascination we identified earlier. Like an ancient Egyptian translated into an art object (neither alive nor dead), and for precisely the same reasons, the achievements of Late Modernism are liable to provoke sensations that can only be characterised as *uncanny*.

Hence, the Daleks, which constitute in miniature form the Late Modernist infrastructures that they represent. In fact, we might go so far as to suggest that their status as *toys* has played no small part in the feelings that they have aroused over the decades: the reader might remember that Freud devotes no small part of his essay on *The Uncanny* to the impression made by children's dolls and automatons. At the start of this section we asked the question: why might Daleks be scary? Like Freud, we can conclude that the answer is that these toys embody not infantile *fears* but rather an infantile *wish*. Such an idea is supported in Terry Nation's own realisation that: 'Adults can see the Daleks as absolute mindless bureaucracy, and children can see them as nice, frightening, antiteddy bear figures'.[39] One can go further: watching Daleks on the television from behind a sofa, with a tiny die-cast Dalek gripped in their hands, such children could be said to threaten to efface the distinction between thought and reality, in a manner consistent with Freud's conception of the uncanny. 'Inside the Dalek is a small, vulnerable, helpless creature', reflects Terence Dicks (script editor), 'and I think for a kid the idea of getting inside a Dalek and then going down to school and blasting all the teachers, or blowing up the school bully, is immensely appealing.'[40]

I would like to close this section by adverting to the prevalence of demonic or superpowered children and adolescents in fiction of the post-war period. Although the *fear of progeny* is hardly a new literary trope, the sheer volume and extremity of imaginative material expressing this peculiar anxiety in the third quarter of the past century must indicate a cause specific to this particular era. The six-year-old Anthony Fremont in Jerome Dixby's short story 'It's a Good Life' (1953) and in the episode of that name in *The Twilight Zone* (1961), the super-children in Arthur C. Clarke's *Childhood's End* (1953), the worshippers of the Beast in Arthur Golding's *Lord of the Flies* (1954), the invaders in John Wyndham's *Midwich Cuckoos* (1957) and its film adaptation *Village of the Damned* (1960), the teenage gang in Anthony Burgess's novel *A Clockwork Orange* (1962) and Stanley Kubrick's film adaptation (1971), the devil child in Ira Levin's novel *Rosemary's Baby* (1967) and in the film adaptation by Roman Polanski (1968), Professor Charles Xavier's mutant schoolchildren in the long-running comic-book series *Uncanny X-Men* (1963–1970), the Star Child in Kubrick's *2001: A Space Odyssey* (1968), the twelve-year-old Regan McNeil in William Peter Blatty's novel *The Exorcist* (1971) and its film adaptation (1973), the 'Homo Superiors' that proliferate in David Bowie's music albums *The Rise and Fall of Ziggy Stardust and the Spiders from Mars* (1972) and *Diamond Dogs* (1974), the perpetually young utopians in John Boorman's *Zardoz* (1974) and Michael Anderson's *Logan's Run* (1976), the worshippers of He-Who-Walks-Between-the-Rows in Stephen King's short story 'Children of the Corn' (1977), Damien in Richard Donner's *The Omen* (1976), the chest-bursting foetus in Ridley Scott's *Alien* (1979), 'V'ger' in *Star Trek: The Motion Picture* (1979) – which conflates Kubrick's Star Child with the Monolith and the space-probe/computer HAL – and (a belated addition, adding its own distinctive twist), Salman Rushdie's *Midnight's Children* (1981), in which the creation of an independent India produces a generation of children endowed with superpowers. One might extend this list by including rather less-fantastical films and fiction, such as Nicholas Rey's *Rebel Without a Cause* (1955), Richard Brooks' *Blackboard Jungle* (1955), Colin MacInnes's *Absolute Beginners* (1958), James Clavell's *To Sir, With Love* (1967), etc., and conclude that such material reflects clearly the excitement and unease provoked by developments associated with the emergence of a new, clearly defined, post-war generation, the so-called Baby Boomers. In part, no doubt, this is correct. But given that the earliest predate any reasonable indication that the children born after the Second World War might initiate the cultural and political insurrection that swept the planet from the late 1950s on, we might decide that the fears and fascination expressed in the film and fiction above might owe rather less to the innate brilliance of the new youth movement than it does to those Late Modernist infrastructures within which, and against which, that generation defined itself. That a militarised Late Modernist state often features prominently in such fictions will not have escaped informed readers. Baby Boomers were *expected* to be the most privileged generation in the history of the world, to be endowed with Promethean gifts, to wield superpowers. With respect to the very real achievements of that generation, and their truly extraordinary economic and political opportunities, such prescience can only be a result of the uncanny effect considered above. The following section now develops this point further, demonstrating how Mumford's 'professional illusionists' propagated a conviction that the post-war generation could expect life to be an infantile wish fulfilled.

The house of the mad

For answers one must go to Marseilles. From here Modernist architects (Le Corbusier, Fernand Léger, Ernö Goldfinger, László Moholy-Nagy) recoiled, in 1933, to Athens on a sea-cruise – for the fourth meeting of the International Congress of Modern Architecture – to consider the future of the urban environment. And there, on a route east out of the city, one can encounter the result, like a stranded liner: l'Unité d'Habitation. A huge white concrete slab looming over a sprawling suburb, the high-rise is held apart from neighbouring houses, and the trees and thundering traffic on the boulevard, by a bristle of heavy-set piloti (a centipedal underbelly) that contrives to suggest a civilisation in flight; or else an impending Laputa, power descending from on high to judge the quick and the dead, a tablet of the law. Proceeding towards the great central wall that connects the main bulk of the building to the ground, mysterious designs appear imprinted upon this surface as shadows that twist in the sun, and the pale-grey mass of the monolith parts to discover a grid on hollow blocks of red, blue, yellow, as in a picture by Mondrian. In the cavity beneath, one enters the comfortable gloom of a lobby, pocked with seashells, as though raised from an ocean bed, shot through with primary colours, daylight filtered through glass brick. Ascending by lift, one encounters a third floor comprising a street-in-the-sky: a luxury restaurant, expensive shops that sell nothing but gewgaws, delicacies and coffee-table books (about architecture and Modernist art), the Hotel Le Corbusier, and around thirty or so businesses – all of them (without apparent exception) being either an architectural or psychiatric practice. The locals call this *la maison des fous* – and this is truly a place to go hungry or mad, to practice an ascetic self-reflexive contemplation. One comes to this building solely in order to reflect upon one's being in this building. And this is precisely what the architect had hoped to provide: 'One would like to think, collect oneself, meditate', remarked Le Corbusier in *The Modulor* (1951), a book produced to publicise the high-rise and its various innovations. The Unité was built as a space in which to reflect on the future, 'a possible awakening in this age of every conceivable ferocity'.[41] This 'great ship' is declared to be a 'convoy of day-to-day happiness', and the piloti are 'heroes in an adventure soon to happen in town-planning'), with the geometric purity and raw concrete surfaces of the Unit being reiterated across the globe, in projects that would constitute the planet's first international infrastructure.[42] If one is to understand Late Modernism, and the post-modernist reaction, one must return to the space of its inception, in order to decipher the mysterious signs that the architect left here as the key to understanding his Radiant City: a Monolith, coloured red and blue, with bronze numbers encrusted upon it (the 'Stele of the Measures'), and the Hieroglyph of a 'Modulor Man', encased in a square of red- and blue-coloured glass, and, keyed into the concrete *brut*, six men, set one on top of the other, next to two undulating, intersecting vectors. 'Three men of bronze filigree, one with arms upraised, the two others superimposed on each other, will proclaim the rule.'[43] Le Corbusier explains that the designs celebrate the 'prowess of the numbers' that generated the Unité. 'I asked the drawing section of the studio to draw up the nomenclature of all the measurements employed in the Marseilles building', he recalled. '*Fifteen* measurements had been enough.'[44] In fact, all the exterior planes, the areas in the interior, floors, ceilings, furniture and fittings are ruled by the systematic application of measures derived from a harmonic scale termed the *Modulor*, with the result that, 'all aspects, and therefore all sensations, are brought into harmony with each other'.[45]

The Modulor was the culmination of Le Corbusier's long campaign for the introduction of mass-produced, standardised components into the construction industry. 'We must strive towards the establishment of a standard in order to face the problem of perfection', wrote Le Corbusier in *La Ville Radieuse* (1927). 'Building should be the concern of heavy industry and the component parts of houses should be mass-produced.'[46] When such schemes were finally realised, twenty years later, Le Corbusier was shocked to discover that his input would not be required:

> The AFNOR [Association Française de Normalisation, the French standards organisation] had been set up under the Occupation as an aid to the reconstruction of the country; industrialists, engineers and architects had banded together to perform the necessary task of standardizing everything pertaining, in particular, to building. Our man was not invited to sit at that table.[47]

Understandably frustrated, Le Corbusier determined to set out his own ideas for a far more ambitious series of standardised

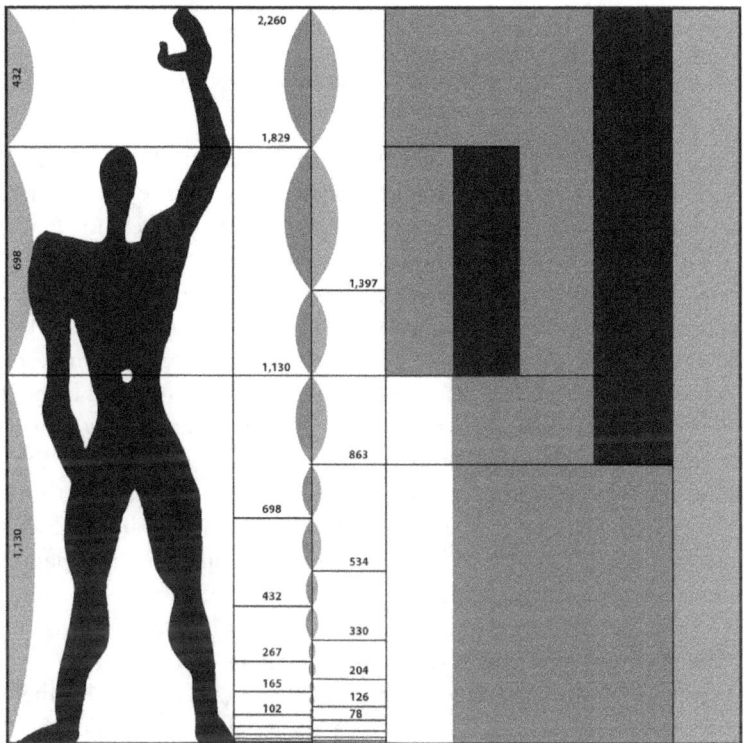

Figure 5.2 Le Corbusier's Modulor Man (1954). (From Le Corbusier's *The Modulor*, trans. Peter de Francia and Anna Bostock, London: Faber and Faber, 1954.)

measures that would restore harmony and proportion to architecture: 'On the day on which the first standardized construction series of AFNOR were published, our man decided to set down in concrete form his ideas on the subject of a harmonious measure to the human scale, universally applicable to architecture and mathematics.'[48] What Le Corbusier proposed, in fact, was no mere measurement system but a harmonic scale of such measures keyed to the human form, as the Golden Ratio corresponds to Vitruvian Man.

> Take a man-with-arm-upraised, 2.20 m. in height; put him inside two squares, 1.10 by 1.10 metres each, superimposed on each other; put a third square astride these first two squares. This third square should give you a solution. The place of the right angle should help

you to decide where to put this third square. With this grid for use on the building site, designed to fit the man placed within it, I am sure you will obtain a series of measures reconciling human stature (man-with-arm-upraised) and mathematics.[49]

The values of the Modulor initially determined by the body of a man 1.75 metres in height, the breakthrough is said to have come when a colleague observed that this was rather a *French* height: 'Have you never noticed that in English detective novels, the good-looking men, such as the policemen, are always six feet tall?'[50] Le Corbusier applied this standard – six feet = 182.88 cm – and found to his delight that the graduations of a new 'Modulor', based on a man six feet tall, translated themselves into round figures in feet and inches. Needless to say, this possessed considerable practical utility, opening up the possibility of a truly international standard measure that would bridge the gap separating the users of the metre from those of the foot and inch. 'The difference is so serious in its practical effects that it creates a wide gulf between the technicians and manufacturers who use the foot-and-inch system and those who work on the basis of the metre', explains Le Corbusier. 'The conversion of calculations from one system into the other is a paralysing and wasteful operation, so delicate that it makes strangers of the adherents of the two camps even more than the barrier of language.'[51] But the Modulor could convert automatically a measurement based on the decimal system (easy to use but devoid of proportion) into imperial units (based on a harmonic scale but fiendishly difficult to calculate with):

> In fact, it makes allies – not of the metre, which is nothing but a length of metal at the bottom of a well at the Pavilion du Breteuil near Paris – but of the decimal and the foot and inch, and liberates the foot-and-inch system, by a decimal process, from the necessity for complicated and stultifying juggling with numbers – addition, subtraction, multiplication and division.[52]

For Le Corbusier this achievement possessed more than merely practical appeal, reconciling the measures associated with the two great manifestations of what he termed 'the spirit of geometry'. 'The foot-and-inch is the incarnation of the great past of the human epic [and] The metre is the bringer of liberation proclaimed at the time of the French Revolution, and of the resources of the decimal system.'⁵³ The former is credited with the creation of Egyptian, Chaldean, Greek and Indian temples and European cathedrals: all are said to be eternal and enduring because they were built according to a measure linked to the human person. 'The names of these tools were: elbow (cubit), finger (digit), thumb (inch), foot, pace, and so forth', says Le Corbusier; 'they formed an integral part of the human body, and for that reason they were fit to serve as measures for the huts, the houses and the temples that had to be built'.⁵⁴ More than that: 'they were infinitely rich and subtle because they formed part of the mathematics of the human body, gracious, elegant and firm, the source of that harmony which moves us: beauty'.⁵⁵ But since the Parthenon, Indian temples and cathedrals, huts and houses, were all built in certain particular places – Greece, Asia, Europe and so forth – there was then no need for any unification of measures: 'As the Viking is taller than the Phoenician, so the Nordic foot and inch had no need to be adapted to the build of the Phoenician, or vice versa.'⁵⁶ With the onset of an international modernity, however, with factory-made goods circulating over the globe, the old measures were necessarily replaced by a standard measure that would possess universality. 'The French Revolution did away with the foot-and-inch system with all its slow and complicated processes', observed Le Corbusier. 'That being done ... The *savants* of the Convention adopted a concrete measure so devoid of personality and passion that it became an abstraction, a symbol: the meagre, forty-millionth part of the meridian of the earth.'⁵⁷ One and a half centuries later, the world is divided into two halves: the foot-and-inch camp and the metre camp.

> The foot-and-inch, steadfast in its attachment to the human body, but atrociously difficult to handle: the metre, indifferent to the stature of man, divisible into half metres and quarter metres, decimetres, centimetres, millimetres, any number of measures, but all indifferent to the stature of man, for there is no such thing as a one-metre or a two-metre man.⁵⁸

The first generates 'upright walls, perceptible surfaces between four walls, the right angle, hallmark of balance and stability', and is called by Le Corbusier 'spirit under the sign of the set-square'. The second produces 'brilliant diagrams, radiating in all directions, or folded in upon themselves in triangles or other polygons, source of spatial amplitude as of subjective and abstract symbols', and is called by Le Corbusier 'spirit under the sign of the triangle and the pentagon (star-shaped or convex), and their volumetric derivations (icosahedron and dodecahedron)' – that is to say, 'architecture under the sign of the triangle'.[59] He concludes:

> I return to this simple reasoning: on the one hand, things which are seen and measured [i.e. *strong objectivity of forms, under the intense Mediterranean sun*] and I think *architecture*; [and], on the other, things thrusting forward into unlimited and intangible worlds [i.e. *limitless subjectivity rising against a clouded sky*] and I think, *metaphysics*. Two consecutive phenomena: the one overtakes the other, and passes it, not, perhaps, without some danger.[60]

In reconciling the two measurement systems used by 'Masters of the Rule' and 'Masters of the Compasses', the Modulor would correct the 'dislocation and perversion of architecture' that began to take hold in the European Renaissance. 'Last summer', Le Corbusier recalled,

> as I was paying for my glass of Pernod at a garden cafe on the banks of the Marne, my eye lingered on the picture on the fifty-franc note held out to me by the waiter: an engraving by M. Leverrier, representing (no doubt) Mansart the architect, compasses in hand, in front of his masterpiece, the Paris observatory.[61]

And he wrote then in his notebook:

> The curse of architecture are the compasses: not those used by Copernicus, but the compasses of the Beaux Arts, indifferent to measures and dimensions, making no distinction between a metre and hundred metre and a kilometre, used in an operation which is abstract, without bones or flesh, without life, without blood. A simple progression, addition, alignment of equal values, offering precision without flavour.[62]

Le Corbusier had always refused to recognise the architecture of that period or the one which followed it: 'I felt at first that I did not agree, and for a long time I was unable to explain to myself why that was so.'[63] Now he concludes that humanist geometricians (with their plans devised with the compasses, on paper, star-shaped) were worlds removed from the basic premise of the problem: the eye's vision. 'Their system was erected outside the medium of visual perception, and those who contemplate their work today cannot, without that visual medium, grasp the subjective intentions with which they claimed to have filled their designs.'⁶⁴ For the built environment is experienced not from above but by the person on the ground:

> His eyes (of which he has two, and not ten or a hundred or a thousand) are placed in the front of his head, within his own face, looking forward; they cannot look sideways or backwards, and are thus incapable of appreciating the dazzling scene around them, with its combinations issuing from the philosopher's polyhedrons ... The human eye is not the eye of a fly, placed within the heart of a polyhedron: it is situated upon the body of a man, in twin position on either side of the nose, at an average height of 1.60m. above ground.⁶⁵

Architecture, Le Corbusier concluded, is *experienced* or *lived*, not as a synchronic phenomenon but as a successive one, 'made up of pictures adding themselves one to the other, following each other in time and space, like music'.⁶⁶ Standing beside those two billowing lines referring to imperial and metric units of length, the 'Modulor Man' is evidently intended to represent, in visionary and semi-mystical terms, Le Corbusier's synthesis of Anglo-Saxon engineering with continental architecture:

> Spark stolen from the flame
> the Gods nourished to
> make the world play ...
> Mathematics! ...
> Here is a fact: the fortunate
> miraculous meeting perhaps of one
> among several numbers has
> furnished men with this tool ...
> Its value resides
> in this: the human body
> has chosen number as its
> admissible vehicle.⁶⁷

Nature + Spirit = Experience. Le Corbusier's dialectical account of architectural space will no doubt sound curiously familiar to readers with even the most casual acquaintance with post-modernist cultural geography. In fact, Le Corbusier's Modulor theory bears more than a passing resemblance to the theoretical framework developed by Henri Lefebvre in his study on *The Production of Space* (1975): his spatial triad of *perceived, conceived* and *lived*.

The first of these categories is, first and foremost, a product of the individual body, resulting in those spatial practices that ensure continuity and cohesion. The second is the conceptual space of the scientist, town planner, engineer and a certain type of artist: *representations of space* which are produced by those who identify what is lived and perceived with what is conceived, and which rise from the order imposed by social relations, ideal and abstract, erasing the historical. And the third category is space as directly lived through images and symbols by its users and inhabitants, passively dominated spaces which the imagination seeks to change and appropriate: *representational spaces*.[68]

The parallel here with Le Corbusier's Modulor theory should be self-evident, and this will be shocking to readers immersed in postmodernist urban theory, precisely because Le Corbusier, and postwar Brutalist architecture, feature so prominently in such work, as an example of everything associated with the second phase in the dialectical process outlined above – termed *Abstract Space* by Lefebvre, *functional metropolis* by Situationist Guy Debord and *the Concept City* by Michel de Certeau. 'Le Corbusier was working towards a technicist, scientific and intellectualized representation of space [i.e. the conceived]', remarks Lefebvre: 'the homogeneity of an architectural ensemble conceived of as a "machine for living in", and as the appropriate habitat for a man-machine'.[69] Said to be the culmination of a variety of abstract thinking about space that began in the Renaissance with René Descartes, Le Corbusier is dismissed (with just enough justice to make the charge sting) as the purveyor of 'a moral discourse on straight lines, on right angles and straightness in general, combining a figurative appeal to nature (water, air, sunshine) with the worst kind of abstraction (plane geometry, modules, etc.)'.[70] The Lettrists and the Situationist International were even less forgiving: 'We will leave Monsieur Le Corbusier's style suitable for factories and hospitals, and no doubt eventually for prison', wrote Ivan Chtcheglov in his 'Formulary for a New Urbanism' (1953). 'Some sort of psychological repression dominates this individual – whose face is as ugly as his conceptions of the world – such that he wants to squash people under ignoble masses of reinforced concrete ... destroying the last remnants of joy. And of love, passion, freedom.'[71] Instead, Situationists would seek out fragments that survive from earlier phases in the history of the city, or – like Constant Nieuwenhuys – attempt to build a "drift city", changing from day to day, an anti-capitalist conception of urban space that depends upon a perpetually impermanent steel infrastructure moving over the ruins of the past, a space for play.[72] In the urban theories of Lefebvre, Debord and Michel De Certeau, the city of the engineer and town planner consistently emerges as a space enforcing order, uniformity and control – but which must (somehow?) be resisted or subverted. This is an apparent paradox often permitted to pass unremarked. For if the extent of the restrictions exerted by the cybernetic city on our personal liberties is such as to prevent meaningful political agency, how is such resistance possible? Indeed, how should one account for *any* activity not conforming to that which is apparently required?

Perhaps, in the words of the British poet Nicolas Spicer, 'No one is paranoid *enough*'.[73] Reaffirming in the very act of rejecting the theoretical framework that had informed the Brutalism of Paris X Nanterre, "practising" (to borrow a term from Lefebvre) Late Modernist architecture in a manner that (albeit surprising) is entirely consistent with the vision of the architect, the student activists who very nearly toppled the Fifth French Republic in May '68 must surely be regarded as that institution's most outstanding success. One is tempted to conclude that Baby Boomers were indeed empowered, or *superpowered*, by the Late Modernist infrastructures in which they were born, raised, educated. This in spite of the fact (or perhaps *because*) they would later attack them with such ferocity. An Oedipal assault – ungrateful recipients of Promethean gifts, promised to their generation by the architects of the postwar world.

In fact, the illusion of order, uniformity and control projected by Late Modernist infrastructures is surely an uncanny effect, produced by the encompassing, and seemingly immovable, theoretical frameworks for explaining reality that dominated intellectual life through the third quarter of the twentieth century, informing, in turn, both Modernist design practice and the first fumbling postmodernist critiques. For instance, the quite striking parallels established above are probably indicative of little beyond a shared taste for Hegelian dialectic (prevalent in the period we are examining, having acquired a new popularity and political impetus through the victories of revolutionary leader Mao Zedong and theoretical work by Frantz Fanon). But this serves only to underscore the extent to which one is hard put to talk of Late Modernist structures *without* employing the terminology and theoretical frameworks chosen by the architect. In the final section, I suggest that if Late Modernist structures might seem to anticipate everything that could reasonably be said about them, this is for the reason that (for some decades after the Second World War) there was no difference between ostensibly *post-modernist* theory and *Late Modernist* practice. (In fact, I would like to suggest that the term *post-modernism* be restricted, in future, to that body of theory and practice informed by the "linguistic turn" prevalent from the 1970s on, with its equivalent in the free-floating exchange rates that characterised neoliberal economics; an idea in keeping with a historically important critique of US-based L=A=N=G=U=A=G=E poetry by the British Late Modernist poet Jeremy Prynne.[74] The French urban theorists considered in this chapter would be regarded as *Late* Modernist, using this new terminology.) If the extraordinary consensus between post- and Late Modernism is often missed, I believe this may be down to the fact that literary critics insufficiently recognise the radical nature of the economic basis that sustained the creative and critical output of the immediate post-war period: the theory and policies of the Cambridge economist John Maynard Keynes.

Voodoo economics

Its author convicted as a nuisance by a grand jury in Middlesex in 1723, Bernard Mandeville's poem *The Fable of the Bees* stands out in the history of the moral sciences for its scandalous reputation. 'Only one man is recorded as having spoken a good word for it', observes the social-liberal economist John Maynard Keynes, 'namely Dr Johnson, who declared that it did not puzzle him, but "opened his eyes into real life very much".'[75] Mandeville's poem set forth 'the appalling plight of a prosperous community in which all the citizens suddenly take it into their heads to abandon luxurious living, and the State to cut down on armaments, in the interests of *Saving*'.[76]

> Now mind the glorious Hive, and see
> How Honesty and Trade agree:

> The Shew is gone, it thins apace;
> And looks with quite another Face,
> For 'twas not only they that went,
> By whom vast sums were yearly spent;
> By Multitudes that lived on them,
> Were daily forc'd to do the same.
> In vain to other Trades they'd fly;
> All were o'er-stocked accordingly.
> The price of Land and Houses falls;
> Mirac'lous Palaces whose Walls,
> Like those of Thebes, were rais'd by Play,
> Are to be let.[77]

In a note explaining the theoretical basis for the poem, Mandeville says that it is an 'error' to assume that a 'prudent economy', while the most certain method to increase an estate when practised by private families, will have the same effect upon a whole nation if pursued generally – that the English, for example, might be much richer than they are if they were as frugal as their neighbours. On the contrary, Mandeville concludes: 'The great art to make a nation happy, and what we call flourishing, consists in giving everybody an opportunity of being employed; which to compass, let a Government's first care be to promote as great a variety of Manufactures, Arts and Handicrafts as human wit can invent; and the second to encourage Agriculture and Fishery in all their branches, that the whole Earth may be forced to exert itself as well as Man.'[78]

> Bare Virtue can't make Nations live
> In Splendour. They that would revive
> A Golden Age, must be as free,
> For Acorns as for Honesty.[79]

'No wonder', remarks Keynes, 'that such wicked sentiments called down the opprobrium of two centuries of moralists and economists who felt much more virtuous in possession of their austere doctrine that no sound remedy was discoverable except in the utmost of thrift and economy, both by the individual and by the state.'[80] In fact, Mandeville's re-evaluation of 'virtue' and 'vice' had recognised that wealth is created by the 'Labour of the People', and can therefore be increased by public and private expenditure that support and expand such Labour. He thereby anticipated the key insight that underpins Keynes's *General Theory of Employment, Interest and Money* (1936) – and thus the economic basis of the post-war consensus, a period lasting until the mid-1970s that British historian Eric Hobsbawm would later designate a 'Golden Age of Capitalism'.[81] As Keynes would later, famously, explain the idea:

> If the Treasury were to fill old bottles with banknotes, bury them at suitable depths in disused coal-mines which are then filled up to the surface with town rubbish, and leave it to private enterprise on well-tried principles of laissez-faire to dig the notes up again (the right to do so being obtained, of course, by tendering for leases of the note-bearing territory), there need be no more unemployment and, with the help of the repercussions, the real income of the community, and its capital wealth also, would probably become a good deal greater than it actually is. It would, indeed, be more sensible to build houses and the like; but if there are political and practical difficulties in the way of this, the above would be better than nothing.[82]

Keynes adds archly that the form of digging holes in the ground known as gold-mining has long been considered a perfectly rational activity (the chief difference being only that the latter adds nothing whatever to the real wealth of the world, since it involves the disutility of labour): 'To dig holes in the ground', paid for out of savings, will increase not only employment, Keynes suggests, but the real national dividend of useful goods and services.[83] Keynes observes:

> In so far as millionaires find their satisfaction in building mighty mansions to contain their bodies when alive and pyramids to shelter them after death, or, repenting of their sins, erect cathedrals and endow monasteries or foreign missions, the day when abundance of capital will interfere with abundance of output may be postponed.[84]

'Pyramid-building, earthquakes, even wars, may serve to increase wealth, if the education of our statesmen on the principles of the classical economics stands in the way of anything better.'[85] Indeed, in a fascinating twist on a passage in the *Communist Manifesto*, Keynes would appear to be suggesting that the bourgeoisie's near-magical powers might be the result of, rather than the force behind, 'wonders far surpassing Egyptian pyramids, Roman aqueducts and Gothic cathedrals', and that the practical inutility of the latter projects (compared with our own highly functional wonders) might even account for the wealth and stability of ancient civilisations (that present so sharp a contrast to the perpetual crises that characterise our own).[86]

Ancient Egypt was doubly fortunate, and doubtless owed to this its fabled wealth, in that it possessed two activities, namely, pyramid-building as well as the search for the precious metals, the fruits of which, since they could not serve the needs of man by being consumed, did not stale with abundance. The Middle Ages built cathedrals and sang dirges. Two pyramids, two masses for the dead, are twice as good as one; but not so two railways from London to York.[87]

'What will you do', it is asked, 'when you have built all the houses and roads and town halls and electric grids and water supplies and so forth that the population of the future can be expected to require?'[88] To which Keynes responds: something new, something extraordinary, something beyond the mere economic survival that has kept the human race fully occupied up to this point. 'Thus we are so sensible, have schooled ourselves to so close a semblance of prudent financiers, taking careful thought before we add to the "financial" burdens of posterity by building them houses to live in, that we have no such easy escape from the sufferings of unemployment'[89] – that is to say, no such easy escape as the Egyptians had in pyramid-building. 'It is not reasonable, however, that a sensible community should be content to remain dependent on such fortuitous and often wasteful mitigations when once we understand the influences upon which effective demand depends.'[90] And in a passage that, again, echoes Marx, Keynes concludes that the "natural" rules of our present conditions are merely 'a fact of observation concerning the world as it is or has been, and not a necessary principle which cannot be changed'.[91]

The General Theory provoked fierce criticism from the moment of its inception, not least from the neoliberal economist F. W. Hayek. In his seminal anti-planning polemic *Road to Serfdom* (1944), Hayek would warn that a move towards public works undertaken on a very large scale might lead to further serious restrictions on the competitive sphere, and that 'in experimenting in this direction, we shall have carefully to watch our step if we are to avoid making all economic activity progressively more dependent on the direction and volume of government expenditure'.[92] In a letter responding to these criticisms, Keynes would point out that even a Hayekian economy would contain some minimal element of central planning (for instance, the enforcement of contracts): and 'as soon as you admit that the extreme is not possible ... you are, on your own argument, done for, since you are trying to persuade us that so soon as one moves an inch in the planned direction you are necessarily launched on the slippery path which will lead you in due course over the precipice'.[93] Hayek's subsequent celebrity as the architect of our contemporary neoliberal economy (having been credited with predicting the phenomenon of stagflation, and cited as an inspiration by Margaret Thatcher) has ensured that his views on the General Theory are now very well known, but perhaps, as a direct result, we are likely to overestimate the extent of his impact upon public perceptions. As Hayek himself subsequently acknowledged in *The Constitution of Liberty* (1960), if we wish to understand the later disillusionment with Keynes's ideas, it is not to the economic but to the imaginative literature that we must look for answers: 'Though the contention that socialism and individual liberty were mutually exclusive had been indignantly rejected by [socialist intellectuals] when advanced by an opponent, it made a deep impression when stated in powerful literary form by one from their own ranks.'[94] Offering us an insight into the origins of the febrile and often, frankly, irrational public discourse that would later overwhelm Keynes's so-called Voodoo economics, Aldous Huxley's *Brave New World* (1932) and George Orwell's *1984* (1949) are also well placed to identify elements in Keynesian thought that anticipate the post- (or rather Late) Modernist critiques of consumer society, together constituting a peculiar – specifically anti-Keynesian – subgenre of the anti-socialist dystopia.

Huxley's *Brave New World* (1932) had initially been conceived following a period living in California, a place which the novelist had regarded with disdain but had recognised as, 'Materially, the nearest approach to Utopia yet seen on our planet'. Disgusted by the vulgarity of the film industry, the 'pneumatic' flappers and 'barbarous' jazz, Huxley decided to expose the flaws inherent to Utopian projects by demonstrating what the realisation of such schemes would be likely to entail: 'a novel about the future – a satire on the horror of the Wellsian Utopia and a revolt against it'.[95] Huxley had once remarked that 'To the Bolshevist idealist, Utopia is indistinguishable from a Ford factory,' and *Brave New World* is extremely unusual in that its primary target would appear to be the capitalist West rather than the Communist East. His World Controller Mustapha Mond, for instance, is evidently modelled on the British industrialist Sir Alfred Mond, first chairman of Imperial Chemical Industries Ltd, whose vast factory at Billingham near Middlesborough Huxley had visited before he started writing *Brave New World*. 'The great ICU factory is one of those ordered universes that exist as anomalous oases of pure logic in the midst of the larger world of planless incoherence.'[96] Undertaking an extensive tour of factories in the wake of the Wall Street crash, Huxley was attuned to how industry was adapting to challenging circumstances (with American-style production lines, as at the Lucas magneto factory in Acocks Green, Birmingham) and was seriously contemplating what a future based on a reconstructed capitalism might look like, at a time when a great many other writers were, quite literally, writing it off. In the novel, Henry Ford's production lines are applied to the mass manufacture of "human resources", and Huxley's inventive speculations concerning the technical practices that might make this possible have been the subject of considerable critical attention over the years, with "Bokanovskification" and "Neo-Pavlonian Conditioning" being related to developments in eugenics and in mass suggestion, respectively, and their application in early-twentieth-century totalitarian regimes. But this critical preoccupation with the technologies involved has obscured perhaps the most brilliant insight underpinning Huxley's dystopia: a recognition that the demand-driven economy would require a fundamentally different moral basis, and that this new morality already existed (was, in fact, at that very moment being written up) in the General Theory of J. M. Keynes. 'Ending is better than mending', insist the Machines. 'The more stitches, the less riches.'[97]

> 'We condition the masses to hate the country,' concluded the Director. 'But simultaneously we condition them to love all country sports. At the same time, we see to it that all country sports shall entail the use of elaborate apparatus. So that they consume manufactured articles as well as transport.'[98]

Thus the ubiquity of Centrifugal Bumble-Puppy: a game requiring a chrome-steel tower containing a rapidly revolving disc that hurls a ball out through one of a series of apertures pierced into the cylindrical casing:

> 'Imagine the folly of allowing people to play elaborate games which do nothing whatever to increase consumption,' cries the Director.

'It's madness. Nowadays the Controllers won't approve of any new game unless it can be shown that it requires at least as much apparatus as the most complicated of existing games.'[99]

Published four years before the completion of *The General Theory*, this inspired satire on Keynesian economics indicates the extent to which Huxley was engaged with that work-in-progress, through conversations either with the economist himself or else with their shared contacts in the Bloomsbury Group. This would certainly serve to account for what is surely Huxley's most extraordinary insight into the moral basis for consumer capitalism: his realisation that Keynes's moral revolution had been thoroughly informed by Freudian theory on the "*Auri Sacra Fames*". As economic historian Robert Skidelsky explains, 'Keynes' thesis was that the engine of capitalism was driven by a neurosis which he calls "love of money" ... 'but this neurosis [had been, up to the present moment] the means to the good, because it [had been] the means to the abundance which will make capitalism unnecessary'.[100] With most wants satiated, Keynes predicted, there would be great changes in the code of morals: 'We shall be able to rid ourselves of many of the pseudo-moral principles which have hag-ridden us for two hundred years, by which we have exalted some of the most distasteful of human qualities into the position of positive virtues', he wrote, in his famous essay "Economic Possibilities for our Grandchildren" (1928), 'love of money' would at last be recognised as 'a somewhat disgusting morbidity, one of those semi-criminal, semi-pathological propensities which one hands over with a shudder to specialists in mental disease'.[101] And Keynes had provided a revealing clue as to what he thought these might be in *A Treatise on Money* (1930), referring readers to a passage in Freud's *Collected Papers* (edited by his friend James Strachey), where Freud had claimed that the baby's 'interest in faeces is transformed into the high valuation of gold and money'.[102] – classical economic theory, and the British ruling class cruelty that this had entailed over centuries, were (Keynes was implying) motivated by infant anal retention.[103] As Skidelsky remarks, such speculations could have aroused only contempt in Keynes's fellow economists: 'Fixed exchanges and sound money, they would have said, were necessary to economic progress.'[104] Being a 'Bloomsbury' himself, Huxley was less dismissive, was prepared to concede that innovations in toilet-training might well precipitate just such a world-historical transition to a society of leisure as that envisaged by Keynes in "Economic Possibilities for our Grandchildren". Here, I believe, we have arrived at the root of that pronounced and apparently irrational fear of progeny in the speculative fiction of the post-war era, the scenes of infant-conditioning in the novel being perhaps the earliest example of this trope. In *Brave New World*, it is suggested that the reason the children of the future will be so unlike us is that they will be products of an utterly alien moral education, informed by the psychoanalytical theories of ' "Our Freud" (as, for some inscrutable reason he chose to call himself whenever he spoke of psychological matters...)', a morality diametrically opposed to the self-denial that we had, for centuries, regarded as virtue: 'Self-indulgence up to the very limits imposed by hygiene and economics', explains the World Controller. 'You can't have a lasting civilisation without plenty of pleasant vices.'[105]

Huxley would also appear to be the source of the widespread idea, developed later by F. W. Hayek in *Road to Serfdom* (1944), that Keynesian economics would produce a fearsome class hierarchy. In fact, Keynes anticipated the 'euthanasia of the rentier' and predicted that an egalitarian society would be achieved by means of his reforms, peacefully, thereby obviating the need for a violent revolution, and Huxley provides no rationale when he asserts otherwise. Such a rationale would be provided by a second, hugely influential Keynesian dystopia, George Orwell's *1984* (1949), which would accept the premises of *The General Theory* only in order to show that Keynesian economics might be made to support, rather than dissolve, a sadistic and hierarchical Big State apparatus:

> an all-round increase in wealth threatened the destruction – indeed, in some sense it *was* the destruction – of a hierarchical society ... In the early twentieth century, the vision of a future society unbelievably rich, leisured, orderly, and efficient, was part of the consciousness of nearly every literate person. And in fact, without being used for any such purpose, but by a sort of automatic process – by producing wealth which it was sometimes impossible not to distribute – the machine did raise the living standards of the average human being very greatly over a period of about fifty years at the end of the nineteenth and the beginning of the twentieth centuries.[106]

In fact, this particular passage in Goldstein's *Theory and Practice of Oligarchical Collectivism*, the book that Winston reads in the novel, bears more than a passing resemblance to Keynes's own experiment in futurology, his essay "Economic Possibilities for our Grandchildren". The twist is that Oceania's ruling elite have chosen *not* to go quietly, and would appear to have accepted the theoretical premises of Keynesian economics so that they might avoid all the practical consequences: 'The problem was how to keep the wheels of industry turning without increasing the real wealth of the world', explains Goldstein. 'Goods must be produced, but they must not be distributed.'[107] In practice (readers will no doubt already be aware) the only way of achieving this is said to be through continuous warfare. 'In principle it would be quite simple to waste the surplus labour of the world by building temples and pyramids, by digging holes and filling them up again, or even by producing vast quantities of goods and then setting fire to them', writes Goldstein, referencing imagery from *The General Theory*. 'But this would provide only the economic and not the emotional basis for a hierarchical society.' On the other hand, 'War, it will be seen, not only accomplishes the necessary destruction, but accomplishes it in a psychologically acceptable way'.[108]

> The essential act of war is destruction, not necessarily of human lives, but of the products of human labour. War is a way of shattering to pieces, or pouring into the stratosphere, or sinking in the depths of the sea, materials which might otherwise be used to make the masses too comfortable, and hence, in the long run, too intelligent. Even when weapons of war are not actually destroyed, their manufacture is still a convenient way of expending labour power without producing anything that can be consumed. A Floating Fortress, for example, has locked up in it the labour that would build several hundred cargo-ships. Ultimately it is scrapped as obsolete, never having brought any material benefit to anybody, and with further enormous labours another Floating Fortress is built.[109]

On one level, Goldstein is entirely correct: Keynes himself believed that we do lack the faith necessary to create pyramids or even cathedrals, while the war god has, sadly, not only retained but perhaps even expanded his cult following. In fact, 'warfare' and 'welfare' are equally important components in the appraisal of the post-war Keynesian society produced by critics such as J. K. Galbraith. But Keynes would have disagreed profoundly with Orwell's suggestion that public spending on military hardware is productive of nothing but waste. Bomb craters, bunkers, trenches and nuclear silos are all varieties of holes in the ground, and one must remember that while it might be more sensible to build houses and such like, Keynes believed this to be at least better than nothing, if the education of our politicians stands (as he thought quite likely) in the way of anything better. The history of the Cold War appears to have proven Keynes right: while the period of massive public spending during and after the War was certainly accompanied by private austerity (in the form of rationing), this would present no impediment to the significant public infrastructure and welfare expenditure for which the era is remembered. Indeed, Britain's welfare state was integral to the efficient management of a mobilised society, with the consumer economy being boosted later by a range of military spin-off technologies: nuclear weapons, radar technology and delta-wing bombers, for instance, resulting in nuclear power stations, microwave ovens and supersonic commercial flight. And much the same would appear to be true of the massive increases in military spending towards the end of the era, in response to civil war in Northern Ireland, the Falklands conflict and increased tension with the USSR. While the Thatcher government was opposed on ideological grounds to public welfare spending, it remained deeply committed to massive public infrastructure projects (London Orbital, the Jubilee Line, MI6 headquarters, etc.) and to the corporate welfare that sustained the conspicuous consumption for which the era is now notorious, memorialised by the glittering towers at Canary Wharf and by miles and miles of luxury flats in the surrounding regenerated Docklands. Indeed, a Keynesian Utopia would ultimately be averted not through military spending but through the extraordinary decision to export surplus capital to China, thereby depriving the manufacturing districts that had traditionally supported the Labour movement while destabilising (if Orwell and Keynes are correct on this point) the last bastion of authoritarian Marxist thought with the all-round increase in wealth that *is* the destruction of a hierarchical society. Only time will tell whether President Nixon's historic trip to China was a geopolitical masterstroke on the part of the West's ruling class, or a catastrophic strategic error: it might be that in curtailing socialism at home, our ruling class have only postponed the inevitable, and eventually face a reckoning greater, and potentially rather less benign, having effectively put the planet's entire working class under communist management: an outcome that even a committed

Marxist reading the *Manifesto* back in the Seventies might have had trouble believing.

Both Huxley's and Orwell's Keynesian dystopias were to prove hugely influential in the English-speaking world, and they can together be seen to account for popular misconceptions of the Keynesian consensus as at once profligate and conducive to the formation of an oppressive and hierarchical State. 'Let Labour's Orwellian nightmare of the Left be the spur for us to dedicate with a new urgency our every ounce of energy and moral strength to rebuild the fortunes of this free nation', proclaimed Prime Minister Thatcher in a speech in 1980. 'If we were to fail, that freedom could be imperilled.'[110] As the novelist Salman Rushdie astutely pointed out, cutting right through the platitudes that have built up around these revered authors, the Huxley of *Brave New World* and the Orwell of *1984* are 'advocating ideas that can only be of service to our masters'.[111] Even so, I would suggest that both authors do retain an edge over more sophisticated, theoretical critiques of the consumer society produced later in the post-war era, in that each recognised that Keynesian philosophy (1) had broken with the theory of capital accumulation as the result of savings, (2) had incorporated the radical theoretical premises of Marx and Freud, and (3) would be integral to the post-war Advanced Industrial Society. Working in close proximity to Keynes's Bloomsbury milieu, Huxley and Orwell were simply in a position to see this, as theorists associated with the Frankfurt School were not. The latter would, consequently, employ a historically distinctive fusion of Marxist critique and Freudian analysis in their cultural criticism without ever once acknowledging the extent to which such theory had been rendered *basic* to post-war Western political economy by the chief architect of that system.

Hence, perhaps the pessimism expressed by Herbert Marcuse in his landmark *One-Dimensional Man* (1964). 'Social theory is concerned with the historical alternatives which haunt the established society as subversive tendencies and forces', Marcuse writes. 'The values attached to the alternatives become facts when translated into reality by historical practice.'[112] That is to say, theoretical concepts *ought* to terminate with social change in a dialectical process, with socialism appearing to be the historical negation of capitalism. But the Western political economy between 1950 and 1975 would confront 'the critique' with a situation that appeared to deprive it of its very basis. 'Contemporary society seems to be capable of containing social change – qualitative change which would establish essentially different institutions, a new direction of the productive process, new modes of human existence', he writes. 'This containment of social change is perhaps the most singular achievement of advanced industrial society.'[113] The dialectic of theory and practice that has motivated the historical process is collapsed by this paralysis of criticism, by a society without opposition, by *One-Dimensional Man*: 'The society of total mobilization, which takes shape in the most advanced areas of industrial civilisation, combines in productive union the features of the Welfare State and Warfare State [and is] an historical freak between organised capitalism and socialism, servitude and freedom, totalitarianism and happiness.'[114] This closing of the political universe entails a condition of post-modernity, the so-called end of history. Frankly acknowledging that his treatise *One-Dimensional Man* will 'vacillate throughout between two contradictory hypotheses', Marcuse insists that forces and tendencies exist that may break this containment, even as he emphasises the extent to which advanced industrial society is capable of containing qualitative change for the foreseeable future: an opinion that would have a formative, enduring (and I believe profoundly problematic) impact upon the New Left.[115] I wish to suggest that we might now be in a position to understand *why* Late Modernist thinkers so profoundly overestimated the immovability and totality of a post-war economic construct which would ultimately prove to be extraordinarily fragile. They had simply missed (as Huxley and Orwell had not) that Keynes, the creative intelligence behind this system, had understood and embraced his role (or rather that of Western capitalism) as the wizard who had summoned the forces of darkness, imagined by Marx. The Keynesians would appear to be in control of such forces *only because* they so fully acknowledged them as their own.

The girl with all the gifts

Ballard's *High-Rise* ends with a vision of children playing in the sculpture garden on the roof of the apartment complex. 'The doors, chained for so long to exclude them, were now wide open', writes

Ballard, and his character Wilder observes 'the geometric forms of the play-sculptures, their vivid colours standing out against the white-walls'.[116] Everything has been freshly painted. The roof is said to be vibrant with light. Hinting at a future beyond anything that the architect Royal might have intended, Wilder's (brief) glimpse of this society of women and children in 'The Blood Garden' tantalises the reader with the question: what will happen to the next generation who will grow up in this haunted house, haunted by a future that has already happened?

This should be easy enough to answer; because I am (figuratively speaking) one of those children glimpsed towards the end of Ballard's novel. I grew up in the shadow of the headquarters building of the Central Electricity Generating Board (CEGB), designed in the 1960s by Birmingham's leading post-war Modernist, John Madin (creator of the iconic Central Library, of the *Birmingham Post and Mail* building and of BBC Pebble Mill). My father worked there. Over thirty-five years, I saw the mid-century Modernist paradigm embodied by that building fall apart.

The CEGB was a sculptural arrangement of three gently curving blocks, a high-rise office block, a long, low building, and a canteen (apparently modelled on the Royal Festival Hall) overlooking a bowling green, clad in solid black granite; with bands of alternating glass window and marble mosaic, the complex stood in the midst of small ponds and smooth lawns, in landscaped grounds, planted with trees. The integrity of the site was marred, initially, by the need for an extension (provided by Madin) that connected the original structures via new glass aerial walkways to a rather squat building on the Stratford Road. In the late 1970s, the increased use of office computers led to over-heating, and so the engineers in charge responded by clapping four giant pipes for air and water against the exterior of the main block: an efficient, albeit brutally jarring, addition that inadvertently anticipated the hyper-Modernist functionalism of Richard Rogers' Lloyd's Building (1986), in which the essential services are placed on the outside of the building (and for precisely the same reasons). In the early 1990s, awash with cash from John Major's privatisation of the CEGB, the engineers again found their buildings too cramped and pushed for an extension on adjacent wasteland, comprising an immense glass pyramid that would flaunt the wealth of their new denationalised company PowerGen (its Promethean logo a fitting image of stolen power). The plan encountered fierce resistance from locals, and so the engineers departed, disgruntled, to a greenfield site in remote rural Warwickshire, selling the headquarters building to a "developer" who promised to repurpose it *only on the condition* that planning permission be granted for a supermarket on a far more valuable site in the town centre, adjoining public parkland, in line with a controversial new method of "regeneration" (pioneered in South Woodham Ferrers), whereby a supermarket would occupy (or replace) the town centre, with public libraries and other public services being removed from existing buildings (sold off for a tidy profit) to new (inferior) units within the privatised civic space. The community that had seen off PowerGen resisted this plan too – and was compelled to watch as the Modernist buildings that had been right at the heart of their town, sustaining their small shopping district, fell into decay. For fifteen long years the deadlock continued, until the developer and his supermarket client were given what they wanted. Permission being granted, plans for repurposing Madin's building were abandoned and a new controversial plan presented to the local community requiring the demolition of all the existing buildings. This would prove to be a gargantuan high-rise filing cabinet for ageing Baby Boomers: an unlovely hulk vainly pretending that it was not a single mass of concrete pocked with windows pushed right to the road's edge, but rather a series of blocks – of varying height, in different colours of brick. Ten years later, ground down by the relentless hostility, by the vandalism, drugs and empty shops, by the weight of living with the urban blight that had been visited (quite deliberately) upon their town, the community was nevertheless shocked by photographs (taken by an enterprising schoolgirl) of a major motion picture then being shot in their town: the grounds of Madin's CEGB headquarters building strewn with rotting corpses, sprouting some species of fungus, the setting for a zombie movie. The developers declared Madin's building an eyesore, having done everything in their power, over twenty-five years, to render it such: and the local community agreed. The building was demolished, and the new post-modernist structure erected. Completed now, this looms over a peculiar traffic island, bristling with colossal metallic poppies, like Martian flora or Triffids, straight out of the science fiction dystopia that had been filmed on this spot only a few years previously.

Colm McCarthy's film adaptation (2016) of M. R. Carey's novel *The Girl With All The Gifts* (2014) presents a haunting cinematic perspective on the derelict state of the post-war Modernist buildings that are the subject of this chapter. Captured on film fifty years after the collapse of the economic model that had created and sustained them, the Post Office Tower in London, Hanley Bus Station in Stoke-on-Trent, and the CEGB headquarters building present images of pronounced urban decay that can be seamlessly intercut with aerial footage of the Ukrainian town of Pripyat, uninhabited since the 1986 Chernobyl disaster. How, one might ask, is such ruination possible in well-to-do Midland towns that have *not* been abandoned for fear of radiation poisoning? The answer, in M. R. Carey's dystopia, is that humanity has been infected and manipulated by a pathogenic fungus that hijacks the central nervous system in much the same way that *Ophiocordyceps camponotifloridani* has been observed to parasitise carpenter ants. Compelling its ant host to move with jerking zombie-like movements, the fungus removes the ant from its nest, drives it twenty-five centimetres up the stem of a plant, then makes it bite down on a leaf vein with abnormal force, to anchor itself as a sporocarp or "fruiting body" sprouts from the head. This will explode, releasing spores to infect other ants. The lifecycle of the fungus in Carey's fiction is similar, the two key differences being that the "fruiting body" will release its spores only when exposed to fire, and that such a release is to wipe out entirely the host species (rather than merely settling on one or two more in order to perpetuate the existence of the parasite). Truth is stranger than fiction, and a fungal infection of our higher brain functions is a perfectly credible way of accounting for the fact that the extraordinary dereliction of the various post-war Modernist buildings we see in this film was only possible because the majority of us *voted for it, repeatedly.*

In Carey's fable, children who have grown up with the fungus have developed a symbiotic relationship with it, which enables them to function as human beings, but they are treated with disgust and fear by the older generation, who are attempting by means of cruel experiments on the children to develop a cure that will permit them to restore the old world. Eventually, Melanie, one of the children – the gifted child referred to in the title – refuses to assist them, and will ignite a fire to initiate the final release of the spores from the fruiting body that has grown up around the Post Office Tower (and the CEGB), thereby putting an end to a world that she believes well beyond saving. Inspired by the myth of Pandora (the girl with all the gifts), Melanie is remembering that Hope is to be found only at the bottom of that tightly sealed jar, only after the fear, misery, anger and despair that were the inevitable consequence of that original Promethean gift (the theft of fire) are permitted to work their course. In McCarthy's movie this is forcefully conveyed by the image of Melanie's beloved teacher (played by Gemma Arterton) educating the symbiont children from inside a sort of box, a portacabin that was a field hospital but now serves as a school. The structure reminded me of the "temporary" wooden classroom huts at the schools I attended as a child, built initially for the generation of post-war Baby Boomers, following the creation of a national state-run system of education, and still in use decades after I had left. Hospitals and schools: the core of Britain's post-war Modernist miracle, and though a little battered, still very much in place, retaining their hold upon the imagination and the affection of the British people, and raising serious questions as to how post-modernist we truly are even now, after decades of neoliberal economics and privatisation. Increasingly rare now, these "temporary" wooden structures represent the earliest iteration of the National Health Service (NHS) and of the UK's system of state comprehensive education and remind us that the imposing, seemingly monumental buildings that we have lost were intended to be equally provisional. Often imprinted with the woodgrain of the shuttering into which the concrete was poured, these Brutalist superstructures might eventually be recognised as the memorialisation, or ossification, of something inherently alive, organic, ephemeral – beautiful fossils produced by a living spirit impressed upon wet mud. These might fall to pieces in our hands, but the spirit remains with us still, kept alive for coming generations, in those cheap Modernist huts. And as long as that remains the case, anything is possible. Because the final Promethean gift is Hope. After every possible post-modernist reversal and blowback, Hope remains at the bottom of the box.

The ancients were divided on the significance of Hope, with some viewing the gift of this small fluttering creature not as an ameliorating blessing but rather as part the curse, designed to prolong the torture inflicted by the other things contained in the jar. In the following chapter we will see how Modernist ambitions persist in the neoliberal era, producing uncanny effects that are extraordinarily potent precisely because they are now so very hard to recognise as such: an enduring basis for contemporary Promethean horror.

Notes

1 J. G. Ballard, *High-Rise* (London: Fourth Estate, HarperCollins, 2014), 3.
2 *Ibid.*, 19.
3 *Ibid.*, 1.
4 By way of illustration, consider the two anthologies that launched Larkin's Movement. Often thought to draw a line under Modernist experiment, Robert Conquest's introduction to *New Lines* (1956) is remarkable for *not* mentioning Modernism at all. The target of this critical intervention is actually the neo-Romantic poetry of the 1940s (Dylan Thomas et al.): 'when the mistake was made of giving the Id, a sound played on the percussion side under a strict conductor, too much of a say in the doings of the orchestra as a whole'. In fact, the attack on Modernism that readers remember occurs only in *New Lines II* (1963), and is evidently taking place at this juncture *because* Conquest has realised that Modernism is far from being a spent force. 'At least the best writers of the 'Twenties were following their own bent and doing something new', he writes: *'the more recent seekers after novelty are not in fact providing it at all, but simply imitating the novelties of a generation or a generation and a half ago'*. But having perceived this new threat to the recently established Movement, Conquest takes issue with Late Modernists – not for being new-fangled, but for being so very old-fashioned. 'It was in the 19th century that architecture got itself into a position rather like that of poetry nowadays', he writes. 'The impulse that produced architects like [William] Butterfield [gothic revival architect, 1814–1900] is extremely comparable to that which produced Pound, an absurdly inflated search for novelty through an attempted blend of the flashier and the more irrelevant features of past schools.' One might even suspect that, while the result of Conquest's critical polemic was to impress upon readers the unsupportable notion that Modernism was a phenomena that belonged properly to the era of Art Nouveau, poets of the Movement had begun to hope that their own writing might be regarded as the literary equivalent to the comprehensive urban renovations then being built by Late Modernist

architects. If this seems unlikely to readers who think the Movement a return to the traditional, consider: the poets who mock Pound for being Art Nouveau, or even gothic revival, lived and worked in masterpieces of Brutalism, such as the Kenneth-Capon-designed University of Essex (poet Donald Davies), which has a library inspired by Kagawa Prefecture and towers that evoke Louis Kahn's iconic Philadelphia Laboratories; and the Brynmor Jones Library at the University of Hull, an astonishing building that resembles nothing so much as the Borg ship on *Star Trek TNG* (Philip Larkin as head librarian had considerable input into Leslie Martin's design). 'All of us were brought up in the tradition of the supposed poetic revolution of the 1920s and 1930s', argued Conquest. It is with this claim to authority (or rather, modernity) that he rejects what is 'only a particular type of American poetry long notorious for obliquity of grammar, vocabulary, structure and sense'. Not everyone in the Movement agreed, and Donald Davie later played a pivotal part in the reassessment of Pound and Bunting, and through his protégé J. H. Prynne, the British Poetry Revival. But Conquest is surely right to suggest that 'All our predilections and original partisanships were for this "modernism"', and this must compel us to reconsider everything we thought we knew of Modernism in relation to this era and to question the process whereby that narrative came into being (periodicity, like canon formation, is never innocent).

5 Frederic Jameson, *Post-Modernism, or The Cultural Logic of Late Capitalism* (London and New York: Verso Books, 1992), 2.
6 Ballard, *High-Rise*, 45.
7 *Ibid.*, 212.
8 *Ibid.*, 28.
9 *Ibid.*, 208.
10 *Ibid.*, 208.
11 *Ibid.*, 50.
12 *Ibid.*, 28.
13 David Whitaker, *Dr Who and the Daleks* (1964), republished by BBC Books (London: Random House, 2011), 39.
14 *Ibid.*, 39.
15 *Ibid.*, 51.
16 Alwyn Turner, *The Man Who Invented th Daleks: The Strange Worlds of Terry Nation* (London: Aurum Press, 2013), 6.
17 Russell T. Davies, quoted by Turner, *The Man Who Invented the Daleks*, 284.
18 Apparently, this point has not escaped the fan community: 'Real Daleks don't climb stairs: they level the building.'

19 Le Corbusier, *The City of To-Morrow and Its Planning* (1929), trans. Frederick Etchells (New York: Dover, 1987), xxiii.
20 Terry Nation, quoted in Turner, *The Man Who Invented the Daleks*, 93.
21 Mumford, *The City in History*, 558–559.
22 *Ibid.*, 560.
23 Herbert Read, 'New Aspects of British Sculpture', exhibition catalogue for the British Pavilion at the XXVI Venice Biennale, 1952.
24 Mumford, *The City in History*, 542.
25 *Ibid.*, 543.
26 *Ibid.*, 546.
27 *Ibid.*, 546.
28 *Ibid.*, 542.
29 Manfred E. Clynes and Nathan S. Kline, 'Cyborgs and Space', *Astronautics* (Sept 1960), 26–27 and 74–75; reprinted in C. H. Gray, S. Mentor and H. J. Figueroa-Sarriera (eds), *The Cyborg Handbook* (New York: Routledge, 1995), 29–34.
30 Mumford, *The City in History*, 546.
31 Le Corbusier, *The City of To-Morrow*, xxiii.
32 *Ibid.*, 178.
33 Sigmund Freud, *Future of an Illusion: Civilisation and Its Discontents* (1930), James Strachey (trans.), *The Standard Edition of the Complete Works*, Vol. XXI, 1927–1931 (London: Hogarth Press, 1961), 91.
34 *Ibid.*, 91.
35 *Ibid.*, 91.
36 Freud, 'The Uncanny', 235.
37 Philip Larkin, 'The Building', *Collected Poems* (London: Faber and Faber, 2003), 136–138.
38 W. B. Yeats, 'Sailing to Byzantium', *The Tower* (1928), A. Norman Jefferies and Warwick Gould (eds), *Yeats's Poems* (Basingstoke, Hampshire, and London: Macmillan, 1996), 301.
39 Quoted in Turner, *The Man Who Invented the Daleks*, 91.
40 *Ibid.*, 92.
41 Le Corbusier, *Modulor 2*, trans. Peter de Francia and Anna Bostock (London: Faber and Faber, 1958), 304.
42 *Ibid.*, 306.
43 Le Corbusier, *The Modulor*, trans. Peter de Francia and Anna Bostock (London: Faber and Faber, 1954), 140.
44 *Ibid.*, 140.
45 *Ibid.*, 78.
46 *Ibid.*, 33.
47 *Ibid.*, 33.

48 Ibid., 34.
49 Ibid., 36–37.
50 Ibid., 56.
51 Ibid., 57.
52 Ibid., 56–58.
53 Ibid., 125.
54 Ibid., 19.
55 Ibid., 19.
56 Ibid., 19.
57 Ibid., 20.
58 Ibid., 20.
59 Ibid., 223.
60 Ibid., 224.
61 Ibid., 222.
62 Ibid., 222.
63 Ibid., 72.
64 Ibid., 72.
65 Ibid., 72–73.
66 Ibid., 73.
67 Le Corbusier, *Le poème de l'angle droit* (1955), Kenneth Hylton (trans.), *Le Corbusier and the Architecture of Reinvention* (London: Architectural Association, 2003), 58–97.
68 Henri Lefebvre, 'Plan of the Present Work', *The Production of Space* (1974), trans. Donald Nicholson-Smith (Oxford: Blackwell, 1991), 1–67.
69 Ibid., 224.
70 Ibid., 224.
71 Ivan Chtcheglov, 'Formulary for a New Urbanism' (1953), Ken Knabb (trans.), *Situationist International Anthology* (Berkeley, CA: Bureau of Public Secrets, 2007), 2.
72 Constant Nieuwenhuys, New Babylon, exhibition catalogue (The Hague: Haags Gemeetenmuseum, 1974).
73 Nicolas Spicer, 'Sea of Teeth', Section III, 'Origin of Divinity', *Landscape With Forgeries* (London: Contraband, 2012), 15.
74 See Richard Owens, 'Dissociations: The McCaffery–Prynne Debate', *Paideuma: Modern and Contemporary Poetry and Poetics*, Vol. 40 (2013), 405–431.
75 J. M. Keynes, *The General Theory of Employment, Interest and Money* (1936), Donald Moggeridge (ed.), *The Collected Writings of J. M. Keynes*, Vol. VII (Cambridge: Cambridge University Press, 1973), 359.
76 Ibid., 360.

77 Bernard Mandeville, *The Fable of the Bees* (1724), ed. Phillip Harth (London: Penguin, 1989), 73.
78 Keynes, *The General Theory*, 360.
79 Mandeville, *The Fable of the Bees*, 76.
80 Keynes, *The General Theory*, 362.
81 'In retrospect it can be seen as a sort of Golden Age, and was so seen almost immediately it had come to an end in the early 1970s.' Eric Hobsbawm, *The Age of Extremes: 1914–1991* (London: Abacus, 1995), 6.
82 Keynes, *The General Theory*, 129.
83 *Ibid.*, 220.
84 *Ibid.*, 220.
85 *Ibid.*, 129.
86 Karl Marx and Friedrich Engels, *The Communist Manifesto* (1848), ed. Gareth Stedman Jones, trans. Samuel Moore (London: Penguin Classics, 2002), 222.
87 Keynes, *The General Theory*, 131.
88 *Ibid.*, 106.
89 *Ibid.*, 131.
90 *Ibid.*, 254, 220.
91 *Ibid.*, 254.
92 F. A. Hayek, *The Road to Serfdom* (New York: Routledge Classics, 2001), 126.
93 Keynes, letter to Hayek, 28 June 1944, quoted by Robert Skidelsky in the abridged one-volume edition of his biography *John Maynard Keynes, 1883–1946: Economist, Philosopher, Statesman* (New York: Penguin, 2005), 273.
94 F. A. Hayek, *The Constitution of Liberty* (London and New York: Routledge Classics, 2006), 223.
95 Aldous Huxley, letter to Mrs Kethevan Roberts, 18 May 1931, published in Letters of Aldous Huxley, ed. Grover Smith (New York and Evanston, IL: Harper and Row, 1969), 348.
96 Aldous Huxley, 'Sight-Seeing in Alien Englands' (1931), David Bradshaw (ed.), *Between the Wars: Essays and Letters* (Chicago: Ivan R. Dee, 1994), 68.
97 Aldous Huxley, *Brave New World* (1932), ed. David Bradshaw (London: Flamingo, HarperCollins, 1994), 19.
98 *Ibid.*, 19.
99 *Ibid.*, 26.
100 Skidelsky, *John Maynard Keynes*, 373.

101 J. M. Keynes, 'Economic Possibilities for our Grandchildren' (1928), Robert Skidelsky (ed.) *The Essential Keynes* (London and New York: Penguin Classics 2016), 84.
102 See J. M. Keynes, *A Treatise on Money*, Vol. II (London: Macmillan, 1930), 258–259. The love of money and anal eroticism are first linked by Sigmund Freud in 'Character and Anal Eroticism' (1908). Anal retention and anal expulsion are considered in Freud's essay 'On Transformations of Instinct as Exemplified in Anal Eroticism' (c. 1917): James Strachey (trans.), *The Standard Edition of the Complete Works*, Vol. XVII (London: Hogarth Press, 1961). Freud's colleague Dr Karl Abraham did much to develop and establish these ideas, in *A Short Study of the Libido* (London: Hogarth Press, 1924).
103 Skidelsky, *John Maynard Keynes*, 34. Also see the note on 907.
104 *Ibid.*, 346.
105 Huxley, *Brave New World*, 34, 216.
106 George Orwell, *1984* (1949), *The Complete Novels* (London and New York: Penguin Classics, 2000), 855.
107 *Ibid.*, 856.
108 *Ibid.*, 856.
109 *Ibid.*, 856.
110 Margaret Thatcher: Speech to Conservative Party Conference: 'The Lady's Not for Turning', 10 October 1980, Thatcher Archive: CCOPR 735/80.
111 Salman Rushdie, 'Outside the Whale', Granta Magazine (1 March 1984).
112 Herbert Marcuse, *One-Dimensional Man: Studies in the Ideology of Advanced Industrial Society* (London: Beacon Press, 1964), xi.
113 *Ibid.*, xii.
114 *Ibid.*, 19.
115 *Ibid.*, xv.
116 Ballard, *High-Rise*, 238.

6

The Mechanical Turk: Enduring misapprehensions concerning artificial intelligence

A system of mirrors

How *does* one picture the Angel of History? We are told his wings are spread. Eyes staring, mouth open, his face turned to the past. 'Where we perceive a chain of events, he sees a single catastrophe which keeps piling wreckage on wreckage and hurls it in front of his feet.'[1] The angel would like to stay, awaken the dead, make whole what was smashed. 'But a storm is blowing from Paradise', observes Walter Benjamin, in his *Theses on the Philosophy of History* (1940); 'it has got caught in his wings with such violence that the angel can no longer close them.'[2] Most commentators picture this creature as a sort of P. B. Shelley, a beautiful and ineffectual revolutionary, beating his luminous wings in the void. 'The storm irresistibly propels him into the future to which his back is turned, while the pile of debris before him grows skyward.'[3] But given that this storm is what *we* call progress, should the Angel be regarded with such immense sympathy, as an icon for the turn to Negative Dialectics on the part of the post-war revolutionary Left? The Marxist scholar and activist Jacob Bard-Rosenberg has argued that 'This famous text is probably Benjamin's most misinterpreted, not least by Americans and other tourists of the Spirit'.[4] The profound shock one cannot but experience on seeing Paul Klee's painting *Angelus Novus* (1920) *after* living so long with the critical consensus must indicate that Bard-Rosenberg is right. Klee's angel is stupid and sly: a Toby-jug fixed to a sparrow. 'And why does no-one mention that he wears a shirt collar and tie?'[5] In fact, Bard-Rosenberg points out, the Angel in the painting bears more than a passing resemblance to a cartoon of a bourgeois man entitled *Hausherr* (1919), drawn by George Grosz *a year before*

Klee painted his Angel.⁶ 'Our angel has become bourgeois', he concludes. 'Certainly a sympathetic bourgeois, but bourgeois nonetheless.'⁷ And Bard-Rosenberg suggests that Benjamin might have been remembering a famous passage in *The Communist Manifesto* where Marx refers to that small section of the ruling class that cuts itself adrift from the rest to join the workers' movement – 'a portion of the bourgeois ideologists who have raised themselves to the level of comprehending theoretically the historical movement as a whole'.⁸ As Bard-Rosenberg points out, 'There is a similarity between those "bourgeois ideologists" who theoretically comprehend the whole historical movement, and the angel who "sees one single catastrophe".'⁹ And though his reading of the angel as bourgeois ideologist might seem uncomfortable, it finds support in other work by Benjamin, such as 'Central Park':

> The course of history, seen in terms of the concept of catastrophe, can actually claim no more attention from thinkers than a child's kaleidoscope, which with every turn of the hand dissolves the established order in a new way. There is a profound truth in this image. The concepts of the ruling class have always been mirrors that enabled an image of order to prevail. – The kaleidoscope must be smashed.¹⁰

Let us begin doing just that. Having been mistaken for so long as a "catastrophist" himself, Benjamin can now at last be brought to bear upon the enormous critical industry that has built up around the "catastrophe", like so much wreckage about the Angel's feet. Acquiring a fresh twist recently with the onset of global financial crisis (the word can be rendered literally as "downturn"), catastrophe has long held the status of an orthodoxy in the conformist thinking that has been part and parcel (Benjamin suggests) of social democracy from the start.¹¹ As Derrida writes:

> Many young people today (of the type 'reader-consumer of Fukuyama' or of the type 'Fukuyama' himself) probably no longer sufficiently realise it: the eschatological themes of the 'end of history,' of the 'end of Marxism,' of the 'end of philosophy,' of the 'ends of man,' of the 'last man' and so forth were, in the '50s ... our daily bread.

He observes that those who continue to abandon themselves to this 'apocalyptic tone in philosophy' with such youthful enthusiasm 'look a little like late-comers, a little as if it were possible to take still the last train after the last train – and yet be late to an end of history'.¹²

Dissolving the established order in a new way, post-modern philosophy perceives history to be a 'single catastrophe' from *after the end*, thereby enabling an image of order to prevail.[13] Thus Jean Baudrillard proposes that 'the *actual* catastrophe may turn out to be a carefully modulated strategy of our species ... may be what allows us to preserve the energy of that *virtual* catastrophe which is the motor of all our processes, whether economic or political, artistic or historical'.[14] At its peak in the 1960s, the "catastrophist" discourse of theorists such as Maurice Blanchot and Lewis Mumford predicted that the coming technological utopia must bring about a perpetual stasis, the end of humankind and historical progress, as every potential future was mapped in advance by ever greater processing power. 'The full-blown, the absolute catastrophe would be a true omnipresence of all networks, a total transparency of all data', declares Baudrillard, 'the culminating point of the development of information and communications, which is to say, death'.[15] And this conviction was to become prevalent again through the 1990s – following the collapse of the Cold War, the decline of socialism, the rise of the internet, and high summer for neoliberalism. In each case, post-modern philosophies had merely followed Hegel in assuming the vantage point of a non-existent future, a total and therefore impossible knowledge, in order to impose upon the past and the present an illusory historical pattern, from which there can be no escape, a retcon that begins from the End.

On the other hand, we have Benjamin's own personal interpretation of historical materialism (which differs from that of Marx with regard to progress and movement). 'Social Democracy thought fit to assign to the working class the role of the redeemer of future generations', observes Benjamin. '[But] this training made the working class forget both its hatred and its spirit of sacrifice, for both are nourished by the image of enslaved ancestors rather than that of liberated grandchildren.'[16] Considering that the Jews were prohibited from investigating the future, and that the Torah and Psalms instruct them in remembrance instead, Benjamin observes that 'This stripped the future of its magic', and empowered the people with a redemptive vision in which 'every second of time was the strait gate through which the Messiah might enter'.[17] For the same reason, 'A historical materialist cannot do without the notion of a present which is not a transition, but in which time stands still and has come to a stop'.[18] In a passage that could have come straight from the philosophy of the English phenomenologist F. H. Bradley, or the poetry of his student T. S. Eliot, Benjamin states that 'A historical materialist approaches his subject only where he encounters it as a monad' (that is to say, a *finite centre of experience* or *point of view* – with even time itself being contained in this *structure* – as a 'precious but tasteless seed' in the 'nourishing fruit of the historically understood'.)[19] 'In this structure [a historical materialist] recognises the sign of a Messianic chance of happening, or, put differently, a revolutionary chance in the fight for the oppressed past.'[20] Exploding the pattern of history, a historical materialist wrests tradition away from a conformism about to overwhelm it, redeeming generations of the downtrodden, and transforming the past here and now in the present. 'As flowers turn toward the sun, by dint of a secret heliotropism, that past strives toward that sun which is rising in the sky of history.'[21]

Benjamin's vision of historical materialism is represented at the start of his essay by the image of Von Kempelen's Mechanical Turk: a chess-playing device dressed as a Turkish sorcerer that appeared to be pure automaton (able to play a winning game of chess, answering each move of an opponent with a countermove), but that was in fact operated by a little hunchback who sat inside the table, concealed by a system of mirrors, guiding the puppet's hand by means of strings. According to Benjamin, one ought to regard historical materialism as the philosophical counterpart to this conjuring trick: 'It can easily be a match for anyone if it enlists the services of theology, which today, as we know, is wizened and has to keep out of sight.'[22] Extending Bard-Rosenberg's reading of the Angel, I believe we should consider the two images in relation to one another – for there are certain strong parallels. In each case there is spirit or mind (a wizened theological force) and there is the matter of history – and, it would seem, between the two, the 'system of mirrors' that serve to obscure, in the first case, the material and, in the second, the spiritual. In fact, the only difference between the two would appear to consist in the outlook of the latter: the spirit is either directing the machine, animating the material of history, or it is propelled through this mechanism, by a moving force that is not believed to be within its control, a victim of its own alienated theological agency. The two images present the same tableau – and this might explain why each has been read in a way that endorses the perspective opposed to that they are said to represent. We have seen that the Angel has been a symbol for the catastrophist viewpoint it was meant to satirise: and it is curious that the Mechanical Turk is so often employed as a symbol for everything embodied, in Benjamin's essay, by the Angel. In work by cyberneticians Claude Shannon and Norbert Wiener, for instance, the Mechanical Turk is represented (in a rhetorical flourish) as precursor to the computer, and thus as harbinger of the processing power that is to bring about the Baudrillardian absolute catastrophe and the End of Man. Of course, such authors harbour no illusions concerning the true nature of the Turk. But I would like to suggest that these playful references are telling nevertheless. For we are now in a position to see that the cybernetic or post-humanist discourses in which they appear labour under the very widespread misapprehensions concerning the philosophy of history that Benjamin attacked. In this chapter I want to find out how the *system of mirrors* in the computational technology embodied by the Mechanical Turk generated orthodoxies of the End in the post-war period: in the social democratic consensus from 1950 to 1975, and then, subsequently, in a paradigm which is, ostensibly at least, post-modern and neoliberal.

The Analytical Engine

A curtain is withdrawn and a machine rolled to within twelve feet of the nearest spectators: a large box of maple wood on castors or brazen rollers. To the back of this a chair is affixed where a figure like a pantomime Turk sits cross-legged; his right arm extended to a chequerboard on the table, his left arm supporting a pipe, the Turk is enveloped in a heavy green cloak – but is discovered to consist of mechanical parts, operated by a larger clockwork engine in the box.[23] Having inspected the compartments containing this mechanism, the spectator engages the Mechanical Turk in a game of chess. The Turk moving the pieces with his left hand, eyes and head rolling in triumph, on putting his enemy into check he will cry '*Échec! Échec!*' Built by Wolfgang von Kempelen for Empress Maria Theresa in 1769, the Turk is said to have won games against Benjamin Franklin and Napoleon Bonaparte, mystifying audiences across Europe and America with a winning streak lasting 84 years. (The Turk's career was terminated by a fire in 1854, in which the mechanism is said to have perished screaming '*Échec!*'.)²⁴ In what is perhaps the most important eyewitness account of the Automaton, produced shortly after seeing the chess player in action while on tour in America in 1836, Edgar Allen Poe suggests that no exhibition of the kind has ever elicited so much speculation. 'Wherever seen it has been an object of intense curiosity, to all persons who think', remarks Poe.

> Yet the question of its *modus operandi* is still undecided ... accordingly we find every where men of mechanical genius, of great general acuteness, and discriminative understanding, who make no scruple in pronouncing the Automaton a *pure machine*, unconnected with human agency in its movements, and consequently, beyond all comparison, the most astonishing of the inventions of mankind.²⁵

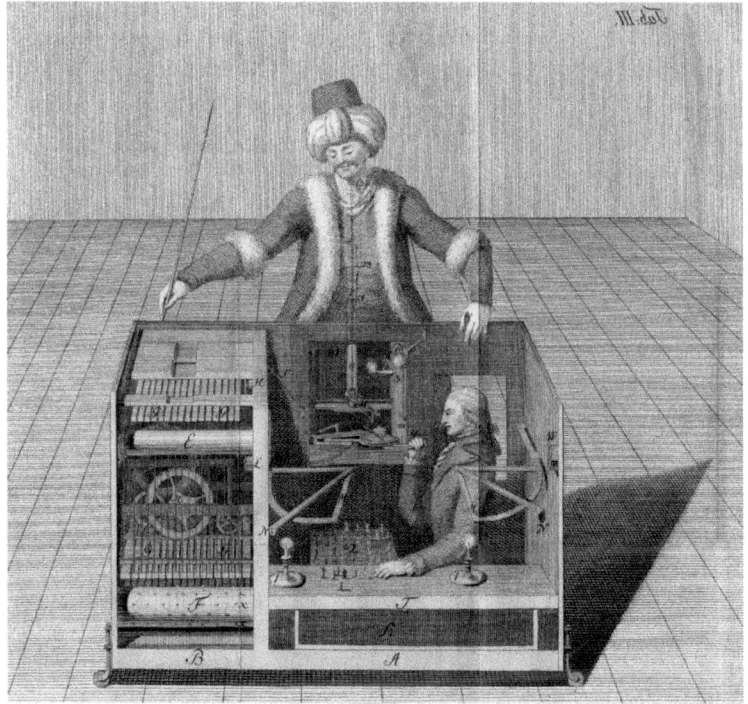

Figure 6.1 The Mechanical Turk as depicted by Joseph Racknitz. (*Ueber den Schachspieler des Herrn von Kempelen und dessen Nachbildung*, Leipzig: Breitkopf, 1789.)

In a rigorous piece of investigative journalism, anticipating the methodology and philosophy of his fictional detective M. Dupin, Poe insists that it is quite certain the operations of the Automaton are regulated by a human agent and nothing else, and goes so far as to assert that the matter is something of a mathematical demonstration, *a priori*. 'Let us place the first move in a game of chess, in juxtaposition with the data of an algebraical question, and their great difference will be immediately perceived.'[26] Recalling the calculating machine developed by Charles Babbage, Poe observes that the arithmetical or algebraical calculations performed by this 'engine of wood and metal', however complex, proceed necessarily and inevitably to the one solution that must follow from the data: 'The second step having been a consequence of the data, the third step is equally a consequence of the second, the fourth of the third, the fifth of the fourth, and so on, and not possibly otherwise, to the end.'[27] But from the first move in a game of chess no step necessarily follows; the uncertainty of each ensuing move increasing, one cannot predict with any accuracy more than a few moves ahead. 'Even granting (what should not be granted) that the movements of the Automaton Chess Player were in themselves determinate, they would be necessarily interrupted and disarranged by the indeterminate will of his antagonist.'[28] So Poe concludes that:

> There is then no analogy whatever between the operations of the Chess-Player, and those of the calculating machine of Mr. Babbage, and if we choose to call the former a pure machine we must be prepared to admit that it is, beyond all comparison, the most wonderful of the inventions of mankind.[29]

Poe could not have known that the concept of the "calculating machine" underpinning his "demonstration" was being rendered obsolete, even as he wrote, by the inception of Babbage's Analytical Engine. In a series of notes that contain the most important information relating to this project, published seven years later in 1843, Ada Lovelace observes that there is 'considerable vagueness and inaccuracy in the minds of persons in general regarding the subject' of Babbage's work. 'There is a misty notion among most of those who have attended at all to it', she writes, 'that *two* "calculating machines" have been successively invented by the same person within the last few years; while others again have never heard but of the one original "calculating machine", and are not aware of there being any extension upon this.' While the first engine developed by Babbage was strictly *arithmetical*, the results it could arrive at lying within a clearly defined and restricted range, the powers of the new Analytical Engine were co-extensive with our knowledge of the laws of *analysis* itself. 'Indeed', remarks Lovelace, 'we may consider the engine as the *material and mechanical representative of analysis* ... the executive manipulation of algebraical and numerical signals.' Inspired by the chains of punched cards employed in mechanised Jacquard looms to regulate the production of complex textile patterns, Babbage had invented a physical system for encoding and uploading a computer program, which anticipated the perforated paper tapes that would later be used to transfer data to the ROM and EPROM on the first mini-computers. 'The bounds of *arithmetic* were ... overstepped the moment the idea of applying the cards had emerged; and the Analytical Machine does not occupy common ground with mere "calculating machines"', concludes Lovelace. 'We may say most aptly, that the Analytical Engine *weaves algebraical patterns* just as the Jacquard-loom weaves flowers and leaves.' Indeed, Alan Turing later acknowledged, the machine is at least potentially an example of the "Universal Logic Machine" he laid the groundwork for in his paper 'On Computable Numbers, with an Application to the Entscheidungsproblem' (1936): and it *could* therefore have run a chess program (like the program he developed while at Bletchley Park during the Second World War) which assigns numerical values to pieces, positions and potential for future positioning then selects the one move with the greatest value and the greatest position-play value.[30]

One cannot but wonder whether Poe might have been the first person to have realised this. Certainly, there is a marked change of emphasis in his next piece of writing about chess, in the preamble to 'The Murders in the Rue Morgue' (1841), which might suggest that Poe had learned of the Analytical Engine in the interim. (Poe could not have read Lovelace's notes, nor Babbage's unpublished description of the Analytical Engine in his 1937 essay 'On the Mathematical Powers of the Calculating Engine', nor the original 1842 Italian-language version of the 'Sketch of the Analytical Engine' produced by L. F. Menabrea, before writing the first of his three stories about Dupin; but he was clearly following Babbage's work with considerable interest, and his story might be a response to information concerning the second engine contained in a letter from Babbage to Quetelet published in *Bulletins de l'Académie Royal des Sciences et Belles-Lettres de Bruxelles* in May 1835 and in a collection of essays called *The Ninth Bridgewater Treatise* in 1837.) On the one hand, chess is no longer thought to be beyond those 'arithmetical or algebraical calculations' one might perform on a machine.[31] In fact, 'to observe attentively', 'to remember distinctly', 'to have a retentive memory' and 'to proceed by the book' are now considered to be the 'sum total of good playing'.[32] But in both 'Murders in the Rue Morgue' and 'The Purloined Letter', Poe takes issue with popular errors relating to the term *analysis*, promulgated by certain mathematicians.[33] 'The faculty of re-solution is possibly much invigorated by mathematical study, and especially by that highest branch of it which, unjustly, and merely on account of its retrograde operations, has been called, as if *par excellence*, analysis.'[34] But to calculate is *not* to analyse. In fact, the 'constructive or combining power' is a 'primitive faculty', so 'frequently seen in those whose intellect bordered otherwise upon idiocy ... as to have attracted general observation among writers on morals'.[35] If this is not generally understood, the 'elaborate frivolity of chess' might help to explain why: 'the pieces have different and bizarre motions, with various and variable values, [and in consequence] what is only complex is mistaken (a not unusual error) for what is profound'.[36] Having rejected 'this particular deception', Poe posits a rather more comprehensive conception of analysis that extends beyond mathematical reason, and the 'pagan fables' of algebra.[37] 'Our player confines himself not at all; nor, because the game is the object, does he reject deductions from things external to the game.'[38] Instead, 'the analyst throws himself into the spirit of his opponent, identifies himself therewith, and not infrequently sees thus, at a glance, the sole methods (sometimes indeed absurdly simple ones) by which he may seduce into error or hurry into miscalculation'.[39] According to Poe, simple games like draughts or whist might, therefore, provide a better means of testing the highest powers of the intellect; in the former, for instance, where the moves are homogenous and far less calculating power is required, advantages are said to be obtained 'by either party only through superior *acumen*'.[40] In the stories that follow, the analytical powers of Dupin would invariably surpass the immense processing or computational power of the Parisian police force: 'His results, brought about by the very soul and essence of method, have in truth, the whole air of intuition.'[41]

Poe's thoughts on chess and analysis were to prove remarkably prescient, anticipating the problems that would preoccupy the mid-twentieth-century pioneers of artificial intelligence. As Poe perceived, chess does in fact require far greater computational power than draughts. 'Not only is the end game different from the middle game in the considerations which are paramount, but the openings are much more devoted to getting the pieces into a position of free mobility, for attack and defence that is the middle game', explains Norbert Wiener in *Cybernetics*. 'The result is that we cannot be even approximately content with a uniform evaluation of the various weighting factors for the game as a whole.'[42] And while it would prove easy enough to programme machines that could play a 'tolerable game' (Turing) or 'a chess not so manifestly bad as to be ridiculous' (Wiener), the shortcomings of what Poe termed 'an exaggeration of *the application* of the one principle or set of principles of search' soon became all too evident.[43] 'You will find that when the same situation comes up twice on the chessboard, your opponent's reaction will be the same each time, and you will find that he has a very rigid personality', says Wiener. 'It is thus not too hard for an expert to get a line on his machine opponent and to defeat him every time.'[44] What was required clearly was a computer which would perform the sort of observations that inform Poe's Analyst. 'Let us suppose [the machine] examines all the previous games which it has recorded on its memory to determine what weighting of the different evaluations of the worth of pieces, command, mobility, and the like, will conduce most to winning', suggests Wiener. 'In this way, it learns not only from its own failures but its opponent's successes.'[45] Unfortunately, 'All this is very difficult to do in chess, and as a matter of fact the full development of this technique, so as to give rise to a machine that can play master chess, has not been accomplished.'[46] And that remains the case today, over fifty years later – as philosopher and Turing specialist B. Jack Copeland has pointed out: 'The huge improvement in computer chess since Turing's day owes much more to advances in hardware engineering than to advances in AI.'[47] The victory of IBM's chess-playing computer Deep Blue over Russian Grand Master

Garry Kasparov was the result not of a learning algorithm but of 256 parallel processors examining 200 million possible moves per second and strategies extending fourteen moves ahead. As Noam Chomsky remarked, the outcome was as meaningful as a bulldozer winning a weight-lifting competition.[48] 'In fact, little or nothing about human thought processes appears to have been learned from the series of projects that culminated in Deep Blue.'[49]

This is *not* the impression people formed at the time. 'As Kasparov suspected, his duel with Deep Blue indeed became an icon in musings on the meaning and dignity of human life', observed Robert Wright in *Time Magazine* (1996); 'he seemed to personify some kind of identity crisis that computers have induced in our species'.[50] In fact, the popular reaction to the triumph of IBM is consistent with a tendency to invest chess-playing computers with deeply rooted anxieties concerning the development of artificial intelligence. The first robot in English literature was 'Moxon's Master' (1893), a chess-playing automaton inspired by Von Kempelen's Turk: 'not more than five feet in height, with proportions suggesting those of a gorilla – a tremendous breadth of shoulders, thick, short neck and broad, squat head, which had a tangled growth of hair and was topped with a crimson fez'.[51] Beginning with the question that preoccupied *Time Magazine* (does a machine think about the work it is doing?), Ambrose Bierce describes how Moxon is murdered one night after beating his creature at its own game:

> the whole room blazed with a blinding white light that burned into my brain and heart and memory a vivid picture of the combatants on the floor, Moxon underneath, his throat still in the clutch of those iron hands, his head thrown backward, his eyes protruding, his mouth wide open and his tongue thrust out; and – horrible contrast! – upon the painted face of his assassin an expression of tranquil and profound thought, as in the solution of a problem in chess![52]

HAL 9000 adopts a similar course of action immediately after playing a game of chess in Stanley Kubrick's *2001: A Space Odyssey* (1968), and the US intercontinental ballistic missile system Joshua suggests that Matthew Broderick might prefer a 'nice game of chess' before settling for global thermonuclear war in John Banham's *War Games* (1983). So, while Poe is surely correct to suggest that what is merely complex is consistently mistaken for what is profound, one cannot but wonder whether this might not itself be a significant mistake, integral to the pervasive cultural unease which has so long surrounded the rise of the machines.

Returning to Freud's famous essay on 'The Uncanny' (1919), readers will recall that particularly favourable conditions for generating an uncanny feeling seem to exist if intellectual uncertainty is aroused as to whether a thing is animate or inanimate.[53] Freud observes that young children will make no sharp distinction between the animate and inanimate, but are especially fond of treating their dolls as if they were alive, and so he speculates that the sense of the uncanny might 'derive not from an infantile fear, but from an infantile wish'.[54] Our inclination to attribute thought to automata might have begun as an insurance against extinction, an attempt to cheat death by investing these physical objects with ego, on the misguided conviction that *thoughts are omnipotent*.

> But these ideas arose on the soil of boundless self-love, the primordial narcissism that dominates the mental life of both the child and primitive man, and when this phase is surmounted, the meaning of the 'double' changes: having once been an assurance of immortality, it becomes the uncanny harbinger of death.[55]

Cultural anxieties generated by artificial intelligence, together with our consistently overrating the significance of its achievements, indicate that what we are dealing with here is an uncanny effect. In this one respect, though they possess no technical similarities, IBM's Deep Blue was no less a conjuring trick than Von Kempelen's Mechanical Turk.

If all this seems inconsequential, note that Turing first conceived of the 'Imitation Game' which has become the foundation for posthumanist philosophies relating to AI *as a game of chess*. Explaining that it is not difficult to devise a program that will play a 'not very bad game of chess', Turing proposes a 'little experiment'. Get three men as subjects for the experiment: A, B, C. Two of these, let us say A and C, are to be rather poor chess players. B is to do no more than work the machine. Two rooms are used, with some arrangement for communicating moves, and a game of chess is to be played between C and either A or the machine B. The point of the experiment is to demonstrate that 'C may find it quite difficult to tell which he is playing'.[56] (According to Turing, this was an idealised form of an experiment he had actually done – probably with the Champernownes at Bletchley Park.)[57] As we shall see, this is remarkably close to the final form of the so-called Turing Test or Imitation Game that would soon follow – and this must have profound implications for how we interpret an experiment widely regarded as an empirical measure for AI. For this supposedly behaviourist or operationalist criterion for thinking is clearly designed to gauge an uncanny effect. 'Playing against such a machine', writes Turing, 'gives a definite feeling that one is pitting one's wits against something alive.'[58]

The Imitation Game

In his famous essay 'Computing Machinery and Intelligence' (1950), Turing sets out to investigate whether machines can think. But for the very reason Descartes refused to consider whether he was a rational animal, Turing proposes to replace this question with another, which is closely related to it but which will be expressed, claims Turing, in relatively unambiguous words. 'This new form of the problem can be described in terms of a game which we call the "imitation game".'[59] This party game is played by three people, a man (A), a woman (B) and an interrogator (C) in a room apart from the other two who may be of either gender. The object of the game for the third player is to determine which is the man and which is the woman; the interrogator will present the other players with a series of questions, and the answers will be mediated in some fashion to ensure the interrogator decides based solely upon the answers provided. The object of the game for the first player is to deceive the interrogator into believing he is the woman, while the object for the second player is to prevent this from happening. 'She can add such things as "I am the woman, don't listen to him!" to her answers, but it will avail nothing as the man can make similar remarks.'[60] Having set out the rules of the game, Turing then invites us to imagine what will happen when a machine takes the part of the man. This is the 'more accurate form of the question' that replaces the original problem: 'Will the interrogator decide wrongly as often when the game is played like this as he does when the game is played between a man and a woman?'[61] And Turing is in no doubt as to what the answer might be: predicting that machines certainly *could* triumph in such a contest, he even speculates that this might happen by the end of the twentieth century. 'I believe that in about fifty years' time it will be possible to programme computers, with a storage capacity of about 10^9, to make them play the imitation game so well that an average interrogator will not have more than 70 per cent. chance of making the right identification after five minutes of questioning.'[62] And though the original question 'Can machines think?' is dismissed as 'too meaningless to deserve discussion', Turing nevertheless affirms his belief that 'by the end of the century the use of words and general educated opinion will have altered so much that one will be able to speak of machines thinking without expecting to be contradicted'.[63]

Debate has raged ever since as to what Turing might have meant, and the critical literature on the Imitation Game comprises a vast and bewildering array of differing interpretations. The matter is complicated by the fact that in the same essay Turing presents a different version of the game, where the computer plays the part of A and the part of B is 'taken by a man'.[64] This has provoked commentators such as S. G. Sterrett in 'Turing's Two Tests for Intelligence' (2000) to distinguish between what he terms (1) the 'Original Imitation Game', in which the objective is for the computer to impersonate the woman, and (2) the 'Standard Interpretation' of the 'Turing Test', in which the objective is to imitate a 'man', with the latter generally being understood to mean *human* rather than *male*.[65] And, though commentators often miss or reject the possibility of such a distinction, there is a general agreement that Turing had really been trying to assess a computer program's ability to imitate a human being. This 'Standard Interpretation' might seem to find support in Turing's later articles and broadcasts, where he says simply that 'The idea of the test is that the machine has to try and pretend to be a man', and that our main problem is to 'programme a machine to imitate a brain'.[66] And it is the 'Standard Interpretation' that has provided the criterion for the Loebner Prize, an annual competition in which computer programs compete for a gold medal and an award of $100,000. The outcomes of such competitions arouse interest far beyond the small community of specialists in AI because it is widely believed that Turing was offering his test as a means of defining the nebulous term *thinking*. 'An especially influential behaviourist definition of intelligence was put forward by Turing', writes psychiatrist Ned Block; and this assumption is shared by philosopher John Searle and physicist Roger Penrose in their own landmark assessments. 'The operationalist would say that the computer *thinks* provided that it acts indistinguishably from the way that a person acts when thinking', writes Penrose 'This viewpoint was argued for very forcefully in a famous article by Alan Turing.'[67] But, as Turing's editor, B. Jack Copeland remarks, Turing says quite explicitly that his aim is *not* to give a *definition* of thinking but rather a '*criterion* for "thinking"'.[68] The result of this emphasis on the 'Standard Interpretation' of the Test as a means of verifying the claims of what Searle and Penrose term 'strong AI' is that the 'Original Imitation Game' is often considered irrelevant or misleading, dismissed by Turing's biographer Andrew Hodges as a 'red herring', and regarded by Turing's editor as part of the protocol for scoring the test: 'Will interrogators decide wrongly as often in man-imitates-woman games as they do in computer-imitates-human games?'[69]

In recent years this critical consensus has come under attack following renewed interest in what Sterret terms the 'Original Imitation Game'. In their recent reception history, Ayse Pinar Saygin, Ilyas Cicekli and Varol Akman note that, while the woman vanishes altogether in the second version of the game which underpins the 'Standard Interpretation', the objectives of A, B and the interrogator remain unaltered. If Turing never explicitly says these have changed, both machine and man must be impersonating a woman.[70] In their opinion, 'The man and the machine are measured in terms of their respective performance against real women'.[71] And they suggest that, though there is an ambiguity in the paper, the change in the second game is intended to stress the point that the simulations are to be compared against each other and not against that which they are simulating. 'On close examination it can be seen that what Turing proposes is to compare the machine's success against that of the man, *not* to look at whether it "beats" the woman in the IG.'[72] Saygin, Cicekli and Akman conclude that 'The crucial point seems to be that the notion of *imitation* figures more prominently in Turing's paper than is commonly acknowledged'.[73]

Though a tiny number of commentators have come to this conclusion, they have failed to recognize purpose and utility in Turing's design. Patrick Hayes and Kenneth Ford, for instance, write that 'he tells us quite clearly to make a program that can do as well as a man at pretending to be a woman', 'a mechanical transvestite', only to support their case that the Test is a blind alley as 'imitating human capabilities should not be the ultimate goal of AI'.[74] But once we accept that the criterion with which Turing replaces the question 'Can a machine think?' is designed to ascertain *not* whether a machine can think but whether a machine can produce a model of a phenomenon at least as convincing as that produced by a man, then the purpose and utility of the Test becomes immediately apparent. Indeed, as Searle observes, 'The idea that computer simulations could be the real thing ought to have seemed suspicious in the first place because the computer isn't confined to simulating mental operations by any means'.[75] Though reality can never be represented exactly by a mathematical model, what we do produce is often sufficient for our purposes; and with the proliferation of cheap and increasingly sophisticated information technology, the use of computers to model scientific, social and economic phenomena has in fact become increasingly prevalent. Only an obsessive preoccupation with a very specific and peculiar conception of AI can have prevented us from seeing that the Imitation Game provides us with the framework necessary for testing the success or the "intelligence" of such simulations: setting the predictions against reality first, then against the performance of proven simulators, in order to ascertain which most closely corresponds to data derived from observations in the laboratory or from the field. If there is any doubt on this score, consider that Turing introduces yet another (and surprisingly overlooked) Imitation Game – in which "humans" do not feature at all. Proceeding on the assumption that the computer to which he has referred throughout performs satisfactorily (i.e. a paper machine: more on this later!), Turing suggests that his Imitation Game could even be reconfigured in a way that might permit one to test programs on the new digital computers. 'The imitation game could then be played with the machine in question (as B) and the mimicking digital computer (as A) and the interrogator would be unable to distinguish them.'[76]

In fact, Turing's criterion for *thinking* would seem to be Poe's criterion for *analytical thought*, for the objective of the machine is to present a convincing simulation and there can be no better measure of success than deception – that is, to 'seduce into error or hurry into miscalculation'.[77] And having established this crucial point, one cannot but wonder whether the huge number of conflicting opinions concerning the meaning and implications of the Test might be significant. Turing was a computer programmer, and thus entirely capable of writing instructions which are not open to misunderstanding; his paper promised a new form of the problem expressed in relatively unambiguous terms. How is the past half-century of incomprehension and interminable argument possible? The use of the misleading and loaded terms "thinking" and "thought" might be merely unfortunate. The resemblance of Turing's Test to the famous Cartesian test for *conscious thought* – in which it is shown that no one could mistake a 'clockwork man' for a human with a soul – might conceivably be dismissed as a devastating blunder.[78] But how to account for his mischievous comments about the future being like the chapters describing the rise of the machines in Samuel Butler's fantasy novel *Erewhon*? '[It] seems probable that once the machine thinking method had started, it would not take long to outstrip our feeble powers', writes Turing. 'At some stage therefore we should have to expect the machines to take control.'[79] An embarrassment to proponents of Strong AI – 'this is comic-strip stuff'[80] – one begins to understand precisely why Turing was seen to *giggle* when he penned 'Computing Machinery and Intelligence'.[81] I believe we should at least be prepared to entertain the possibility that the enormous confusion surrounding the Turing Test is something rather more than a mere accident. The very imprecision of the Imitation Game has helped to produce an environment in which interrogators are regularly seduced into serious errors regarding the ontological status of computers. Indeed, Turing's article itself might be regarded as a program of sorts, one that has won game after game (invariably mistaken for a passage in Descartes), a mechanism for dissimulation with a track record equal to that of the Mechanical Turk.

Once this is accepted, further mysteries concerning the Imitation Game begin to fall into place. Consider the "Gödel Argument" set out by the philosopher John Lucas in his famous article 'Minds, Machines and Gödel' (1961), which is developed at length by Roger Penrose in *The Emperor's New Mind* (1989) and *Shadows of the Mind* (1994). As Penrose notes, in proving that no algorithm exists for deciding whether or not an algorithm run on a Turing machine is going to stop, Turing himself had shown that there can be no general algorithm for deciding mathematical questions:[82] 'By Gödel's famous theorem or some similar argument [i.e. Church-Turing], one can show that however the machine is constructed there are bound to be cases where the machine fails to give an answer, but a mathematician would be able to.'[83] And so, Lucas and Penrose conclude, the human mind *cannot* be explained as an algorithm running on a Turing machine. Indeed, in Copeland's view, it is virtually impossible to say what mathematical conception of the mind is available to someone who endorses the Gödel Argument – 'because the objection, if sound, could be used equally well to support the conclusion, not only that the mind is not a Turing machine, but also that it is not any one of a very broad range of machines.'[84] How is this apparent contradiction in Turing's thought possible? Penrose merely concludes that 'There is perhaps some irony in the fact that this aspect of Turing's own work may now indirectly provide us with a possible loophole to his own viewpoint concerning the nature of mental phenomena.'[85] I would go considerably further and suggest that it is quite unthinkable that the mathematician who established the existence of non-computable numbers could have been suggesting in all seriousness that the human mind is an algorithm. In fact, Turing can be seen to have anticipated that the original, imprecise form of his question might provoke what he termed the 'Mathematical Objection', and we are now in a position to understand his response. Citing the mathematicians who have worked for centuries on the question of whether Fermat's last theorem is true or not, Turing jokes that 'The short answer to this argument is that although it is established that there are limitations to the powers of any particular machine, it has only been stated, without any sort of proof, that no such limitations apply to the human intellect'.[86] But Turing insists that he does not 'think this view can be dismissed quite so lightly', and his careful response is not what might be expected of a proponent of Strong AI.[87] Turing sets out procedures whereby a machine might be made to appear as though it had overcome the Decision Problem – permitted to risk mistakes for the sake of experiment and provided with a memory bank where the results can be stored, a program could modify itself over time, effectively becoming a different machine, thereby avoiding the problem altogether. Turing's machine would not have overcome the Mathematical Objection, but this deficiency would no longer be apparent to the average interrogator. As Turing says, his contention is merely that 'machines can be constructed which will simulate the behaviour of the human mind very closely'.[88] Evidently, the point to all this has nothing to do with substantiating the claims of Strong AI. Turing is concerned primarily with the production of a machine that will effectively simulate the natural phenomenon that is at once the most familiar to us and the most challenging to model, the human mind. And this may explain why Turing is prepared to countenance what he terms *faking* – predetermining some of the decisions that must be made by a machine in order to hasten and control its education and development.[89]

> It would be quite easy to arrange the experiences in such a way that they automatically caused the structure of the machine to build up to a previously intended form, and this would obviously be a gross form of cheating, almost on a par with having a man inside the machine.[90]

Finally, I would like to suggest we are now in a position to resolve one of the most puzzling aspects of the 'Chinese Room'. In this famous attack on the Turing Test and the related claims of Strong AI, Searle (1980) imagines he is locked into a room and given counters marked with Chinese symbols together with a set of instructions (in English) on how to manipulate them.[91] Searle then passes a version of the Turing Test, providing appropriate responses to questions from outside the room (written in Hanzi) merely by referring to his table of instructions – while doggedly insisting that he does not understand one word of Chinese! 'For the purposes of the Chinese, I am simply an instantiation of the computer program.'[92] According to the proponents of Strong AI, Searle has proven that he understood what was written in Chinese, but to Searle it is quite obvious he has not. 'I have inputs and outputs that are indistinguishable from those of the native Chinese speaker and I can have any formal program you like, but I still understand nothing.'[93] Searle's thought experiment has generated a vast critical literature, but what is perhaps the most curious aspect would seem to have attracted relatively little comment. The fact is that, far from being a modification of the Turing Test (a subversive substitution of a philosopher for a computer), Searle has described precisely the scenario that Turing had in mind. It will be remembered that a digital computer is to play against another 'discrete state machine' which has already played the Imitation Game – and this could hardly be anything other than the sort of *human computer* Searle jokes about. 'The idea behind digital computers may be explained by saying that these machines are intended to carry out any operations which could be done by a human computer', writes Turing. 'The human computer is supposed to be following fixed rules; he has no authority to deviate from them in any detail.'[94] Elsewhere, Turing refers to this combination of a human with written instructions as a *paper machine*: 'A man provided with paper, pencil, and rubber, and subject to strict discipline, is in effect a universal machine.'[95] And it is clear that Turing's earliest thoughts concerning the Imitation Game arose from experience with the experimental chess programs run on such paper machines: 'One can produce "paper machines" for playing chess.'[96] Even Turing's self-adjusting algorithms were run on *himself* and not a digital computer: 'I made a start on the latter but found the work altogether too laborious at present', he explains. 'When some electronic machines are in actual operation I hope that they will make this more feasible ... instead of having to work with a paper machine as at present.'[97] It is safe to conclude that the position on Strong AI frequently attributed to Turing can hardly have been held by a man who had worked for so many years locked up in a Chinese Room. Indeed, we can begin to understand why Turing's surprise at the results produced by his machines is quite so pronounced. As the sentient CPU at the heart of such a machine, Turing would often have found himself performing operations, following his own written instructions, that he could never have anticipated. 'Certainly the machine can only do what we do order it to perform, anything else would be a mechanical fault', he remarks. 'But there is no need to suppose that, when we give it its orders we know what we are doing, or what the consequences of these orders are going to be.' He concludes that: 'One does not need to be able to understand how these orders lead to the mechanism's subsequent behaviour, any more than one needs to understand the mechanism of germination when one puts a seed in the ground.'[98]

The analogy is suggestive. One could argue that agriculture is a sort of self-adjusting routine, run on human hardware for millennia, evolving in response to environmental pressures without much in the way of conscious innovation, producing outcomes that no one could have foreseen at inception. If we repeat the error of anthropomorphising *thought*, we might speculate that while machine intelligence cannot be an ego it might nevertheless be a *person*, in the original sense of that term: a virtual entity sustained by a cultural practice – i.e. *persona ficta*. For just as men make '*Automata*' that move themselves with 'springs and wheels as doth a clock', so 'by Art' men have created 'that great LEVIATHAN' called the State, 'which is but an Artificial Man', 'in which the *Sovereignty* is an Artificial *Soul*'.[99] This position would be congruent with what is called the Virtual Mind Reply to Searle's Chinese Room, but would only perpetuate the Promethean error we seek to disentangle. Turing himself expressed the hope that digital computing machines would eventually stimulate a considerable interest in symbolic logic and mathematical philosophy (noting that the language in which one communicates with the machines, i.e. the language of instruction tables, forms a sort of symbolic logic).[100] For this reason I would like to close this section by suggesting that the clearest conception of what such a *machine for thinking* might be in essence is to be found not in the Ultron computers of sci-fi, but in the thoroughly low-tech "Glass Bead Game" imagined by Hermann Hesse in *Das Glasperlenspiel* (1943).

> A reader who chanced to be ignorant of the Glass Bead Game might imagine such a Game pattern as rather similar to the pattern of a chess game, except that the significances of the pieces and the potentialities of their relationships to one another and their effect upon one another multiplied many-fold and an actual content must be ascribed to each piece, each constellation, each chess move, of which this move, configuration, and so on is the symbol.[101]

Inspired by Leibniz's unrealised fantasy of a universal language (which would eventually culminate, via that philosopher's engagement with the *I Ching* or *Book of Changes*, in the binary code), the Glass Bead Game is a cultural practice unique to the university province of Castalia: a metalanguage that began as a game, but that developed over time into a sophisticated medium capable of comprehending the arts and sciences, permitting players to construct models of those thought processes through which humans interpret reality: 'a language of symbol and formulas, in which mathematics and music played an equal part, so that it became possible to combine astronomical and musical formulas, to reduce mathematics and music to a common denominator, as it were.'[102] Like Leibniz, the inventor of the game has taken inspiration from the prevalent misconception of Hanzi script as a system of ideograms; and the one Glass Bead Game described in any detail in the book is based on the ritual Confucian pattern for the building of a house.[103] In this context, it might be amusing to relate that this Chinese Room is performed for the Magister Ludi by an assistant *who speaks no Chinese!* ('It was far too late for him to learn it now.') And, as with Turing's early coding, the final program is run on a *human machine*.

> With a luminous golden stylus he delicately inscribed character after character on the small tablet before him, and the same characters promptly appeared in the script of the Game, enlarged a hundredfold, upon the gigantic board on the rear wall of the hall, to be spelled out by a thousand whispering voices, called out by the Speakers, broadcast to the country and the world.[104]

The fate of the hunchback

One might expect the Prime Radiant, the computer in Isaac Asimov's *Foundation Trilogy* (1942–1953) to be rather more high-tech: a near-contemporary (in real time) of the monkish Castalia, the Galactic Empire possesses nuclear power and star-cruisers and energy-shields. So it comes as something of a surprise to find (in the final part of the trilogy) that the Prime Radiant is really little more than a big whiteboard. 'First, a pearly white, unrelieved, then a trace of faint darkness here and there, and finally, the fine neatly printed equations in black, with an occasional red hairline that wavered through the darker forest like a staggering rillet.'[105] Since their fleeting appearance on the pocket calculator of Hari Seldon the psychohistorian in the first book, the symbols projected by the Prime Radiant have been modified by a series of *human computers*, who have made alterations to the program according to instructions in response to external data. 'It was a room which, through the centuries, had been the abode of pure science – yet it had none of the gadgets with which, through millennia of association, science has come to be considered equivalent', explains Asimov. 'It was a science, instead, which dealt with mathematical concepts only, in a manner similar to the speculation of ancient, ancient races in the primitive, prehistoric days before technology had come to be; before Man had spread beyond a single, now-unknown world'.[106] Like Castalia's Glass Bead Game, psychohistory is considered the culmination of a Leibnizian symbolic logic: but where the Masters of Castalia have decisively rejected that 'philosophy of history of which Hegel is the most brilliant and also most dangerous representative', psychohistorians of the Second Foundation have applied their skills in computer programming to the historical process, modelling with apparent success the entire history of a Galactic Empire over tens of thousands of years.[107] In fact, the series of crises, and the dialectical progression, predicted by psychohistorians cannot fail to recall the historical materialism of Marx; while the Seldon Plan to alleviate the worst of the coming catastrophe is entirely in keeping with the mania for planning that characterised the era from 1925 to 1975 (from Lenin's New Economic Plan and Le Corbusier's urbanism to the Keynesian stimulus package and China's Great Leap Forward). 'Psychohistory was the quintessence of sociology', explains Asimov; 'it was the science of human behaviour reduced to mathematical equations.'[108] This is said to be possible because, while individual human beings are unpredictable, the reaction of human mobs can be treated statistically. 'The larger the mob the greater the accuracy that could be achieved', claims Asimov. 'And the size of the human masses that Seldon worked with was no less than the population of the Galaxy, which in his time was numbered in the quintillions.'[109] If the determinism in this vision of history is (ostensibly) now a thing of the past, the suggestion that sociology might eventually come to be regarded as 'that branch of economics that deals with the reactions of human conglomerates to fixed social and economic stimuli' can be seen to have proven most prescient, anticipating the application of humanity's ever greater processing power to the problems of macroeconomic management over the latter half of the twentieth century.[110] 'Someday there will exist a unified social science of the kind that Asimov imagined', insists Paul Krugman, neo-Keynesian and Nobel Prize-winning economist, in his introduction to the folio edition of *The Foundation Trilogy* (2012), 'but for the time being economics is as close to psychohistory as you can get'.[111]

The groundwork for this development was laid before the advent of computing shortly before the Second World War, with the attempt to reconcile the General Theory of John Maynard Keynes with the orthodox neo-classical approach (based on the Enlightenment faith in a rational subject) that took place in a meeting at Oxford in 1937 – when Roy Harrod and J. E. Meade presented mathematical models of the General Theory. In the view of economic historian Warren Young, this is the most important meeting in the history of economics, and it represented a parting of the ways within the General Theory Group over 'whether the approach they were developing was a determinate system which could be expressed in the form of simultaneous equations or a system fraught with uncertainty and animal spirits'.[112] The triumph of the 'mathematically elegant' approach came about through the publication of the paper 'Mr Keynes and the Classics: A Suggested Reinterpretation' by John Hicks in *Econometrica* that same year, with its formal representation of Keynesian macroeconomics – the IS-LM diagram. According to Robert Skidelsky, 'This determinate system in which the "authority" could act on the multiplier by fiscal policy ... gave economists a potentially key position at the centre of government'.[113] As refined further by Alvin Hansen ("the American Keynes"), "Keynesian" economics laid the foundation for the unprecedented era of prosperity that would follow the Second World War, the "Golden Age of capitalism" that would last until the early 1970s, and which held out the possibility that a managed economy might effect an arrest in the historical process, the prospect of a post-historic future in which the agency and even the integrity of the human subject must eventually suffer corrosion: 'The nuclear reactor is the seat of the power', remarks cultural historian Lewis Mumford, in a diatribe that perfectly captures the anxieties of this era: 'radio transmission and rocket flight their angelic means of communication: but beyond these minor agents of divinity the Control Room itself, with its Cybernetic Deity, giving His lightning-like decisions, and His infallible answers: omniscience and omnipotence, triumphantly mated by science'.[114]

But, like the Seldon Plan in the *Foundation Trilogy*, this heroic attempt to control the future was ultimately undermined by an inability to reduce what is uncertain to the calculable status of what is known. A result that might have been predicted by Keynes himself, whose writing (from his first treatise on probability through to *The General Theory*) had repeatedly attacked attempts to deal with the present that cannot acknowledge how little we know concerning the future. 'If we speak frankly, we have to admit that our basis of knowledge for estimating the yield ten years hence of a railway, a copper mine, a textile factory, the goodwill of a patent medicine, an Atlantic liner, a building in the City of London, amounts to little and sometimes to nothing; or even five years hence', admits Keynes; 'human decisions affecting the future, whether personal or political or economic, cannot depend on strict mathematical expectation, since the basis for making any such calculations does not exist'.[115] If the necessity for action and decision compels us, as 'practical men', to do our best to overlook this awkward fact, to behave as though we could calculate the probability of prospective advantages and disadvantages, we should never, as theorists, lose sight of the flimsy foundation upon which we build. 'All these pretty, polite techniques, made for a well-panelled board room and a nicely regulated market, are liable to collapse', he writes. 'At all times the vague panic fears and equally vague and unreasoned hopes are not really lulled, and lie but a little way below the surface.'[116] Further developing such insights, the post-Keynesian philosopher and economist G. L. S. Shackle would suggest, like Benjamin before him, that the expectations produced by the patterns we project onto time are *kaleidic*. 'Like the symmetrical pattern of colours in the kaleidoscope, they can be changed comprehensively and radically by a slight shock or twist given to the instrument.'[117] Having fashioned the concepts that produce the appearance of an orderly system, 'the economist ought to bear in mind that his conjuring tricks have their element of illusion, which he must not allow to deceive himself, despite the strong temptation'.[118] And in a passage that has remarkable parallels to that describing the Angelus Novus in Walter Benjamin's critique of social democracy, Shackle would insist that:

> The inspired creative power, the original Promethean gift, *original* in its continuous power of perhaps *ex nihilo* contribution to history, which drives the human affair along, is incompatible with foreknowledge ... For how should there be knowledge, in every present moment, of what men are about to *originate* in the extreme sense, to draw from the void?[119]

The bourgeois subject, still moving blindly into the abyss, is propelled here – beyond the history it is constructing – not by the storm of progress but by its own innate Promethean fire. Drawing on subjectivist or "Austrian School" thinking that had been sidelined in the Golden Age, a generation of theorists and politicians in the United Kingdom would accordingly seek to eliminate structures perceived to embody a futile or even counterproductive attempt to second-guess the future, in the belief that this would allow the 'gift of choice' a free (and invisible) hand. Sustained by good fortune that could not have been predicted (e.g. North Sea oil, the availability of Chinese labour, the collapse of the Soviet Union, the development of the internet), neoliberal economics has survived recessions that might have been avoided (and that really ought to have sunk it), proceeding (like the hunchback in Asimov) to discredit the very notion of long-term planning.

How, then, was the neoliberal paradigm "captured" (like Asimov's hunchback) by the machine it set out to destroy, succumbing to delusions that had seized upon social democracy before it? 'What we may be witnessing is not just the end of the Cold War, or the passing of a particular period of post-war history', claimed Francis Fukuyama in his landmark essay 'The End of History' (1989), 'but the end of history as such: that is, the end point of mankind's ideological evolution and the universalization of Western liberal democracy as the final form of human government.'[120] One might have thought that the slogan "There is no alternative" had no place in an economic system which claims to be maximising our potential for free choice. What, beyond mere political expediency, might account for such a glaring contradiction? In his *Machine Dreams: How Economics Became a Cyborg Science* (2001), the economic historian Philip Mirowski has traced in great detail the process whereby the US military's cybernetic technology began to be applied to economics in the post-war era, and while centres such as the Chicago School play an important part in this story (employing a British approach to operational research that possesses a Seldon-esque tone of surety: 'large bodies of men and equipment behave in an astonishingly regular manner'), it is the work conducted by the father of cybernetics John von Neumann at the RAND Corporation that proves to be central.[121] 'From Nash equilibria to "psychological" experimental protocols, from "scratchpad wars" to computer simulations, from dynamic programming to evolutionary dynamics, from "rational decision theory" to automata playing games, all constitute the *fin-de-siècle* economic orthodoxy', and, Mirowski concludes, 'in each case, RAND was there first'.[122]

Evaluating von Neumann's most important contribution, the *Theory of Games and Economic Behaviour* (1944), Shackle observes that it must appear perfectly suited to the radical subjectivist paradigm:

> [Keynes's] ultimate vision, or discernment, of the chaotic in the business world might have been extended and opened out, made explicit and anatomised in detail, by the authors of the Theory of Games, had they happened to achieve some spasm of radical doubt. But on the contrary, by an extraordinary paradox, the Theory of Games turned out to be a supreme intellectual effort to defend the rationality of conduct in face of a recognition that business, and life in general, is a conflict of cutthroat ferocity.[123]

In fact, Mirowski precisely captures the radically empiricist outlook at RAND when he notes that there, war was considered just another problem in logic, and so too politics and economics: 'Hence they sought out people who really believed deep down that rationality was algorithmic and did not treat cognitive considerations in what they considered a cavalier manner.'[124] As Shackle complained, in *Epistemics and Economics* (1972):

> The Theory of Games of von Neumann and Morgenstern makes conduct rational despite the head-on collision of interests, by supposing that this is the conflict, not of real life in the fog of deliberately engendered uncertainty and misconception, but instead the conflict of a *game with known rules ... surprise*, the most powerful and incisive element in the whole art of war, is eliminated by the theoretical frame itself; and novelty, the *changing* of what appeared to be the rules of the game, the continually threatening dissolution of the conditions and circumstances in which either player may suppose himself to be operating, is eliminated also, by the supposition that each player, like a chess player of super-human intellectual range, knows everything that can happen.[125]

In spite of this fact, the cybernetics pioneered by RAND, including but extending far beyond game theory, has become an intrinsic and ever more important part of our twenty-first-century economic reality. In order to establish why this might be (and what might result) I conclude by considering one of the most influential varieties of economic "war-gaming" – scenario planning. Developed by Herman Kahn at the Hudson Institute (from his work undertaken for the US military at the RAND Corporation), scenario planning was used to extraordinary effect in the early 1970s by Royal Dutch Shell, enabling that corporation to respond effectively to the formation of OPEC (Organization of the Petroleum Exporting Countries), the resulting oil crisis 1973–1974 and the break-up of the USSR. In each case, Shell's scenario planning had described these possibilities beforehand: a fact that appears rather less remarkable once it is understood that scenario planning requires the development of not just one plan for the future, but a large number of such plans for *alternative futures*, and not on the off-chance that one proves applicable, but rather as a means of sharpening a manager's ability to perceive a pattern in events that depart from conventional expectations, and to recognise the extent to which their choices shape outcomes. 'By considering alternative futures, we begin to see that the future is shaped not only by the past but by what we think is possible and by the choices we make.'[126] In short, scenario planning seems perfectly suited to a neoliberal paradigm that emphasises radical subjectivity: and it should come as no surprise to find that the technique has been taken up by a great many corporations and institutions hoping to emulate Shell's success.

Interestingly, there is some disillusion with scenario planning. According to Shell, 'perhaps the single greatest driver of this dissatisfaction is a widely held yet misguided expectation that scenario planning readily and directly improves strategic decision making'.[127] The adaptation of the technique by Phillip Bobbitt, law professor, political historian and national security advisor to Carter, Bush and Clinton, in his blockbuster book on war, law and the course of history, *The Shield of Achilles* (2002) must present us a case in point. In this book Bobbitt posited three alternative approaches to a shared set of trends, drivers and emergencies: 'The Meadow with its impatient and ruthless naturalism, The Park with its bureaucratic Cartesianism, The Garden with its understated but iron insistence on harmony.'[128] Insisting that this is not a futurology, Bobbitt explains that it is about *present choices*. 'Taken individually, these decisions show how essential human agency is to any account of history (even an historical account of the future) and yet how confined our choices can become as a consequence of precedent-setting decisions.'[129] But if this was truly the intention, the way this scenario planning is framed could not be more misleading. For the same three alternative versions of the "market state" have just been described (in the chapter preceding this) as the inevitable outcome of the "long war" between the three competing systems of the nation state (communism, fascism, liberalism). In fact, we are led to believe, the market state is to be regarded as the next phase in a recurring historical pattern that resembles nothing so much as the familiar Hegelian triad (the chief difference being that synthesis follows here not from dialectic but from a non-determined three-way conflict)! 'The pattern of epochal wars and state formation, of peace congresses and international constitutions, has played out for five centuries to the end of the millennium just past', writes Bobbitt. 'But if the pattern of earlier eras is to be repeated, then we await a new, epochal war with state-shattering consequences.'[130] Far from permitting us to realise our own agency, Bobbitt's alternative futures come freighted with crippling dogmas, and this is because they are being used to illustrate, rather than to throw into question, his hugely controversial thesis. 'The importance of this idea in our present period of transition is that we can shape the next epochal war if we appreciate its inevitability and also the different forms it may take.'[131] As Shackle observed of game theory, the way the choice is being framed here permits us no choice at all.

And, unfortunately, Bobbitt's misleading scenario planning might well have had extraordinarily serious consequences – for *The Shield of Achilles* has had a profound and acknowledged impact on foreign policy.[132] Perplexing to most at the time, the British prime minister Tony Blair's conviction there was a *real and present danger* that Saddam Hussein might give weapons of mass destruction (WMDs) to Al-Qaeda, while admitting that the association between them was loose makes perfect sense once it is realised that foreign policy was being based (as foreign secretary Jack Straw explained) not on what we knew (hindsight) but on what we could not (foresight), following to the letter the prescription for Bobbitt's preferred future – the entrepreneurial fantasy-world of The Meadow.[133]

Careful investigative work ... was responsible for uncovering an Iraqi attempt to use the terrorist network [Al-Qaeda] for a nuclear attack – actually a conventional explosive that would disseminate radioactive materials, the so-called dirty bomb – against the city of Washington in 2007 ... Ultimately Iraq is blamed and this provided the decisive impetus for an invasion. A slightly different coalition [not the G-9] was organised to provide an expeditionary force ... This new expeditionary force, composed of troops hitherto delegated to NATO commands by the United States, Germany, and the United Kingdom, launched an airborne assault, seizing Baghdad, and meeting up with an amphibious offensive from the Persian Gulf, joined by overland elements of the same force from Kuwait.[134]

'The Kaleidoscope has been shaken', declared Tony Blair, in his famous speech at the Labour conference in October 2001, shortly after the 9/11 attacks. 'The pieces are in flux. Soon they will settle again. Before they do, let us re-order this world around us.'[135] Apparently referencing Shackle, Blair would seem to have missed the philosopher's warning that those who resort to such 'conjuring tricks' should not permit themselves to be deceived by their own illusions, 'despite the strong temptation'.[136]

CGI

The endurance of such misconceptions regarding computer modelling in the era of neoliberalism is evident in what is the most influential and fully realised Promethean horror to emerge from this period, Michael Crichton's *Jurassic Park* (1990), and Steven Spielberg's film adaptation (1993). What one remembers is the Promethean ambition of entrepreneur John Hammond and genetic scientist Henry Wu as they use cloning technologies to resurrect prehistoric monsters. But much of the horror here arises not from the dinosaurs alone, but from the feeling of helplessness that characters experience on being trapped in over-engineered, hyper-integrated, dysfunctional technological environments. Even the door locks are controlled centrally (an intrinsic flaw) and fail the moment the system goes down. Entire sections of the book consist of nightmarish blocks of computer code that engineer John 'Ray' Arnold must scour as he searches for the 'White Rabbit' that hacked his system.

Lewis Mumford's critique of the Late Modernist cybernetic city proves to be readily adapted to spaces created by corporations that had privatised and repurposed those Cold War information technologies. But like Late Modernist theorists considered in the previous chapter, Crichton can also be seen to reiterate, to a significant degree, the very Promethean illusion of order that he is attempting to attack.

'Who could have imagined it would turn out this way?' asks John Hammond. 'Apparently, Malcolm', replies Ellie Sadler.[137] In fact, much of the book is devoted to rockstar mathematician Dr Ian Malcolm's exposition of chaos theory, which originally grew out of a realisation that while the behaviour of complicated systems cannot be predicted, we can identify regularities in the complex variety of a system's behaviours. 'That's why chaos has become a very broad theory that's used to study everything from the stock market, to rioting crowds, to brain waves during epilepsy', explains Malcolm. 'Any sort of complex system where there is confusion and unpredictability. We can find an underlying order. Okay?'[138] Since Jurassic Park is just such a system, Malcolm asserts, it too will eventually show unpredictable behaviour.

'You know this because of...'

'Theory,' Malcolm said.

'But hadn't you better see the island, to see what he's actually done?'

'No. That is quite unnecessary. The details don't matter. Theory tells me that the island will quickly proceed to behave in unpredictable fashion.'

'And you're confident of your theory.'

'Oh, yes,' Malcolm said. 'Totally confident.' He sat back in the chair. 'There is a problem with that island. It is an accident waiting to happen.'[139]

As the engineer John 'Ray' Arnold points out, there's a paradoxical *certainty* here concerning *unpredictability* in complex systems – while decrying the limitations of older mathematical techniques for modelling reality, Malcolm is in fact doing precisely that, and is only innovating in that he is using computers to generate models of far more complicated systems than would otherwise be possible.

'Malcom's just another theoretician', Arnold says. 'Sitting in his office, he made a nice mathematical model, and it never occurred to him that what he saw as defects were actually necessities.'[140] Instabilities in a mechanical system, that might result in it spinning out of control, are actually essential to living systems, which might seem stable but are in fact never in equilibrium. 'Everything is moving and changing', says Arnold. 'In a sense, everything is on the edge of collapse.'[141] But this means only that the system is healthy and responsive, and according to Arnold this is something that Malcolm never understood. ' "Look", Arnold said. "The proof is right here." He pointed to the screens. "In less than an hour," he said, "the park will be back on line." '[142]

Of course, we all know how that works out. Arnold himself is messily dispatched by a velociraptor while attempting to get the main power back on, having failed to realise that the park has been running for some hours on auxiliary, with the electric fences down as result. Arnold's mistake is to consider the park a living rather than a mechanical system, in which, as he says, slight instabilities do matter immensely: 'A little wobble can get worse until the whole system collapses.'[143] As the lawyer Gennaro correctly observes, this is not a mistake that Malcolm would make because he is well aware that the animals in Jurassic Park are *not exactly real*. 'We haven't *re-created* the past here', confesses Dr Henry Wu. 'What we've done is *reconstruct* the past – or at least a version of the past.'[144] Indeed, the discovery that dinosaurs *cannot* be cloned using the techniques in the book (as DNA would not survive intact even in blood-sucking insects trapped in amber), together with the now rather outdated appearance of Spielberg's on-screen dinosaurs, has led the online fan community to speculate that the story concerning the recovery of viable dinosaur DNA was contrived by Wu to conceal from the visitors (and perhaps from John Hammond himself) the true and indeed the only possible way one might reconstruct living dinosaurs: modification of a closely related species (a chicken) with gene-editing software to create an animal resembling what we imagine a particular dinosaur might have been like. 'You said yourself, John, this park is entertainment', Henry Wu says. 'And entertainment has nothing to do with reality. Entertainment is antithetical to reality.'[145] Not a zoo but a theme park, John Hammond's final project is not so very unlike the flea circus that, in the cinematic adaptation, he remembers taking to Covent Garden on first coming down from Scotland: 'There were no fleas, of course...'

Only take Dr Wu's insight through to its logical conclusion, and one can see that the proof required by Arnold, while painfully lacking in the novel, might be found in the movie: not in the *plot* of the movie, which merely follows that of the novel, but in the fact of its existence, its critical and commercial success. For Spielberg's blockbuster is a realisation not merely of Crichton's novel, but of Hammond's scheme *within* that novel, for a theme park capable of provoking awe and wonder, presenting spectators with the sublime spectacle of apparently living dinosaurs. Itself the product of a big and complicated system (the Hollywood production process), the movie generates *illusions of chaos* through the groundbreaking use of computer-generated images (CGI), and is thus at once the reiteration and refutation of Malcolm's ideas. It is worth asking, were Jurassic Park to be actually realised, physically, as a theme park ride, whether it would *not* incorporate some scenario in which the ride broke down and all the dinosaurs escaped, threatening to kill all the visitors. One need only look to the British theme park Alton Towers, where every major ride seems to be premised on some sort of dystopian catastrophe (Nemesis, Oblivion, Smiler, Th13teen, Wicker Man, etc.), unintentionally lending the place something of the apocalyptic grimness of Banksy's parodic *Dismaland*. The motion picture reiterates the catastrophic narrative in Malcolm's computer models even as it contradicts them by realising John Hammond's Promethean ambition in the most magnificent way: *illusions of chaos* contained within *ordered images*.

This chapter has shown that even paper machines are capable of projecting patterns that can overwhelm our faith that there is human agency (whether it be that of the revolutionary class or that of the bourgeois subject) in shaping our own history. And this is the very real danger involved in computer modelling: not that a model might predict the future but that we might allow it to *determine* the future by believing in the prediction; binding ourselves to a pattern of thought that is not reality but ratiocination, we risk a restriction on our capacity to think out new options, and to take control. And while computer simulations, as opposed to linear modelling, might seem to make no claims to veracity, this chapter has shown that these have proven more than capable of seducing policy-makers

Figure 6.2 Images of chaos. The Heighway Dragon Curve or the Harter-Heighway Dragon, also known as the Jurassic Park Dragon. First investigated by NASA physicists John Heighway, Bruce Banks and William Harter, and described by Martin Gardner in his *Scientific American* column 'Mathematical Games' in 1967. Iterations of the fractal appear at the beginning of each chapter in the novel *Jurassic Park*. (Image drawn by Dr Philip Gressman for the Internet Fractal Archive, University of Pennsylvania.)

into serious errors too. Indeed, this chapter has discovered that Turing, like Poe before him, believed that this should become the *standard test* for effective forms of artificial intelligence. In this respect, Malcolm's prophecies of chaos (and the catastrophic narratives predicted by his many real-world counterparts) are surely, in spite of their anti-Promethean, anti-scientific, anti-Modernist fervour, perfect Promethean illusions. For predicting the collapse of all big and complicated systems is emphatically *not* the same thing as acknowledging *uncertainty* in the manner that Keynes and Shackle advocated. On the contrary, it is yet another example of a mathematical model being mistaken for reality, and it is perhaps the most insidious, because it appears to endorse rational reservations about the limitations of mathematical modelling, while constituting precisely such a mathematical model itself – one that taps into and reiterates our oldest, most irrational prejudices against science and modernity. Christopher Marlowe's *Doctor Faust*; J. W. von Goethe's *The Sorcerer's Apprentice*; Mary Shelley's *Frankenstein*: since the beginning of the modern era there has been a predisposition to believe the very worst of our modern Prometheans, and computer-generated models of reality that pander to this old pessimism are thus already well placed to pass for the real thing. 'Malcolm's models are all phase-space shapes on a computer screen', says Arnold. Appearing at the head of each chapter (and apparently generated on the fractal principle that structures on a very large scale will reiterate the smaller forms they contain) Malcolm's intricately formal, non-linear, computer-generated patterns could not better illustrate Benjamin's concept of *catastrophe* as nothing more than a child's kaleidoscope, 'which dissolves the established order in a new way, while enabling an image of order to prevail'.[146]

Notes

1 Walter Benjamin, 'Theses on the Philosophy of History' (1940), *Illuminations*, trans. Harry Zorn (London: Random House, 1999), 245.
2 *Ibid.*, 245.
3 *Ibid.*, 245.
4 Jacob Bard-Rosenberg, 'Angelic Satire: Benjamin on Standstill and Marx on Movement', paper presented at Historical Materialism Conference, Birbeck College, London, 8 November 2015.
5 *Ibid.*
6 *Ibid.*
7 *Ibid.*
8 Karl Marx and Frederick Engels, *The Communist Manifesto* (1848), Robert C. Tucker (trans.), *The Marx-Engels Reader* (New York: W.W. Norton, 1978), 481.
9 Bard-Rosenberg, 'Angelic Satire'.
10 Walter Benjamin, 'Central Park', Edmund Jephcott and Howard Eiland (trans.), *Selected Writings: 1938–1940, Vol. 4* (Cambridge, MA: Belknap Press, 2003), 164.
11 Benjamin, 'Theses', 250.
12 Derrida, Specters, 16–17.
13 Benjamin, 'Theses', 253.
14 Jean Baudrillard, *The Transparency of Evil*, trans. James Benedict (New York: Verso, 1993), 69.
15 *Ibid.*, 68.

16 Benjamin, 'Theses', 257.
17 *Ibid.*, 255.
18 *Ibid.*, 254.
19 *Ibid.*, 254.
20 *Ibid.*, 254.
21 *Ibid.*, 246.
22 *Ibid.*, 245.
23 Edgar Allan Poe, 'Maelzel's Chess-Player', *Southern Literary Journal*, Vol. 2 (April 1836), 318–326.
24 Gerald M. Levitt, *The Turk, Chess Automaton* (McFarland & Co., 2000), 97, 27–42.
25 Poe, 'Maelzel's Chess-Player', 318–326.
26 *Ibid.*, 318–326.
27 *Ibid.*, 318–326.
28 *Ibid.*, 318–326.
29 *Ibid.*, 318–326.
30 'The idea of a digital computer is an old one. Charles Babbage, Lucasian Professor of Mathematics at Cambridge from 1828 to 1839, planned such a machine, called the Analytical Engine, but it was never completed. Although Babbage had all the essential ideas, his machine was not at that time such a very attractive prospect. The speed which would have been available would be definitely faster than a human computer but something like 100 times slower than the Manchester Machine, itself one of the slower of the modern machines. The storage was to be purely mechanical, using wheels and cards.' Alan Turing, 'Computing Machinery and Intelligence' (1948), *The Essential Turing*, ed. B. Jack Copeland (Oxford: Clarendon Press, 2004), 446. Also, see his essay on 'Chess' (1953), 573.
31 Poe, 'Maelzel's Chess-Player', 318–326.
32 Poe, 'Murders in the Rue Morgue' (1841), *Selected Tales* (Penguin: London, 2007), 118.
33 *Ibid.*, 350.
34 *Ibid.*, 118.
35 *Ibid.*, 119.
36 *Ibid.*, 119.
37 *Ibid.*, 350.
38 *Ibid.*, 118.
39 *Ibid.*, 119.
40 *Ibid.*, 119.
41 *Ibid.*, 119.
42 Norbert Wiener, *Cybernetics: Or Control and Communication in the Animal and the Machine* (Cambridge, MA: MIT Press, 1948, 1961), 173.

43 Turing, *The Essential Turing*, 570. Wiener, *Cybernetics*, 164. Poe, 'The Purloined Letter', *Selected Tales*, 348.
44 Wiener, *Cybernetics*, 165.
45 *Ibid.*, 172.
46 *Ibid.*, 172.
47 Turing, *The Essential Turing*, 566.
48 Noam Chomsky, *Language and Thought* (London: Moyer Bell, 1993), 93.
49 Turing, *The Essential Turing*, 566.
50 Robert Wright, 'Can Machines Think?', *Time Magazine* (25 March 1996).
51 Ambrose Bierce, 'Moxon's Monster' (1893), *Can Such Things Be?* (Fairfield, IA: 1st World Books, 2006), 65.
52 *Ibid.*, 65.
53 Sigmund Freud, 'The Uncanny' (1919), David McLintock (trans.), *The Uncanny* (Penguin: London, 2003), 135.
54 *Ibid.*, 141.
55 *Ibid.*, 142.
56 Turing, *The Essential Turing*, 431.
57 See Turing', 'Chess', and also B. Jack Copeland's introduction, in *The Essential Turing*, 562–575.
58 *Ibid.*, 412.
59 *Ibid.*, 441.
60 *Ibid.*, 441.
61 *Ibid.*, 441.
62 *Ibid.*, 449.
63 *Ibid.*, 449.
64 *Ibid.*, 448.
65 See S. G. Sterrett, 'Turing's Two Tests for Intelligence', *Minds and Machines*, Vol. 10 (2000), 541–559, reprinted in J. H. Moor (ed.), *The Turing Test* (Dordrecht: Kluwer, 2003).
66 Turing, *The Essential Turing*, 495, 485.
67 Roger Penrose, *The Emperor's New Mind* (Oxford: Oxford University Press, 1989, 1999), 7.
68 Turing, *The Essential Turing*, 435.
69 Andrew Hodges, *Alan Turing: The Enigma* (New York: Simon and Schuster, 1983), 415; Turing, *The Essential Turing*, 435.
70 Ayse Pinar Saygin, Ilyas Cicekli and Varol Akman, 'Turing Test: 50 Years Later', *Minds and Machines*, Vol. 10 (2000), 467.
71 *Ibid.*, 467.
72 *Ibid.*, 467.
73 *Ibid.*, 467.

74 See Judith Genova, 'Turing's Sexual Guessing Game', *Social Epistemology*, Vol. 8, No. 4 (1994), 313–326. Also, Patrick Hayes and Kenneth Ford, 'Turing Test Considered Harmful', *Proceedings of the Fourteenth International Joint Conference on Artificial Intelligence*, Vol. 1 (1995), 972–977.
75 John R. Searle, 'Minds, Brains and Programs', *Behavioral and Brain Sciences*, Vol. 3, No. 3 (1980), 417–457.
76 Turing, *The Essential Turing*, 448.
77 Poe, *Selected Tales*, 119.
78 Descartes, *Discourse*, 103.
79 Turing, 'Intelligent Machinery, A Heretical Theory' (c. 1951), *The Essential Turing*, 475.
80 *Ibid.*, 470.
81 'I remember him reading aloud to me some of the passages – always with a smile, sometimes with a giggle.' R. Gandy, 'Human versus Mechanical Intelligence', Millican and A. Clark (eds.), *Machines and Thought: The Legacy of Alan Turing*, vol. I (Oxford: Clarendon Press, 1996), 125.
82 Penrose, *The Emperor's New Mind*, 83.
83 Turing, *The Essential Turing*, 473.
84 *Ibid.*, 468.
85 Penrose, *The Emperor's New Mind*, 46.
86 Turing, *The Essential Turing*, 451.
87 *Ibid.*, 451.
88 *Ibid.*, 473.
89 *Ibid.*, 475.
90 *Ibid.*, 473.
91 Searle, 'Minds, Brains and Programs'.
92 *Ibid.*, 420.
93 *Ibid.*, 420.
94 Turing, *The Essential Turing*, 444.
95 *Ibid.*, 416.
96 *Ibid.*, 412.
97 *Ibid.*, 428.
98 *Ibid.*, 485.
99 Thomas Hobbes, *Leviathan: Or, The Matter, Form and Power of a Common-wealth, Ecclesiastical and Civil* (London: Andrew Crooke, 1651), 10.
100 Turing, *The Essential Turing*, 392.
101 Hermann Hesse, *The Glass Bead Game* (1943), trans. Richard Winston and Clara Winston (London: Vintage Classics, 2000), 114.
102 *Ibid.*, 28.

103 *Ibid.*, 230.
104 *Ibid.*, 248.
105 Isaac Asimov, *Foundation Trilogy* (London: Everyman's Library, 2010), 494.
106 *Ibid.*, 493.
107 Hesse, *The Glass Bead Game*, 331.
108 Asimov, *Foundation*, 411.
109 *Ibid.*, 411.
110 *Ibid.*, 17.
111 Paul Krugman, 'Incidents from My Career', available online at: http://web.mit.edu/krugman/www/incidents.html (accessed 7 December 2023).
112 Warren Young, *Interpreting Mr Keynes: The IS-LM Enigma* (Boulder, CO: Westview Press, 1987), 10.
113 Skidelsky, *John Maynard Keynes*, 546–548.
114 Mumford, *The City in History*, 452.
115 Keynes, *The General Theory*, 149–150, 162–163.
116 Keynes, *The Essential Keynes*, 265–266.
117 G. L. S. Shackle, *Epistemics and Economics: A Critique of Economic Doctrines* (Cambridge: Cambridge University Press, 1972), reprinted with additional material by New Brunswick, NJ: Transaction Publishers, 1992), 183.
118 *Ibid.*, 10.
119 G. L. S. Shackle, *Imagination and the Nature of Choice* (Edinburgh: Edinburgh University Press, 1979), 131.
120 Francis Fukuyama, 'The End of History?', The National Interest (Summer 1989).
121 Philip Mirowski, *Machine Dreams: Economics Becomes a Cyborg Science* (Cambridge: Cambridge University Press, 2008), 204.
122 *Ibid.*, 214.
123 Shackle, *Epistemics and Economics*, 161.
124 Mirowski, *Machine Dreams*, 215.
125 Shackle, *Epistemics and Economics*, 161.
126 *Public Global Scenarios 1992–2020* (Shell International Petroleum Company, 1992), 2.
127 See Peter Schwartz, *The Art of the Long View: Planning for the Future in an Uncertain World* (New York: Currency Doubleday, 1991).
128 Philip Bobbitt, *The Shield of Achilles: War, Peace, and the Course of History* (London: Penguin, 2002), 722.
129 *Ibid.*, 728.
130 *Ibid.*, xxvii.
131 *Ibid.*, xxiv.

132 'It may be written by an academic but it is actually required reading for political leaders.' Tony Blair, jacket review for Philip Bobbitt's *Terror and Consent: The Wars for the Twenty-First Century* (London: Allen Lane, 2008).
133 See Tony Blair's speech to the House of Commons (18 March 2003), and Jack Straw's speech to the Foreign Policy Centre: 'Reordering the World' (25 March 2002). 'What we need is not so much a diplomacy of hindsight, but rather a diplomacy of foresight.' Both are available in full online at: www.theguardian.com/politics/2003/mar/18/foreign policy.iraq1 and www.theguardian.com/politics/2002/mar/25/foreign policy.thinktanks (accessed 7 December 2023).
134 Bobbitt, *The Shield of Achilles*, 730–731.
135 Tony Blair's speech to the Labour Party Conference, as reported in the *Guardian* (2 October 2001).
136 *Ibid.*, 10.
137 Michael Crichton, *Jurassic Park* (New York: Ballantine Books, Random House, 2015), 391.
138 *Ibid.*, 83.
139 *Ibid.*, 84.
140 *Ibid.*, 276.
141 *Ibid.*, 276.
142 *Ibid.*, 277.
143 *Ibid.*, 277.
144 *Ibid.*, 136.
145 *Ibid.*, 136.
146 Benjamin, 'Central Park', 164.

7

The Promethean altar: Prospects of atonement in twenty-first-century science fiction

Reptiles of the mind

There are the usual stage properties: 'The outline of some fantastic chemical laboratory is seen, with weird mixtures bubbling, coloured solutions (or solutions that glow in the dark).'[1] And a very familiar protagonist: a 'magician intent on what he is doing, with a large book in his hand ... is bent over a mortar and is jamming a pestle into it, watching very closely.'[2] The motive is precisely what one might have predicted: 'creation of new energy ... A man like ourselves, though different because it will beyond the human imagination.'[3] There are warnings and ominous signs to indicate that this Mad Scientist's activities threaten the very fabric of Nature: 'The stars are out in daytime ... The night is filled with thousands of suns ... The earth trembles beneath our feet ... The sea shudders and throws strange creatures on the land.'[4] Then, amid bright explosive flashes, sirens, screams and blasting lights, there appears the expected Monster: 'A crouched figure is seen covered in red flowing skins like capes.'[5] Inevitably, the strange new creature turns against his creator, and is banished with the latter's dying breath to caves in the cold North, 'to make some horrible life of its own'.[6] But this Mad Scientist is neither Doctor Faustus nor Doctor Frankenstein nor Doctor Herbert West but the spirit of primordial evil in the foundational myth of the so-called "Nation of Islam", and the Monster that he has unleashed upon the world is thus nothing other than the original White Man.

> The figure is absolutely cold white with red lizard-devil mask which covers the whole head and ends up as a lizard spine cape ... The smoke is clearing, and the white thing hops and shudders, vomiting

occasionally, and trying to make other explanatory speech-like sounds, but all that comes out intelligibly is the same phrase 'White! White! White!' Then he gurgles off into unintelligible 'explanations'.[7]

Amiri Baraka's dramatisation of the Yakub myth in his play *A Black Mass* (1966) is remarkable for the intensity of its poetic language and musical accompaniment (courtesy of Sun Ra), but I would suggest it owes its shocking power to the extent to which the poet has brought this story into alignment with that of Prometheus-Faust-Frankenstein. Reiterating all-too-familiar tropes nearly point for point, Baraka harnesses – or rather, subverts or *detournes* – the immense cultural resonance of an archetype central to European notions of modernity. *A Black Mass* is so profoundly disturbing because the story it is retelling in no way differs from that which Europeans have been telling concerning themselves for a great many centuries. T. S. Eliot once speculated that European culture had suffered from a 'dissociation of sensibility' he believed to have set in some point during the early seventeenth century, and Baraka's Monster embodies that dissociation, that dialectic: 'The compassionless abstractions, the opposites ... A heart full of numbers and cold formulae ... Asking God's questions and giving animal answers ... This beast is the twisted thing a man would be, *alone* ... without his human soul.'[8] An unresolved conflict of mind and body, human and beast, lacking the synthesis that would make up a whole human soul, Baraka's White Monster is (like the Modernist) a thing of time: 'I have created time', says Jacoub. 'Now I will create a being in love with time ... From beyond the powers of natural creation, I make a super-natural being.'[9]

Freud once suggested that there could be no clear distinction between the first type of the uncanny and the second, and this is all too clear in the case of Jacoub, since the Promethean horror projected by the Necromancer is inextricably bound up with his gothic revival (a pre-human, reptilian past), which must (as in all good stories of this kind) finally overwhelm him. It is not merely the power projected by the Necromancer that terrifies, but the prospect of that power failing in the act of being realised. And this, I would suggest, is why the tradition of Promethean horror is likely to thrive in the twenty-first century, even as the ambitions of mid-century Modernism recede ever further into the past. Long after we have lost faith in the capacity of the modern mind to exert control and order over our lives, society and environment, we are convinced in the nemesis that is the punishment for hubris, retain our atavistic fear of the vengeance of the gods. We believe that the period designated "anthropocene", for instance, will necessarily entail an era of cosmic horror; we expect to suffer, like the criminal Titan, centuries exposed to hostile skies. 'The sins of fathers are visited on their children to the third and fourth generation', writes Horace Walpole in his preface to the first gothic novel *The Castle of Otranto* (1764), adding wryly: 'I could wish [that the author] had grounded his plan on a more useful moral than this.'[10] Certainly, Baraka's work possesses extraordinary topicality in the era of the Black Lives Matter movement, the toppling of nineteenth-century statues (of Walpole's friends), together with campaigns to decolonise the curriculum, indicating that Promethean horror will continue to retain its purchase for as long as legacies of the Enlightenment remain contested.

In this final chapter, we examine three twenty-first-century literary texts which each represent a different approach to the Promethean tropes reviewed in this book, and that give us some indication as to how we can reasonably expect to see such tropes handled in the near future. In so doing, this chapter should resolve those questions that have arisen in this study relating to Modernism and to post-modernism, outlining new ways of understanding these contested phenomena in, and in relation to, the twenty-first century. We will begin with a book that takes us back to the Promethean myth's point of origin, those undying fires in the regions east of the Caucasus Mountains, feeding on the petroleum that oozes out of the ground, the black blood of the earthbound Titan ...

Tellurian insurgencies

'To the north lies Zorzania', writes the Venetian explorer Marco Polo, in his *Travels* (1300), 'near the confines of which there is a fountain of oil which discharges so great a quantity [that] In the neighbouring country no other is used in their lamps, and people come from distant parts to procure it.'[11] Likewise, in Sir John Mandeville's *Travels* (1536) we read of a great marvel in a kingdom called Abchaz: 'For a province of the country that hath well in circuit three journeys, that men clepe Hanyson, is all covered with darkness, without any brightness or light; so that no man may see ne hear, ne no man dare enter into him.'[12] And black smoke rises to this day on Yanar Dag, the Fire Mountain, in what is now Azerbaijan, and in the sacred Fire Temple at Baku, said to have been built for an unknown cult centuries before it spread into Persia and India, evolving into Zoroastrianism in the former, and into Vedic Hinduism in the latter. It was in this region that the Hebrew Bible, drawing no doubt on traditions of great antiquity, placed the first invention of the metallurgical arts that initiated the Bronze Age; and Prometheus, father of these science, is said to be punished for his impiety in the mountainous regions to the west; on Mount Elburz according to the Greeks, and on Mount Kazbek according to the Georgians, where Prometheus / Amirani remains still, accompanied by a little dog that is slowly, over the centuries, licking away his chains...

Shelley declared *Prometheus Unbound* at the start of the nineteenth century; the ensuing Industrial Revolution might indicate that the poet was quite correct (though in a way he could not have imagined), and the nations have continued, as they did in Marco Polo's day, to resort to this region and to the regions to the south to procure the black blood of the fallen Titan, but in ever greater quantities, to the extent that one struggles to imagine our civilisation without petroleum coursing through pipelines, smoke spewing into the air. We are become the spectral embodiment of the Promethean spirit, a demonic possession. As fossilised sunlight, removed from the Earth's atmosphere, over millions of years, by the carbon-scrubbing action of plant life, is restored by the fires of industry, temperatures are rising again – to those once enjoyed by the planet's primordial inhabitants. Might Prometheus be the ghost of extinct ecosystems, rising from the earth after aeons of slumber to punish the planet with plague and fire?

This is the premise of Reza Negarestani's *Cyclonopaedia: Complicity with Anonymous Materials* (2008), in which a young American woman attempts to decipher disordered notes containing Negarestani's attempt to interpret, through the framework provided by Lovecraftian weird fiction, horror movies and French post-modernist theory, the renegade Iranian archaeologist Dr Hamid Parsani's book *Soorat-zoda-ee az Iran-e-Bastan: 9500*

Sal Nabood-khanie (*Defacing Ancient Persia: 9500 Years Call for Destruction*). The latter posits that the Middle East is a sentient entity, present in the petroleum that courses into the West through oil pipes, fuelling and escalating the transgressive impetus of Western war machines towards the utter degradation of the Earth into the ultimate desert – which is, ironically, the very objective of the Wahhabi and Taliban jihadis with which these machines clash in the "War on Terror", for whom every erected thing, so to speak, every verticality, is an idol, and the desert, as militant horizontality, the promised land of the divine. As Negarestani explains:

> Those Mecca-nomic agencies of War on Terror who consider everything that is not desert a violation against the all-consuming hegemony of God crave for the desert as a ground independent of Earth and its inhabitants; but what they actually achieve, and passively cooperate with, is the Tellurian insurgency of the Earth towards [what] Ibn Hamedani calls ... the 'Mother of All Plagues' ... They want God but what they get is the Tellurian Omega – the incinerating immanence with the Sun and the Earth's core assembled on an axis which knows nothing of authoritarian divine and monopolistic convergence, the Hell-engineering Axis of the Earth.[13]

Indeed, via a series of compelling, and heavily theorised, readings of cultural artefacts ranging from the Sumero-Assyrian demon Pazuzu in William Peter Blatty's horror *The Exorcist* (1971) to the story of Ashemoga the Cook in the poet Ferdowsi's Persian epic *Shahnameh* (*The Book of Kings*, c. 1010 CE), Negarestani concludes that monotheisms were infested from the outset with the beliefs of mysterious peoples, already living on the Iranian plateau, who knew nothing but demons: magi or magicians. 'These pre-Aryan sorcerous people regarded everything as an avatar of horror, of a radical Outside; even the fertilizing forces of nature such as wind, rain, thunder, soil and growth were *Daivas* (demons)', says Negarestani. 'Life was *Druj* itself, the Mother of Abominations, the radical Outside', and was thus believed to be 'external to survival, lurking beneath it as the ultimate Unlife'.[14] For them, survival could only be achieved by feeding the Outside, was itself an occult practice for feeding its avatars: 'They believed that survival fed an unthinkable Abomination, an ultimate outsider their Zoroastrian descendants called Druj.'[15] In the obsessive racial purity that the invading Aryans sought to maintain, in their long migrations, through the exclusiveness and restrictiveness of monotheistic religion, the ancient sorcerers perceived strategic potential for establishing contact with the Outside, by becoming what it hungers for the most:

> When the unclean spirit is gone out of a man, he walketh through dry places, seeking rest, and findeth none. Then he saith, I will return into my house from whence I came out; and when he is come, he findeth it empty, swept, and garnished. Then goeth he, and taketh with himself seven other spirits more wicked than himself, and they enter in and dwell there: and the last state of that man is worse than the first.[16]

Likewise, in the Persian *Vendidad*, every sanitary practice and act of closure is characterised as effective against one demon, but as equally likely to invoke legions more: 'purify yourself from all defects, attend numerous hygiene courses, develop a quotidian and institutionalised life-style, evade all defilement both physically and mentally .... you must just try to make A Good Meal out of yourself for the Life-Satan and its avatars', writes Negarestani. 'In this way the Life-Satan is strategically lured to tear you to shreds.'[17] And so the indigenous crowds surrendered themselves to the invading Aryans, supported their beliefs, fortified their reign, intensified the mania for purity, aiding them to develop ever greater restrictions. 'In fact, the Aryan's paranoia for purity combined with their ruthless hegemonic policies was a perfect carrier for the sorcerous experiments of these indigenous crowds whose sole inclination was communicating with the Outside'.[18] In this way, Zoroastrianism became the original vehicle for the sabotaged Aryanism of the Iran plateau, with every monotheism that has emerged since being infested with the same fifth column, secretly in league with the Fallen God under the surface to restore the Earth and the Sun to their original primordial state of undifferentiated material chaos (*Tiamaterialism*).

'The mission of monotheism was to fuse with planetary events in order to transform everything into a sacrificial meal for the Outside', Negarestani concludes. 'But the problem with the Outside is that the more you feed it, the more it asks for.'[19] Whether one endeavours to placate the Outside, in the manner of an ancient sorcerer, by maintaining "radical schizoid" openness to it, or whether one seeks to exclude it with a reactionary and paranoid system of thought, the destination remains the same, and the latter approach might even get you there faster. 'Does the ancient fetishistic paranoia that Lovecraft vividly diagrams in his stories have only one side, that associated with artless paranoia and racism?' asks Negarestani, in what is certainly a rhetorical question. 'Or does it have another edge whose dominant function is that of cutting itself open, reinventing itself as an ultimate polytics for communicating with the Outside – a schizotrategic two-edged blade?'[20] And so (having framed the question in these familiar post-modernist terms) one is led to the inescapable conclusion that the most radical political philosophy possible *must* be the most reactionary and paranoid. If you really want to achieve a truly post-modernist state of schizophrenic openness, such as that promoted by Deleuze and Guattari, become a Wahhabi or Taliban jihadist and/or strive to maintain Aryan racial purity. As the philosopher Graham Harman remarks dryly, 'Reading Negarestani is like being converted to Islam by Salvador Dali.'[21]

The horror of the *Cyclonopedia* consists in the apparently inescapable nature of its argument; no matter what we say or do, we are on an inevitable trajectory towards the Ultimate Desert, the Mother of Abominations. But (one hopes) this is satire, theory-fiction, jargon-heavy and packed with absurd neologisms, this is surely a *reductio ad absurdem* of some of the more fashionable theories to emerge from the 1960s, designed to show precisely where we will end up, philosophically and politically, if we follow to its logical conclusion Deleuze and Guattari's reiteration (within their post-modernist paradigm) of the radical empiricist or psychological philosophy of Schopenhauer, Nietzsche, James, Bergson and Freud. The vertiginous terror that the book produces lasts for precisely as long as one indulges the philosophy. But, as Freud himself pointed out, 'The division of the psychic realm into the conscious and the unconscious is the fundamental premiss of psychoanalysis', and psychoanalysis is only possible once one has chosen to believe in that fundamental article of faith. 'To most people whose education is grounded in philosophy [i.e. phenomenology], the idea of a psychic realm that is not also a conscious one is so incomprehensible as to seem an absurdity easily refuted by plain, straightforward logic', admits Freud:

> If I were able to imagine every last person with an interest in psychology reading this essay, then I should not be one whit surprised

to find a number of those readers calling a halt right now and refusing to read another word – for here at once is the first shibboleth of psychoanalysis.[22]

As we have seen previously, Freud believed that he himself, and other psychoanalysts, might eventually come to be considered to possess uncanny power, and in persuading readers that the unconscious might have a will of its own, he might have been re-enacting the very procedure for producing an uncanny effect that he had himself described: the last in a long tradition of scientist-magicians, who extend back beyond the "shame totem" Frankenstein, and the necromancers of eighteenth-century German gothic horror, to the natural philosophers who might well have started it all (T. S. Eliot's 'dissociation of sensibility'), Descartes, Spinoza, Locke, Berkley, Hume and, perhaps most pertinent here, political revolutionary, Birmingham "Lunar Man" and Unitarian preacher, the Reverend Joseph Priestley.

The terrible sermon

The fear that monotheism might be tainted or undermined by sorcerers seeking to connect with the Schopenhaurian Thing-in-Itself or Will or Force is also the premise of Stephen King's late classic Promethean horror *Revival* (2014), a novel which harks right back to the inception of the anti-gothic tradition we have traced, to the necromancers and magicians that terrified the ancient regimes of Europe. And perhaps further, to the historical figure who might well have inspired such tales of political revolution and scientific malpractice, radical Unitarian preacher Joseph Priestley, with his daring electrical experiments, his support for revolution and his extraordinary treatise, *Disquisitions relating to Matter and Spirit* (1777), which speculated that the universe might have a purely material basis; that spirit is either nothing, or nothing but some form of matter; and that powers of attraction and repulsion are nothing apart from but are essential to matter. Like Freud, Priestley speculated that misconceptions concerning the soul had arisen among the ancient Egyptians as a result of the uncanny effects generated by their burial practices; and he concluded (somewhat like Negarestani) that Christianity had been corrupted by Oriental philosophy: 'the notion of the soul being a substance distinct from the body, was originally part of the system of *heathenism*, and was from thence introduced into Christianity, which has derived the greatest part of its corruptions from this source'.[23] Priestley expected that his materialist philosophy would be denounced as atheism, but the uncanny power of his fictional progeny goes beyond any reaction that might be attributed to mere doctrinal disapproval and owes its inception, I suggest, to "double-think" on the part of his readers, who might have been swayed by this materialist vision of the universe without being able to shake the notion that there must be some numinous *thing* behind what would be considered appearances or phenomena in Kant's system, but which are here the material facts themselves. Priestley speaks derisively of the Oriental belief that every intellect is but a portion of the *great soul of the universe*, but Arthur Schopenhauer's conception of the World as Will and Idea is similar to this, and has its source in the same, early translations of the Hindu *Vedas* that Priestley consulted. Might Priestley's vulgar materialism be haunted by its radical empiricist counterpart? By the ghost of itself that matter had acquired in the course of passing through phenomenological philosophy? Seeking to exorcise the Christian religion of spirit, might Priestley have rendered matter itself uncanny? Like the Jewish golem, or the homunculi of Paracelsus, his vision of the universe unsettles us because a thing which we are accustomed to think of as inert or dead is moving without the means of animation; one remains convinced that there must be a soul and can only regard with misgiving the conjurer who has presented us with this Frankenstein's Monster.

This is the case in King's novel, which is remarkable in that its main character harks right back to what I consider to be the inception of modern Promethean horror within this profound crisis opened up in Protestant Christianity. King's novel traces the misadventures of the small town preacher Charles Jacobs, who loses his faith in (the Christian) God after the tragic death of his wife Patsy and infant son Morrie in a horrific traffic accident. But if he renounces his faith in Christ, this disaster only reaffirms Jacobs' deeper faith in natural science: 'If you want truth', he declares in his final terrible sermon, 'a power greater than yourselves, look to the lightning – a billion volts in each strike, and a hundred thousand amperes of current, and temperatures of *fifty thousand degrees Fahrenheit.* There's a higher power in that, I grant you.'[24] Even before his public renunciation of Christianity, sermons and Sunday School lessons are peppered with unsettling technical jargon relating to electronics: an exposition of the Trinity develops into one concerning the workings of a car battery, and a device ostensibly designed to illustrate the miracle of Christ walking on water is remarkably chiefly for being brilliantly lit with electrical lamps – an optical illusion with a battery-powered Jesus Christ hardly likely to inspire faith (or to be more precise, faith in anything but natural science) in those children who are shown this Promethean trick. Embarking on a career as a carnival magician, then as a faith healer, Jacobs performs miracles that are, we eventually learn, the results of his studies into the *potestas magnum universum* ("force that powers the universe"); the secrets to which are contained in several 'Forbidden Books': *The Mysteries of the Worm, Book of Apollinius, Book of Albertus Magnus, Lemegeton, Clavicula Salmonis* and *The Grimoire of Picatrix* (the last of these, along with *De Vermis Mysteriis*, the inspiration for Lovecraft's *Necronomicon*). '[T]he Forbidden Books deal with POWER, and how to obtain it by means that combine alchemy (which we now call "science"), mathematics, and certain nasty occult rituals.'[25] Pastor Jacobs would seem to believe that, through his manipulation of the *potestas magnum universum*, he might eventually be able to apprehend the Thing-in-Itself, and acquire the power to reanimate the dead, enabling him to resurrect his wife and child.

The result of this exercise in Promethean necromancy is just as horrific as one might expect. 'The whole living world was an illusion', relates King's protagonist Jaimie Morton. 'What I'd thought of as reality was nothing but a scrim, as flimsy as an old nylon stocking. The true world was behind it.'[26] At the risk of spoiling the big reveal for any readers who have yet to enjoy the novel for themselves, King's description of this Otherworld is well worth quoting in full:

> Basalt blocks rose to a black sky punched with howling stars. I think those blocks were all that remained of a vast yet ruined city. It stood in a barren landscape. Barren, yes, but not empty. A wide and seemingly endless column of naked human beings trudged through it, heads down, feet stumbling. This nightmare parade stretched all the way to the distant horizon. Driving the humans were antlike

creatures, most black, some the dark red of venous blood. When humans fell, the ant-things would lunge at them again, biting and butting, until they gained their feet again. I saw young men and old women. I saw teenagers with babies in their arms. I saw children trying to help each other along. And on every face was the same expression of blank horror.

They marched beneath the howling stars, they fell, they were punished and chivvied to their feet with gaping but bloodless bite wounds on their arms and legs and abdomens. Bloodless because these were the dead. The foolish mirage of earthly life had been torn away and instead of the heaven preachers of all persuasions promised, what awaited them was a dead city of cyclopean stone blocks below a sky that was itself a scrim. The howling stars weren't stars at all. They were *holes*, and the howls emerging from them came from the true *potestas magnum universum*. Beyond the sky were *entities*. They were alive, and all-powerful, and totally insane.[27]

Combining elements from the cosmic horror of H. P. Lovecraft, the scientific romances of C. S. Lewis (his incomplete story, 'The Dark Tower') and mid-century monster movies (the giant ants), King's preacher-magician-scientist utilises the power of electricity to discover the world *as it really is*, underneath the phenomena we experience, within the bubble of mind or spirit. 'Lightning had smashed the door on a lock that was never supposed to be opened', relates Morton, 'and Mother came through.'[28] Matrix, matter, material, Negarestani's Mother of Abominations, a vision of the Thing-in-Itself: a pantheistic entity comprising all beings that have ever existed in time. A titanic spider-like being, enormous black legs ending in vast claws covered in human faces, begins to tear through holes in the sky. 'One idea saved my sanity', says Morton, 'and I still cling to it: the possibility that this nightmare landscape was itself a mirage.'[29] In the same way that the narrator's faith in the world of appearances is shaken by the magician, so this noumenal "reality" is dispelled when Morton chooses the existential *leap of faith* necessary to negate it. This is presumably why the all-powerful Mother 'wanted one thing and one thing only: to silence the voice of negation'.[30] As in King's earlier novel *It* (1986), a simple act of faith, conceived of in Kierkegaardian fashion, as a negation, as a refusal to believe in the monster, produced by the unconscious, spells its swift demise. '*No!* I shouted again. *No, no, no, no!*'[31]

Faith is often a struggle in King's work; the leap of faith necessary to negate Evil is so difficult because while the Evil appears so strong, the Good is already hollowed out, discredited and corrupted by agents of Evil. The Lovecraftian nightmare of a numenal Thing behind the world that we take for granted is overwhelming, and the Promethean illusion is not easily dispelled. But what scope for Promethean horror in fiction that *has* taken that leap of faith, that believes in the omniscient power of the Logos, or Word? In post-modernist literature that (as defined earlier) follows the "linguistic turn" whereby our reality is understood to be constructed (in a reiteration of the phenomenology that Derrida so loved) as discourse, as generated within and by the matrix of language, a semiotic system of signs? What might a post-modern Prometheus look like? Here we turn to our final text, which presents us with the potential for just that. Though it might appear radical empiricist, an inversion of Lovecraft merely in that embraces rather than rejects as a source of horror the Thing-in-Itself, I will argue that Nnedi Okorafor's *Lagoon* (2014) depicts not the material universe but the matrix of language which creates and sustains it, and that such a reading must profoundly complicate its apparently Post-Humanist purpose.

The cthulucene

Describing a first-contact situation in Lagos, Nigeria, Nnedi Okorafor's *Lagoon* (2014) might appear to extend and reconceptualise the cosmic horror of H. P. Lovecraft, in which entities predating our universe are aroused by evil or misguided Promethean figures who dare probe the terrible secrets contained in the *Al Azif* (عزيف الجن, *Jinn's Song*) or *Necronomicon* (*Book of the Dead*). Composed by Abdul Alhazred, a mad poet of Sana'a in Yemen who flourished during the time of the Ummayed caliphate (700 CE), the book is said to have been transcribed from the annals of the Great Ones, Deep Ones, Elder Things, the Great Race and Mi-Go. Given that these appear to be cephalopods, sarcopterygii, echinoderms, barnacles and crustaceans, respectively, one can only imagine Lovecraft's horror had he lived to read *Lagoon*. 'Suddenly the octopus grows brilliant pink-purple and straightens all its tentacles …, and what look like boney spokes erupt from its soft head.'³² A swordfish grows spikes of cartilage along its spine as though it were an 'ancestral creature from the deepest ocean caves of old.'³³ The ocean water is now said to be able to heal the worst human illnesses and cause a hundred more illnesses not yet known to humankind: 'It is more alive than it has been in centuries and it is teeming with aliens and monsters.'³⁴ And perhaps most terrifying (for those approaching this novel *after* Stephen King's *Revival*) it is eventually revealed that the narrator of the novel is, in fact, Udide, the great spider-god that lurks in a cave beneath the metropolis. 'I have been here for centuries and I will be here for centuries more', she tells us, shortly before resurfacing to welcome the new age of monsters. 'I roll onto my back and place my hairy feet to the earth above me. I feel the vibrations of Lagos.'³⁵

But what would surely cause Lovecraft most distress is that Okorafor's *Lagoon* evinces none of the disgust for such cosmic horror which one encounters in early-twentieth-century weird fiction but maintains a radical openness and generosity throughout, presenting readers with perhaps the most complete illustration in imaginative fiction of what the post-humanist critic Donna Haraway has termed 'The Chthulucene' – named not after Lovecraft's misogynist racial-nightmare monster Cthulhu (note spelling difference), but rather after 'the diverse earthwide tentacular powers and forces and collected things with names like Naga, Gaia, Tangoroa (burst from water-full Papa), Terra, Haniyasuhime, Spider Woman [Udide?], Pachamama, Oya, Gorgo, Raven, A'akuluujjusi, and many more' – and which refers to 'potential multi-species assemblages that include people'.³⁶

> 'My' Chthulucene, even burdened with its problematic Greek-ish rootlets, entangles myriad temporalities and spatialities and myriad intra-active entities-in-assemblages – including the more-than-human, other-than-human, inhuman, and human-as-humus. Even rendered in an American English-language text like this one, Naga, Gaia, Tangoroa, Medusa, Spider Woman, and all their kin are some of the many thousand names proper to a vein of SF that Lovecraft could not have imagined or embraced – namely, the webs of speculative fabulation, speculative feminism, science fiction, and scientific fact.³⁷

Like Haraway, who attains the Chthulucene through her earlier 'Cyborg Feminism', embracing her hybridity as a human-informed-

The Promethean altar   211

by-military-technology, Okorafor envisages her own *multi-species assemblage* coming about through the intervention of (Promethean) information technology. 'We *are* technology', says Adodele, the visitor from beyond the stars; 'WE ARE CHANGE.'[38] Consisting of millions of microscopic metallic balls that assume different forms at will, Ayodele sacrifices herself at the end of the novel, disintegrating, dispersing and integrating herself into every living thing, in a symbiotic relationship, in order to facilitate interconnection and communication through a planetary network, or (if you will) world wide web.

But Okorafor's perspective as a Nigerian novelist necessarily complicates such a reading in a rewarding way, for it is strongly implied that the alien visitors are the latest and purest iteration of a series of waves of information technology that have already transformed Nigerian society. Aside from the transformed creatures in the lagoon, all the new mutants and ancient gods that we encounter are said to have existed as such before the aliens arrived and triggered merely latent superpowers, with each of these being demonstrably the embodiment of imperial institutions. The marine biologist, with her supernatural ability to participate in marine life in a manner consistent with the Cthulucene, is working both in a discipline and in an education system established by the British. The soldier, with his super-strength, is part of a military and police system that is also a legacy of the Empire, recruiting primarily from the Hausa, one of the "warrior-races" identified by the British, in the course of developing national security infrastructures. And while a Christian preacher who embodies Britain's third cultural legacy in Nigeria (Christianity) has something like the superpower of communication practised to a significantly greater degree by the third of the new mutants, it is a Ghanaian rapper who is ultimately chosen: an outsider to Nigeria, it perhaps significant that this third figure should embody another, later form of cultural imperialism to that embodied by the rest, the superpower of Western media.

Nor are the collective entities, Haraway's *interactive entities-in-assemblages*, quite the natural sources of cosmic horror they might first appear. Udide, the Great Spider, is already there beneath the city, waiting; and like her child, the Bone Collector – a personification of Nigeria's (Ballardian) fast and deadly roads, 'paths to the future, always hungry for blood' – she might well be the embodiment or personification of earlier imperial networks. 'I've knitted their stories and watched them knit their own crude webs', says Udide. 'They came in boats that creaked a desperate song and brought me something I'd never have imagined.'[39] Certainly, Haraway's cataloguing of Cthonic entities reiterates imperial procedures for data-capture and analysis, attempts to collect and classify indigenous beliefs in an anthropological system so that equivalences and differences might be established, in order to develop the measures necessary for a system of exchange. With their basis in webs of speculative fabulation, speculative feminism, science fiction, and scientific fact (rather than in Schopenhauer's Will, which Lovecraft's fictions represent), Naga, Gaia, Medusa, Udide and the rest, are monsters, or rather, chimeras, produced by the academy – that is to say, by international institutions for the production of knowledge that are the very modus operandi of imperialist exploitation. Indeed, this may be what makes the apparent embrace of the Thing-in-Itself possible; for this is no longer alien, but is evidently a phenomenon generated by human thought. And if the horror provoked by *Cyclonopedia* consists in the idea (troubling to Christians and Muslims) that monotheism might be infected by the Outside, here there is potential for horror in the fact that those who would open themselves to the Outside cannot transcend the "prison-house of language"; attempting to embrace the Mother, they find only the Word. Here the horror consists not in the potency of the numenal Thing-in-Itself but in its paucity, all too readily identified as a product of Western imperialism, a Promethean illusion. Only imagine how those benevolent, paternalistic and non-consensual transformations effected by aliens might eventually come to be regarded (within this fictional universe) by future generations of post-colonial critics ...

Prometheus unbound

I began this book in Birmingham, having returned to the city where I had grown up, to inspect the ruins of John Madin's Library and his CEGB headquarters, and the site, apparently under the terraced house in which my grandparents had lived, where the Rev.

The Promethean altar

Joseph Priestley's house had stood prior to its immolation, by a Church-and-King mob, following that revolutionary figure's vocal support for the French Revolution. And I found answers in that most Promethean of cities to questions that had perplexed me since I first traced Hawksmoor's ghostly ley lines through the East End in London and perceived an affinity with the brutal force of Modernist high-rises by Lubetkin, Goldfinger, Chamberlin, Powell and Bon. Since then I have sought out Amirani on Mount Kazbek; and I conclude with this prospect of the Temple of the Sacred Fire in Baku and a pilgrimage to Yanar Dag, the real Mount Doom. Having come so far, it is fitting to end the book by re-evaluating the mythic figure whose story embodies the cluster of related hopes and fears that have animated the literature we have studied. What is Prometheus? And what might the tragedy of the rebel Titan have to say to us today, after the Promethean energy of Modernism has been diminished, if not entirely overwhelmed, by the horror and revulsion which inevitably seem to follow such gratuitous brilliance?

In this spot, where one can look East as well as West, one can see what Prometheus might have meant: that his story comprises the components of a sacrificial system that constituted the medium for communication between humanity and the powers of the natural world. Keeper of the Sacred Flame (*Atar*) preserved by Zoroastrian priests, personified as *Agni* in Vedic Hinduism, the fire god whose invocation was a preliminary to any offering, Prometheus is the intermediary that converts the material that is to be sacrificed (i.e. rendered holy) into spirit. He is thus analogous to (and in Hinduism and in most varieties of European paganism, presumably the substitution for) the liminal figure of the eagle (or vulture) that is essential to the funerary practice of sky burial that continues to be performed to this day in Mumbai, in the "Towers of Silence". Indeed, one wonders whether the reformation initiated by Zarathustra might not have been prompted by revulsion at the pollution of the Sacred Fire necessitated by animal sacrifice and human cremation. Is this why those *Prometheid* peoples (to use Marr's term) who ventured west were haunted by a conviction that the fire they used in religious rituals was misappropriated (the altars desecrated with bones and fat)? However that might be, there is no mistaking the dysfunctional quality of the sacrificial mechanism in Greek myth: the guardian of the Sacred Flame is a thief, the offering is a cheat and the eagle that should translate the remains of the faithful into the heavens has become an instrument of torment, tearing the liver. It is often said that the liver torn from Prometheus each morning by the emissary of Zeus is the only organ in the human body capable of growing back. But I would suggest that the choice of this particular organ was something more than medical contingency. In the ancient world the liver was believed to be the seat of prophecy. Having compiled centuries of data on the appearance of entrails extracted from sheep in the compendium *Bārûtu*, haruspices in Mesopotamia and Etruria considered the marks on entrails to be associated with archetypal types of recurring historical events and believed they could predict the future by referencing newly acquired signs against those on record.[40] The liver held a special place within this discipline, regarded as "the seat of the soul" and closely related to the power of sight, eyes being the windows of the soul. The decision to extract the liver is therefore significant. Zeus is torturing Prometheus to learn the secret of his overthrow, known only to the Titan whose name means "foresight". Evidently, Zeus hoped to discover this secret on the liver brought him each morning. No mere lump of meat, the Promethean liver would have appeared to the eyes of this initiate like those clay models of the liver fashioned in Sumer and Etruria: resembling first-generation gaming consoles, ergonomic objects covered in strange signs, these *are* an alien form of information technology. And like every other component in that deranged sacrifice, this act of haruspicy is not working as it should; the Promethean liver should reveal the future, but (as Shackle observed) the original Promethean gift is freedom, and this is the power to determine the future. The rebel Titan possesses foresight only because he alone and no power on Earth or in Heaven can know what he will make of the future, from one moment to the next.

    This is, I believe, the root of the '*dissociation of sensibility*' which T. S. Eliot once diagnosed, that split between body and mind which would assume such titanic proportions in the centuries since the Renaissance, manifesting itself in the "two traditions", as empiricism and idealism, psychology and phenomenology, in the dialectical process that constitutes the modern era, with Modernism being the series of attempts to effect a synthesis of the two, to effect a reconciliation of matter and spirit. There is always a gap, a difference, between body and soul because, for as long as we are alive, there is always this freedom to choose *to become* something other than that which we *are*.

Prometheus achieved a reconciliation of the two by making his choice, enabling Zeus to save himself by preventing the conception of a super-Achilles that might have destroyed Olympus rather than Troy; and one can see how this could be interpreted as surrender, as a recantation of our existential freedom, as a defeat. The poet Percy Bysshe Shelley saw it this way, composing his own version of the (lost) Aeschylean play *Prometheus Unbound*, rather than accept the idea that Prometheus might have sought for a reconciliation with the divine tyrant. But is the decision all that it might first appear? Prometheus is unbound not by God but by Hercules, the Son of God – that is to say, another human-god hybrid, an alternative super-Achilles, who must be seen to embody precisely that cosmic revolution that the old magician had first hoped for when he raised his race of homunculi from the mud and blood of primordial giants. Formerly fashioned from a race of monsters, an abomination, the human form is now divine, at one with the supernatural powers. And being the Titan possessing foresight, Prometheus would know that Hercules would himself ascend the funeral pyre and submit his mortal body to the flames, so that, purged of all but his immortal part, he might take up his appointed place in the Heavens: a human pattern imposed upon the stars (and the ghost of the mortal in Hell); the synthesis of body and mind; the dialectic dissolved by the analytical properties of an alchemical process. Was it for this purpose that the supernatural powers permitted Prometheus to be released?

Though not determined by, we are yet part of, this planet's complex systems and ourselves constitute one of its many feedback mechanisms. Though we can make of this world what we will, what we will can only ever be that which this world requires of us (although it might, at some point, no longer require *us*, nor our Promethean gift). For instance, the restoration of a portion of the carbon dioxide removed from the Earth's atmosphere by plant life (locked into petroleum, coal, gas and peat) might well have averted a long slow slide into a terminal Ice Age (see Figure 7.1):

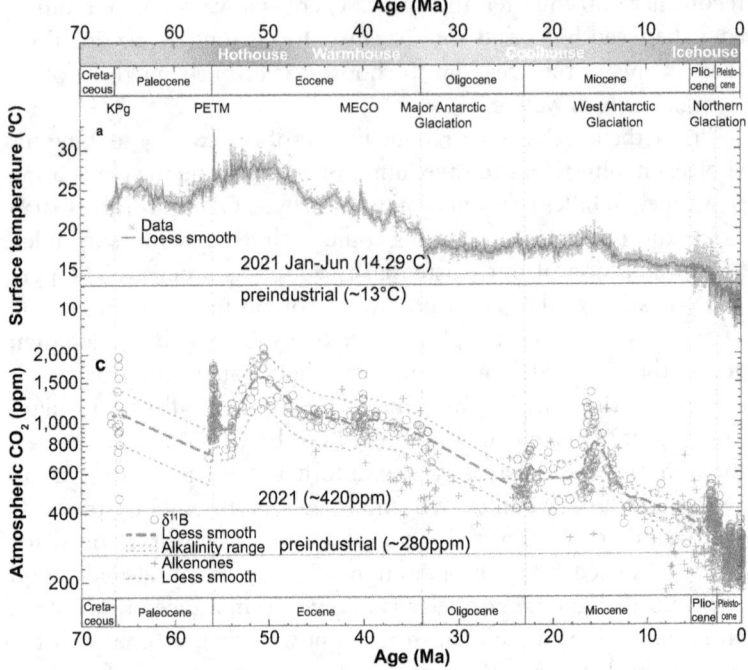

Figure 7.1 Charts showing the correlation between changes in global temperatures and the percentage of carbon dioxide in the atmosphere over millions of years. (J. W. B. Rae, 'Cenozoic CO2 and Global Climate', *Annual Review of Earth and Planetary Sciences*, Vol. 49 (2021), 609–641.)

And so our Industrial Age might be said to have served like the heat-absorbing black daisies in Prof. James Lovelock's famous model, which flourish in the cold conditions produced by the heat-reflecting white daisies, and in so flourishing raise the temperature to a point that results in their own decline, thus permitting the white daisies to flourish again.[41] To acknowledge this simple fact is to see at once the appalling arrogance of both those who are for and those who are against the "modern Prometheus" – but who are alike in sharing the same misguided conviction that the human species in general, and modern Western industrial society in particular, is something apart from, antagonistic to, the natural world. But to suggest that even modern Western industrial society might be an integral part of this planet's feedback mechanisms (in an expanded version of Lovelock's "Gaia hypothesis") is *not* to encourage complacency. On the contrary, the salient point about the black daisies is that they will barely survive their own essential intervention (and will be saved only by the feedback loop which will be produced in turn by the white daisies). Let us hope we do not awake to find one day that, like the black daisies, we have only restored an equilibrium to Gaia by creating the conditions for our own extinction.

Notes

1 Amiri Baraka, *A Black Mass* (1966), republished in *Four Revolutionary Plays* (London: Marion Boyars, 2000), 37.
2 *Ibid.*, 37.
3 *Ibid.*, 43.
4 *Ibid.*, 44.
5 *Ibid.*, 46.
6 *Ibid.*, 52.
7 *Ibid.*, 48.
8 *Ibid.*, 51–52.
9 *Ibid.*, 42–43.
10 Horace Walpole, *The Castle of Otranto* (1765), republished in Peter Fairclough and Mario Praz (eds), *Three Gothic Novels* (London: Penguin Classics, 1986), 41.
11 Marco Polo and Rustichello da Pisa, *Description of the World* (c. 1300), Benjamin Colbert (trans.), *The Travels of Marco Polo* (Ware, Hertfordshire: Wordsworth Editions, 1997), 16.
12 John Mandeville, *The Travels of Sir John Mandeville*, XXVIII (London: Macmillan, 1900), 171.
13 Reza Negarestani, *Cyclonopedia: Complicity with Anonymous Materials* (Melbourne: re.press, 2008), 18–19.
14 *Ibid.*, 210.
15 *Ibid.*, 212.
16 Matt. 12:43–45.
17 Negarestani, *Cyclonopedia*, 200.
18 *Ibid.*, 212.
19 *Ibid.*, 213.
20 *Ibid.*, 213.
21 *Ibid.*, i.
22 Sigmund Freud, 'The Ego and the Id' (1923), Mark Edmundson (ed.) and John Reddick (trans.), *Beyond the Pleasure Principle and Other Writings* (London: Penguin Classics, 2003), 105.

23 Joseph Priestley, *Disquisitions relating to Matter and Spirit* (London: J. Johnson, 1777), 31.
24 Stephen King, *Revival* (London: Hodder & Stoughton, 2014), 68.
25 *Ibid.*, 309–310.
26 *Ibid.*, 351.
27 *Ibid.*, 351.
28 *Ibid.*, 351.
29 *Ibid.*, 351.
30 *Ibid.*, 351.
31 *Ibid.*, 351.
32 Nnedi Okorafor, *Lagoon* (London: Hodder & Stoughton, 2014), 6.
33 *Ibid.*, 6.
34 *Ibid.*, 6.
35 *Ibid.*, 228.
36 Donna J. Haraway, *Staying with the Trouble: Making Kin in the Chthulucene* (Durham, NC, and London: Duke University Press, 2016), 101.
37 *Ibid.*, 101. 'Less simple was deciding how to spell Cthulucene so that it led to diverse and bumptious chthonic dividuals and powers and not to Chthulhu, Cthulhu, or any other singleton monster or deity. A fastidious Greek speller might insist on the "h" between the last "l" and "u"; but both for English pronunciation and for avoiding the grasp of Lovecraft's Cthulhu, I dropped that "h". This is a metaplasm.' Haraway, *Staying with the Trouble*, 169.
38 Okorafor, *Lagoon*, 220, 112.
39 *Ibid.*, 291.
40 For details on the Bārûtu see Westen Holz and Ulla Koch, *The Babylonian Liver Omens: The Chapters Manzazu, Padanu and Pan Takalti of the Babylonian Extispicy Series Mainly from Assurbanipal's Library* (Copenhagen: Museum Tusculanum Press, 2000).
41 See James Lovelock, *The Ages of Gaia: A Biography of Our Living Earth* (London: Bantam Books, 1990).

Select bibliography

Ackroyd, Peter. *Hawksmoor* (London: Penguin, 1985, 1993).
Agrippa, Cornelius. *De Occulta Philosophia* (1533). James Freake (trans.), *Three Books of Occult Philosophy* (London: Printed by R. W. for Gregory Moule, 1651).
Allan, John. *Berthold Lubetkin: Architecture and the Tradition of Progress* (London: RIBA Publications, 1992).
Anderson, Henning. Reconstructing Prehistorical Dialects: Initial Vowels in Slavic and Baltic, *PS E-SE, 7.25: Proto-Baltic ERŽ-IL-A- 'Stallion'* (Berlin: Mouton de Gruyter, 1996).
Anker, Peder. 'The Bauhaus of Nature'. *Modernism/Modernity*, Vol. 12, No. 2 (2005).
Aristotle. *Ethics*. Jonathan Barnes (ed.), *The Complete Works* (Princeton, NJ: Princeton University Press, 1984).
Aristotle. *Politics*. B. Jowett (trans.), *The Politics of Aristotle*, Vol. 1 (Oxford: Clarendon Press, 1885).
Ashley-Montagu, M. T. "Knowledge of the Ape in Antiquity". *Isis*, Vol. 32, No. 1 (1940).
Asimov, Isaac. *Foundation Trilogy* (London: Everyman's Library, 2010).
Ballard, J. G. *High-Rise* (London: Fourth Estate, HarperCollins, 2014).
Baraka, Amiri. *A Black Mass* (1966). Republished in *Four Revolutionary Plays* (London: Marion Boyars, 1998).
Bard-Rosenberg, Jacob. 'Angelic Satire: Benjamin on Standstill and Marx on Movement'. Paper presented at Historical Materialism Conference, Birbeck College, London, 8 November 2015.
Baudrillard, Jean. *The Transparency of Evil*. Trans. James Benedict (New York: Verso, 1993).
Benjamin, Walter. 'Central Park'. Edmund Jephcott and Howard Eiland (trans.), *Selected Writings: 1938–1940, Vol. 4* (Cambridge, MA: Belknap Press, 2003).
Benjamin, Walter. 'Theses on the Philosophy of History' (1940). *Illuminations*, trans. Harry Zorn (London: Random House, 1999).
Black, David. *Helen Macfarlane: A Feminist, Revolutionary Journalist and Philosopher in Mid-19th Century England* (Lanham, MD: Lexington Books, 2004).

Black, David (ed.) and Macfarlane, Helen (trans.), *Red Republican* (London: Unkant, 2014).
Blair, Tony. Speech to the House of Commons. *Guardian* (18 March 2003).
Blair, Tony. Speech to the Labour Party Conference. *Guardian* (2 October 2001).
Bobbitt, Philip. *Shield of Achilles: War, Peace, and the Course of History* (London: Penguin, 2002).
Bobbitt, Philip. *Terror and Consent: The Wars for the Twenty-First Century* (London: Allen Lane, 2008).
Boulle, Pierre. *Planet of the Apes* (1963). Ed. Brian Aldiss, trans. Xan Fielding (London: Penguin, 2001).
Byron, George Gordon. *Don Juan (1819-1824)*. Ernest Hartley Coleridge (ed.), *The Poetical Works of Lord Byron* (London: John Murray, 1905).
Carpenter, Humphrey. *J. R. R. Tolkien: A Biography* (Boston: Houghton Mifflin Harcourt, 2000).
Chomsky, Noam. *Language and Thought* (London: Moyer Bell, 1993).
Chtcheglov, Ivan. 'Formulary for a New Urbanism' (1953). Ken Knabb (trans.), *Situationist International Anthology* (Berkeley, CA: Bureau of Public Secrets, 2007).
Cicero, *De Oratore*. Trans. E. W. Sutton and H. Rackham (Loeb Classics: London, 1942).
Clery, E. J. 'The Genesis of "Gothic" Fiction'. Jerrold E. Hogle (ed.), *The Cambridge Guide to Gothic Fiction* (Cambridge: Cambridge University Press, 2003).
Clynes, Manfred E. and Kline, Nathan S. 'Cyborgs and Space'. *Astronautics* (Sept 1960); reprinted in C. H. Gray, S. Mentor and H. J. Figueroa-Sarriera (eds), *The Cyborg Handbook* (New York: Routledge, 1995).
Crichton, Michael. *Jurassic Park* (New York: Ballantine Books, Random House, 2015).
Darwin, Charles. *The Descent of Man* (1871). Ed. James Moore and Adrian Desmond (London: Penguin, 2004).
De La Ruffiniere Du Prey, Pierre. 'Hawksmoor's "Basilica After the Primitive Christians": Architecture and Theology'. *Journal of the Society of Architectural Historians*, Vol. 48, No. 1 (Mar 1989).
Defoe, Daniel. *Colonel Jack* (1722). Ed. Samuel Holt Monk (London: Oxford University Press, 1965).
Defoe, Daniel. *Robinson Crusoe* (1719). Ed. J. M. Coetzee (Oxford: Oxford University Press, 1997).
Defoe, Daniel. *A Tour thro' the Whole Island of Great Britain* (1724–1727). Ed. P. N. Furbank, W. R. Owens and A. J. Coulson (New Haven, CT: Yale University Press, 1991).
Derrida, Jacques. *The Animal That Therefore I Am*. Ed. Marie-Louise Mallet, trans. David Wills (New York: Fordham University Press, 2008).
Derrida, Jacques. *Specters of Marx: The State of the Debt, the Work of Mourning, and the New International*. Trans. Peggy Kamuf (London: Routledge Classics, 2006).

Descartes, René. *Discourse on Method and Other Writings*. Trans. F. E. Sutcliffe (London: Penguin, 1968).
Dixon, R. M. W. *The Rise and Fall of Languages* (Cambridge: Cambridge University Press, 1997).
Downes, Kerry. *Hawksmoor* (London: Praeger, 1970).
Du Chaillu, Paul. *Explorations and Adventures in Equatorial Africa: With Accounts of the Manners and Customs of the People, and of the Chase of the Gorilla, the Crocodile, Leopard, Elephant, Hippopotamus, and Other Animals* (London: J. Murray, 1861).
Eliot, T. S. '*Ulysses*, Order, and Myth' (1923). Frank Kermode (ed.), *Selected Prose* (London: Faber, 1975).
Engels, Friedrich. *The Condition of the Working Class in England* (1845). Ed. Victor Kiernan and Tristram Hunt (London: Penguin, 2009).
Etlin, Richard A. *Symbolic Space* (Chicago: University of Chicago Press, 1994).
Evelyn, John. *Character of England, As It Was Lately Presented in a Letter, to a Noble Man of FRANCE*, 3rd edition (London, 1659).
Freud, Sigmund. 'Character and Anal Eroticism' (1908). James Strachey (trans.), *The Standard Edition of the Complete Works*, Vol. XVII (London: Hogarth Press, 1961).
Freud, Sigmund. 'The Ego and the Id' (1923). Mark Edmundson (ed.) and John Reddick (trans.), *Beyond the Pleasure Principle and Other Writings* (London: Penguin Classics, 2003).
Freud, Sigmund. *Future of an Illusion: Civilisation and Its Discontents* (1930). James Strachey (trans.), *The Standard Edition of the Complete Works*, Vol. XXI, 1927–1931 (London: Hogarth Press, 1961).
Freud, Sigmund. *The Interpretation of Dreams* (1913), trans. A. A. Brill (London: Wordsworth Classics, 1997).
Freud, Sigmund. *On Murder, Mourning and Melancholia* (1913). Ed. Maud Ellman, trans. Shauen Whiteside (London: Penguin, 2005).
Freud, Sigmund. 'On Transformations of Instinct as Exemplified in Anal Eroticism' (c. 1917). James Strachey (trans.), *The Standard Edition of the Complete Works*, Vol. XVII (London: Hogarth Press, 1961).
Freud, Sigmund. 'The Uncanny' (1919). David McLintock (trans.), *The Uncanny* (Penguin: London, 2003).
Freud, Sigmund. 'The Uncanny' (1919). James Strachey (trans.), *The Standard Edition of the Complete Psychological Works* (London: Hogarth Press, 1955).
Fukuyama, Francis. 'The End of History?' The National Interest (Summer 1989).
Gandy, R. 'Human versus Mechanical Intelligence'. P. Millican and A. Clark (eds.), *Machines and Thought: The Legacy of Alan Turing*, Vol. I (Oxford: Clarendon Press, 1996).
Garth, John. *Tolkien and the Great War: The Threshold of Middle-Earth* (Boston: Houghton Mifflin Harcourt, 2003).

Genova, Judith. 'Turing's Sexual Guessing Game'. *Social Epistemology*, Vol. 8, No. 4 (1994).
Gott, Ted. 'It Is Lovely To Be a Gorilla, Sometimes: The Art and Influence of Emmanuel Fremiet, Gorilla Sculptor', Joseph Burke Lecture 2006. David R. Marshall (ed.), *Art, Site and Spectacle: Studies in Early Modern Visual Culture* (Melbourne: Fine Arts Network, 2007).
Gutheim, F. A. 'Building for Beasts'. *Magazine of Art*, Vol. 29 (Oct 1936).
Haraway, Donna J. *Staying with the Trouble: Making Kin in the Chthulucene* (Durham, NC, and London: Duke University Press, 2016).
Hart, Vaughan. *Nicholas Hawksmoor: Rebuilding Ancient Wonders* (New Haven, CT, and London: Yale University Press, 2002).
Hayek, F. A. *The Constitution of Liberty* (London and New York: Routledge Classics, 2006).
Hayek, F. A. *The Road to Serfdom* (New York: Routledge Classics, 2001).
Hayes, Patrick and Ford, Kenneth. 'Turing Test Considered Harmful'. *Proceedings of the Fourteenth International Joint Conference on Artificial Intelligence*, Vol. 1 (1995).
Hegel, G. W. F. *Aesthetics*. Trans. T. M. Knox (Oxford: Clarendon Press, 1974).
Hesse, Hermann. *The Glass Bead Game* (1943). Trans. Richard Winston and Clara Winston (London: Vintage Classics, 2000).
Hobbes, Thomas. *Leviathan: Or, The Matter, Form and Power of a Common-wealth, Ecclesiastical and Civil* (London: Andrew Crooke, 1651).
Hodges, Andrew. *Alan Turing: The Enigma* (New York: Simon and Schuster, 1983).
Hogle, Jerrold E. 'Introduction'. Jerrold E. Hogle (ed.), *Cambridge Guide to Gothic Fiction* (Cambridge: Cambridge University Press, 2003).
Holz, Westen and Koch, Ullah. *The Babylonian Liver Omens: The Chapters Manzazu, Padanu and Pan Takalti of the Babylonian Extispicy Series Mainly from Assurbanipal's Library* (Copenhagen: Museum Tusculanum Press, 2000).
Home, Stewart. *Mind Invaders* (London: Serpent's Tail, 1997).
Homer. *Iliad*. Samuel Butler (trans.), *The Iliad of Homer* (London: Longmans, Green and Co., 1898).
Huxley, Aldous. *Brave New World* (1932). Ed. David Bradshaw (London: Flamingo, HarperCollins, 1994).
Huxley, Aldous. *Letters of Aldous Huxley*. Ed. Grover Smith (New York and Evanston, IL: Harper and Row, 1969).
Huxley, Aldous. 'Sight-Seeing in Alien Englands' (1931). David Bradshaw (ed.), *Between the Wars: Essays and Letters* (Chicago: Ivan R. Dee, 1994).
Hylton, Kenneth. *Le Corbusier and the Architecture of Reinvention* (London: Architectural Association, 2003).
Jameson, Frederic. *Post-Modernism, or The Cultural Logic of Late Capitalism* (London and New York: Verso Books, 1992).
Jardine, Lisa. *On a Grander Scale: The Outstanding Life of Sir Christopher Wren* (New York: HarperCollins, 2002).

Joyce, James. *Finnegans Wake* (London: Faber and Faber, 1939).
Kehoe, Louise. *In This Dark House* (New York: Schocken Books, 1995).
Keynes, J. M. 'Economic Possibilities for our Grandchildren' (1928). Robert Skidelsky (ed.), *The Essential Keynes* (London and New York: Penguin Classics 2016).
Keynes, J. M. *The General Theory of Employment, Interest and Money* (1936). Donald Moggeridge (ed.), *The Collected Writings of J. M. Keynes*, Vol. VII (Cambridge: Cambridge University Press, 1973).
Keynes, J. M. *A Treatise on Money*, Vol. II (London: Macmillan, 1930).
King, Stephen. *Revival* (London: Hodder & Stoughton, 2014).
Kruchenykh, Aleksei. 'Declaration of Transrational Language'. Anna Lawton and Herbert Eagle (trans.), *Words in Revolution: Russian Futurist Manifestoes 1912–1928* (Washington, DC: New Academia Publishing, 2005).
LaGrandeur, Kevin. *Androids and Intelligent Networks in Early Modern Literature and Culture: Artificial Slaves* (New York: Routledge, 2013).
Larkin, Philip. 'The Building'. *Collected Poems* (London: Faber and Faber, 2003).
Laugier, Marc-Antoine. *An Essay on Architecture* (1755). Trans. Wolfgang Herrmann (Santa Monica, CA: Hennessey & Ingalls, 1985).
Le Corbusier. *The City of To-Morrow and Its Planning* (1929). Trans. Frederick Etchells (New York: Dover, 1987).
Le Corbusier. *The Modulor*. Trans. Peter de Francia and Anna Bostock (London: Faber and Faber, 1954).
Le Corbusier. *Modulor 2*. Trans. Peter de Francia and Anna Bostock (London: Faber and Faber, 1958).
Lefebvre, Henri. 'Plan of the Present Work', *The Production of Space* (1974). Trans. Donald Nicholson-Smith (Oxford: Blackwell, 1991).
Levitt, Gerald M. *The Turk, Chess Automaton* (McFarland & Co., 2000).
Lewis, Wyndham. *Time and Western Man* (1927). Ed. Paul Edwards (Santa Rosa, CA: Black Sparrow Press, 1993).
Linebaugh, Peter. 'Karl Marx, the Theft of Wood, Working Class Composition'. *Crime and Social Justice*, Vol. 6 (Autumn–Winter 1976).
Lovecraft, H. P. 'Herbert West – Reanimator' (1922). Stephen Jones (ed.), *Necronomicon: The Best Weird Tales of H. P. Lovecraft* (London: Gollancz, 2008).
Lubetkin, Berthold. 'Dudley Zoo'. Unpublished transcript, c. 1938. Royal Institute of British Architects (RIBA), Lubetkin's Papers, Box 1, LuB/25/4.
Lubetkin, Berthold. Notes for 'Samizdat'. RIBA, Lubetkin's Papers, Box 1, LuB/25/4.
MacDonald, George. *The Princess and the Goblin* (Edinburgh: Strahan and Co., 1872).
MacNeice, Louis. *Zoo* (London: Michael Joseph, 1938).
Mandeville, John. *The Travels of Sir John Mandeville* (London: Macmillan, 1900).

Marcuse, Herbert. *One-Dimensional Man: Studies in the Ideology of Advanced Industrial Society* (London: Beacon Press, 1964).
Marr, Nikolai Yakovlevich. 'Predislovie k Jafetičeskomu Sborniku, t. V' (1927). *Izbrannye raboty, Tom. 1: Ètapy razvitija jafetičeskoj teorija* (Leningrad: Izdat: GAIMK, 1933).
Marx, Karl. Letter to Engels, 23 February 1851. *Marx and Engels Collected Works*, Vol. 38 (London: Lawrence and Wishart, 1982).
Marx, Karl. *Scorpion and Felix: A Humoristic Novel*, published in *Book of Verse* (1837). Available online at: www.marxists.org/archive/marx/works/1837-pre/verse/verse41.html.
Marx, Karl and Engels, Friedrich. *The Communist Manifesto* (1848). Ed. Gareth Stedman Jones, trans. Samuel Moore (London: Penguin Classics, 2002).
Matthews, W. K. "The Japhetic Theory". *The Slavic and East European Review*, Vol. 27, No. 68 (1948).
Miles, Robert. 'The 1790s: Effulgence of Gothic'. Jerrold E. Hogle (ed.), *The Cambridge Companion to Gothic Literature* (Cambridge: Cambridge University Press, 2003).
Mirowski, Philip. *Machine Dreams: Economics Becomes a Cyborg Science* (Cambridge: Cambridge University Press, 2008).
Moore, Alan and Campbell, Eddie. *From Hell* (London: Knockabout, 2000).
Mumford, Lewis. *The City in History* (New York: Harbinger, 1961).
Negarestani, Reza. *Cyclonopedia: Complicity with Anonymous Materials* (Melbourne: re.press, 2008).
Newman, William. *Promethean Ambitions: Alchemy and the Quest to Perfect Nature* (Chicago: University of Chicago Press, 2004).
Nieuwenhuys, Constant. *New Babylon*. Exhibition catalogue (The Hague: Haags Gemeetenmuseum, 1974).
Okorafor, Nnedi. *Lagoon* (London: Hodder & Stoughton, 2014).
Orwell, George. *1984* (1949). *The Complete Novels* (London and New York: Penguin Classics, 2000).
Owens, Richard. 'Dissociations: The McCaffery–Prynne Debate'. *Paideuma: Modern and Contemporary Poetry and Poetics*, Vol. 40 (2013).
Paracelsus. 'A Book of Nymphs, Sylphs, Pygmies and Salamanders, and on the Other Spirits' (1566). Henry E. Sigherist (trans.), *Four Treatises of Theophrastus von Hohenheim Called Paracelsus* (Baltimore, MD, and London: Johns Hopkins University Press, 1941).
Paracelsus. *De Natura Rerum* (1572). A. E. Waite (trans.), *The Hermetic and Alchemical Writings of Paracelsus* (London: James Elliott and Co, 1894).
Penrose, Roger. *The Emperor's New Mind* (Oxford: Oxford University Press, 1989, 1999).
Pietz, William. 'The Problem of the Fetish'. *RES: Anthropology and Aesthetics*, Vol. 9 (Spring 1985).
Pliny, *The Natural History*. Trans. John Bostock and H. T. Riley (London: Taylor and Francis, 1855).

Poe, Edgar Allan. 'Maelzel's Chess-Player'. *Southern Literary Journal*, Vol. 2 (April 1836).
Poe, Edgar Allan. 'The Murders in the Rue Morgue' (1841). Graham Clarke (ed.), *Tales of Mystery and Imagination* (London: Everyman, 1993).
Polo, Marco and da Pisa, Rustichello. *Description of the World* (c. 1300). Benjamin Colbert (trans.), *The Travels of Marco Polo* (Ware, Hertfordshire: Wordsworth Editions, 1997).
Pound, Ezra. *The Cantos* (London: Faber, 1987).
Priestley, Joseph. *Disquisitions relating to Matter and Spirit* (London: J. Johnson, 1777).
Read, Herbert. 'New Aspects of British Sculpture'. Exhibition catalogue for the British Pavilion at the XXVI Venice Biennale, 1952.
Rohman, Carrie. *Stalking the Subject: Modernism and the Animal* (New York: Columbia University Press, 2008).
Rossetti, Christina. *Goblin Market and Other Poems* (London: Macmillan, 1862).
Rushdie, Salman. 'Outside the Whale'. *Granta Magazine* (1 March 1984).
Savage, Thomas S. 'Notice of the External Characters and Habits of Troglodytes Gorilla, a New Species of Orang from the Gaboon River' and Jeffries Wyman, 'Osteology of the Same'. *Boston Journal of Natural History*, Vol. 5, No. 4 (Dec 1847).
Saygin, Ayse Pinar, Cicekli, Ilyas and Akman, Varol. 'Turing Test: 50 Years Later'. *Minds and Machines*, Vol. 10 (2000).
Schivelbusch, Wolfgang. *The Railway Journey: The Industrialization of Time and Space in the Nineteenth Century* (Leamington Spa, Warwickshire: Berg Publishers, 1986).
Schwartz, Peter. *The Art of the Long View: Planning for the Future in an Uncertain World* (New York: Currency Doubleday, 1991).
Scott, Walter. *Letters on Demonology and Witchcraft* (London: John Murray, 1830).
Searle, John R. 'Minds, Brains and Programs'. *Behavioral and Brain Sciences*, Vol. 3, No. 3 (1980).
Shackle, G. L. S. *Epistemics and Economics: A Critique of Economic Doctrines* (Cambridge: Cambridge University Press, 1972).
Shackle, G. L. S. *Imagination and the Nature of Choice* (Edinburgh: Edinburgh University Press, 1979).
Shelley, Mary. *Frankenstein; or, The Modern Prometheus* (London: Penguin Classics, 2003).
Sinclair, Iain. *Lud Heat and Suicide Bridge* (London: Granta, 1998).
Skidelsky, Robert. *John Maynard Keynes, 1883–1946: Economist, Philosopher, Statesman* (New York: Penguin, 2005).
Sørenson, Preben M. *The Unmanly Man: Concepts of Sexual Defamation in Early Northern Society* (Odense: Odense University Press, 1983).
Speiser, Ephraim Avigdor. 'Introduction to Hurrian'. *The Annual of the American Schools of Oriental Research*, Vol. 20 (1940).

Speiser, Ephraim Avigdor. *Mesopotamian Origins: The Basic Population of the Near East* (Philadelphia: University of Pennsylvania Press, 1930).
Speiser, Ephraim Avigdor. 'Studies in Hurrian Grammar'. *Journal of the American Oriental Society*, Vol. 59, No. 3 (Sept 1939).
Spicer, Nicolas. *Landscape With Forgeries* (London: Contraband, 2012).
Stepanov, N. 'Esperanto kaj Esperanto-Movado en Sovetunio' ('Esperanto and the Esperanto Movement in the Soviet Union'). *Esperanto USA*, 4 (1991).
Sterrett, S. G. 'Turing's Two Tests for Intelligence'. *Minds and Machines*, Vol. 10 (2000). Reprinted in J. H. Moor (ed.), *The Turing Test* (Dordrecht: Kluwer, 2003).
Straw, Jack. Speech to the Foreign Policy Centre: 'Reordering the World'. *Guardian* (25 March 2002).
Thatcher, Margaret. Speech to Conservative Party Conference: 'The Lady's Not for Turning', 10 October 1980. Thatcher Archive: CCOPR 735/80.
Tolkien, J. R. R. *The Annotated Hobbit: Revised and Expanded Edition*. Ed. Douglas A. Henderson (Boston: Houghton Mifflin Harcourt, 2002).
Tolkien, J. R. R. *The Hobbit* (London: Unwin Hyman: London, 1989).
Tolkien, J. R. R. *Letters from Father Christmas*. Ed. Baillie Tolkien (London: HarperCollins, 2015).
Tolkien, J. R. R. *The Letters of J. R. R. Tolkien*. Ed. Humphrey Carpenter (London: HarperCollins, 2006).
Tolkien, J. R. R. *The Lost Road and Other Writings*. Ed. Christopher Tolkien (London: HarperCollins, 2002).
Tolkien, J. R. R. *The Lord of the Rings* (London: HarperCollins, 1995).
Tolkien, J. R. R. *Morgoth's Ring*. Ed. Christopher Tolkien (London: HarperCollins, 2002).
Tolkien, J. R. R. *The Peoples of Middle-Earth*. Ed. Christopher Tolkien (London: HarperCollins, 2002).
Tolkien, J. R. R. 'Philology: General Works'. *The Year's Work in English Studies*, Vol. V (London: Oxford University Press, 1924).
Tolkien, J. R. R. *Sauron Defeated*. Ed. Christopher Tolkien (London: HarperCollins, 2002).
Tolkien, J. R. R. *The Treason of Isengard*. Ed. Christopher Tolkien (London: HarperCollins, 2002).
Tolkien, J. R. R. *The War of the Jewels*. Ed. Christopher Tolkien (London: HarperCollins, 2002).
Tolkien, J. R. R. 'Words, Phrases and Passages in Various Tongues in *The Lord of the Rings*'. Christopher Gilson (ed.), *Parma Eldalemberon*, 17 (Los Angeles: Mythopoetic Society, 2007).
Trotter, David. *Circulation: Defoe, Dickens, and the Economics of the Novel* (Basingstoke, Hampshire: Macmillan, 1988).
Tuite, Kevin. 'The Rise and Fall and Revival of the Ibero-Caucasian Hypothesis'. *Historiographia Linguistica*, Vol. 35, No. 1 (2007).
Turing, Alan. *The Essential Turing*. Ed. B. Jack Copeland (Oxford: Clarendon Press, 2004).

Turner, Alwyn. *The Man Who Invented the Daleks: The Strange Worlds of Terry Nation* (London: Aurum Press, 2013).
Vico, Giambattista. *The New Science* (1744). Trans. David Marsh (London: Penguin, 2013).
Wall, Cynthia. *The Literary and Cultural Spaces of Restoration London* (Cambridge: Cambridge University Press, 1998).
Walpole, Horace. *The Castle of Otranto* (1765). Peter Fairclough and Mario Praz, (eds), *Three Gothic Novels* (London: Penguin Classics, 1986).
Watkins, Alfred. *The Old Straight Track* (London: Abacus, 1970).
Webb, Sydney. *Socialism in England* (Harmondsworth: Penguin, 1974).
Whitaker, David. *Dr Who and the Daleks* (1964). Republished by BBC Books (London: Random House, 2011).
Wiener, Nobert. *Cybernetics: Or Control and Communication in the Animal and the Machine* (Cambridge, MA: MIT Press, 1948, 1961).
Wolfe, Carey (ed.). *Zoontologies* (Minneapolis: University of Minnesota Press, 2003).
Wren, Christopher, Wren, Christopher Junior and Wren, Stephen. *Parentalia: Or, Memoirs of the Family of the Wrens ... Chiefly of Sir Christopher Wren* (London: T. Osborn and R. Dodsley, 1750).
Yates, Frances. *The Art of Memory* (Chicago: University of Chicago Press, 1966, 2001).
Yeats, W. B. *Yeats's Poems*. Ed. A. Norman Jefferies and Warwick Gould (Basingstoke, Hampshire, and London: Macmillan, 1996).
Young, Warren. *Interpreting Mr Keynes: The IS-LM Enigma* (Boulder, CO: Westview Press, 1987).
Zuckerman, S. *The Social Life of Monkeys and Apes* (London: Routledge and Kegan Paul, 1981).

Index

Ackroyd, Peter 11, 18, 24, 27
Adûnaic 100–101
Agrippa, Cornelius 5–8
Akeley, Carl (explorer) 50
aliens 81, 127, 210–212
analysis 57–58, 165–167
Analytical Engine 164–165, 193n.30
Anderson, James 16, 28
Angel of History / Angelus Novus 158–159, 161–162, 182
animal 47–49, 54–58, 60–67, 70, 123, 170, 189, 199, 213
Anker, Peder 46, 60, 62
apes, 47–48, 56–59, 61–67
   in art and cinema 51–55
   as capable of imitating human personality 56–59
   the discovery of the gorilla 49–50
   as embodiment of the human "bestiality" of the "Id" 54–55, 62–63
   as homunculi 50, 67, 198–199
   in London Zoo 45–47
   see also Imitation Game; mimesis
Aristotle 8–9, 47–48
artificial body *see* automatons; cyborg
artificial intelligence (A. I.) 7–9, 12, 167–169, 178, 191
   see also computers

artificial language 90, 93, 99, 178
   see also Black Speech
artificial life 6–7
   Frankenstein's Monster 1–4, 6–7, 9, 198–199
   golems 8, 84, 206
   homunculus 7, 50, 215
   see also orcs
Asimov, Isaac 9, 179–180, 183
Atlantis 100–101
Austrian School economics 139–140, 143, 183
automatons 8–9, 76, 125, 161, 163–164, 168–169, 178, 184
   see also Mechanical Turk

Babbage, Charles 164–166, 193n.30
Babel / Babylon / Baghdad 121–121, 135, 187, 214
Baby Boomers 126, 135, 149, 151
Ballard, J. G. 111–112, 116–117, 121–122, 147–148
Baraka, Amiri 198–200
Bard-Rosenberg, Jacob 158–159, 161
baroque style, the 11, 12, 18, 25–26, 28–29, 39–41
Benjamin, Walter 13, 158–162, 182, 192
Bentham, Jeremy 103
Bergson, Henri 70, 204

Index

Bierse, Ambrose 168
Birmingham 82–83, 113, 141, 148, 205, 212
Black Speech
   characteristics 90–95
   invented by Morgoth 91
   origins (speculative) 90
   resemblance to the speech of the Wild Men 85–86
   resemblance to Georgian 99
   resemblance to Hurrian 95–96
   significance of these parallels 86–89, 96–100
   see also artificial language
Blair, Tony 186–187, 197n.132, 197n.133
Bloomsbury Group 142, 146
Bobbitt, Phillip 185–187
Boulle, Pierre 58–59
Bowie, David 113, 127
Brandt, Georg 79
Brutalism 12, 25, 27, 112, 114–117, 123–124, 134–135, 151, 213
Burgess, Anthony 100, 126
Butler, Samuel 8, 174

carbon economy see fossil fuel
Carey, M.R. 150–151
Carroll, Lewis 96
Cartesian see Descartes
catastrophe 158–162, 180, 190–192
Catling, Brian 22
Caucasian 52, 95, 97–99, 201
Certeau (de), Michel 134–135
Chaillu (du), Paul 50
Chamberlain, Joseph 83
chaos Theory (a.k.a. Complexity Theory) 188–192
Chartism 77, 82
chess 161–169, 177–178, 184
Chicago School (of economics) see Austrian School economics
China 145, 176–179, 181, 183

Chomsky, Noam 168
Chtcheglov, Ivan 134
Cicero 16
Clarke, Arthur C. 9, 125
Cold War 145, 160, 184, 188
commodity fetish see fetish
communism 61, 75, 77–78, 83, 88–89, 101–103
computers 148, 165, 167–168, 170–171, 173, 190, 192
   anxieties relating to 9, 168
   computer-chess 169–170, 178
   computer-generated Images (CGI) 77, 190–192
   computer-modelling 13, 172–173, 179–180, 184, 187–190
   as monsters 126, 168, 178
   paper-machines or human computers 176–177, 179
   as prothesis 8–9, 123, 161, 178
   as uncanny 161, 169–170
   see also Analytical Engine; artificial intelligence; Imitation Game; Mechanical Turk
Conlang see artificial language
Copeland, B. Jack 167, 172, 174
Crichton, Michael 187–190
cybernetics 9, 122–124, 135, 162, 167, 181, 183–184, 189
cyborgs 2, 8–9, 76–77, 123–124, 183, 210–212
   see also Daleks

Daleks 118–122, 124–125
   see also cyborgs
Darwin, Charles 11, 50, 55–56, 61, 64, 71, 205
Debord, Guy 18, 134–135
Defoe, Daniel 20, 33, 36–39
Deleuze and Guattari, 204
demonization see shame totem
Derrida, Jacques 47–49, 55, 76, 78, 83, 103, 159–160, 209
   see also Modernism

Descartes, René 47–49, 56–57, 70, 134, 170, 174, 205
détournement 104, 199
  see also shame totem
dialectic 70, 98, 133–134, 135, 146–147, 158, 180, 186, 199, 215
Dick, Philip K. 49
Disraeli, Benjamin 80
dissociation of sensibility 70, 199, 205, 214
Dixon, R.M.W. 95, 98
Doctor Who 118–119
double (doppelganger) 33, 40, 76, 123–124, 169
Downes, Kerry 23, 25
Drúedain / Drûg-hu 85–86, 88

Egypt 26–28, 124, 131, 138–139, 205
  see also magic; magician; mummies
Eliot, George 75
Eliot, T. S. 11, 70, 88, 112, 161, 199, 205, 214–215
end of history see history of the world
Engels, Friedrich 75, 82
Enlightenment 10–13, 18–19, 33, 40, 47, 66–67, 71, 76, 83, 181, 200
Esperanto see artificial languages
Evelyn, John 29
extinct ecosystems 198–199, 201, 215
  see also fossils

Fanon, Frantz 136
Farrel, Terry 40
Fauskanger, Helge 90–94
fetish 76, 83, 86, 88, 103–104, 110n.107, 204
  see also matter
fire-maps see planning
fossil fuels 120, 185, 200–202, 215–216
  see also extinct ecosystems; industrial revolution
fossils 127, 151, 189
Frankenstein, Victor 1–7, 10, 192, 198–199, 206
  see also Mad Scientist
Frankfurt School 146–147
freedom 13, 66, 134, 146, 214–215
  see also Promethean gifts
Freemasons 10, 18, 28, 40
Fremiert, Emmanuel 50–53, 60, 72n.18
Freud, Sigmund
  on anal retentiveness 121, 143, 157n.102
  on animal totems 54–55, 62
  culmination of the Schopenhauerian tradition in western philosophy 70–71, 204
  forms part of the mid-century synthesis effected by Keynes 12, 104, 143, 146
  might be mistaken for a magician or illusionist 71, 35, 204–205
  on prosthetics, doubling and automatons as origin of the uncanny 123–125, 169
  on the two types of the uncanny 34–35, 39, 169, 199
Fukuyama, Francis 159, 183
futurism 45, 99–100, 122
Futurology see planning; Promethean, foresight and gift

Gaia 210, 212, 217
Galvani, Luigi 4–6
game theory 184, 186
geist see spirit
Gemora, Charlie 52–53, 56, 59
Georgia 13, 97–100, 201
Germany 5, 9–10, 39, 75, 77–78, 87, 89, 108n.57, 187, 205
Gibbon, Edward 26

Glass Bead Game 178–180
goblins 75–81, 84, 86–89, 91,
    101–104
    see also orcs
Goethe (von), J.W. 192
Goldfinger, Ernö 113, 127, 213
Golding, Arthur 125
golems see artificial life
gorillas see apes
Gorilla House 45–47, 59, 63–67
gothic 9–11, 18–19, 24–27, 31–35,
    39–40, 138, 152–153n.4,
    199–200, 205
Great Fire of London 17, 19,
    28–31, 33.
Greene, Robert 8
Grosse, Karl 10, 40
Grosz, George 159

Habermas, Jurgen 10–11
Hanno the Carthaginian 49–50,
    68–69
HAL 9000 see IBN
Haraway, Donna 122, 210,
    211–212
    see also Modernism
Hatherley, Owen 115, 117
Hawksmoor, Nicholas 11, 12, 18–
    19, 21–29, 34, 38, 40, 213
Hayek, F. W. 139–140, 143
    see also liberalism; Modernism
Hegel, G. W. F. 27, 70, 86, 97,
    102, 135, 160, 180, 186
Hercules 215
Hesse, Hermann 178–179
hieroglyphs 28, 98, 128
history of the world 78, 86,
    158, 161
    as cyclical 98, 99
    as dialectical process 70,
        146–147
    the end of history as the
        collapse of the dialectic of
        theory and practice
        146–147, 159–160, 183
    as predictable 180–181, 186,
        190–191

as seen in terms of catastrophe
    159–160, 162
as undetermined 160, 182, 190
Hobbes, Thomas 178
Hobsbawm, Eric 13, 138
Home, Stewart 18, 27
Homer 8
homunculus see artificial life
Huxley, Aldous 55, 140–143,
    146–147

IBN 167–168
Illuminati see Freemasons
illusionists see magician; simulacra;
    mimesis
imitation see mimesis
Imitation Game
    interpretations of the Turing
        Test 171–172
    Mathematical Objection
        174–176
    original Imitation Game
        170–171
    origins in chess programme
        169–170
    reinterpretation of the Turing
        Test by Saygin, Cicekli
        and Akman 172–173
    Searle's Chinese Room
        argument 176–177
    true purpose of the Imitation
        Game 173–174
    Virtual Mind Reply to
        Searle's Chinese Room
        argument 177
    see also mimesis
Indo-European languages (a.k.a.
    Prometheid) 71, 85, 87,
    96–98, 101–102
industrial revolution 82–83, 201
    see also fossil fuels;
        mass-production
International Style see Le Corbusier

Jackson, Peter 77
James, William 70–71
Jameson, Frederic 114

Japhetic theory 96–101
Jesuits 9–10, 40
Johnson, Samuel 103, 136
Jones, Inigo 27, 32
Jonson, Ben 31
Joyce, James 99, 112

kaleidics / kaleidoscope 159, 182, 187, 191–192
Kasperov, Garry 168
Kahlert, Carl Friedrich 10, 40
Kehoe, Louise 64–65
Kempelen (von), Wolfgang 161–163, 168–169
Keynes, John Maynard
  effects a synthesis of the two traditions represented by Marx and Freud 12, 104
  General Theory of Employment, Interest and Money 137–138
  inspired by Bernard Mandeville 136–137
  on Marx 138–139
  neo-liberal critiques by F.A. Hayek and G.L.S. Shackle 139, 182, 184, 191
  reinterpretation of General Theory by John Hicks and Alvin Hansen 181
  science-fiction sub-genre of anti-Keynesian dystopia 12, 140, 146
    Huxley, Aldous 140–143
    Orwell, George 143–145
  significance of the synthesis is overlooked by Frankfurt School 136, 146–147
  template for post-war consumer / welfare-warfare economies 120, 180, 144–145
  see also liberalism
King, Stephen 13, 126, 205–209, 210
King Kong (1933) 54, 59
Klee, Paul 158–159

Kobold 79
  see also goblins; orcs
Kropotkin 61
Krugman, Paul 180
Kubrick, Stanley 125–126, 168

LaGrandeur, Kevin 8–9
Larkin, Philip 124, 152, 153n.4
Laugier, Marc-Antoine 35–37
Le Corbusier 41, 111–114, 119–120, 122, 127–134, 180
Lefebvre, Henri 114, 133–135
Leibniz, G. W. 178
Lévi-Strauss, Claude 67
Levin, Ira 125
Lewis, C.S. 77, 81, 208
Lewis, Matthew 9
Lewis, Wyndham 11, 70–71
Ley Lines 21–22, 27
Loebner Prize *see* Imitation Game
Logos 47, 56–57, 67, 209
Lovelock, James 216–217
liberalism 9–10, 13, 23, 80–83, 186
  neoliberalism 136, 139–140, 151–152, 160, 162, 183, 185, 187
  social liberalism 12, 83, 88, 115, 136, 140, 145, 147, 159–160, 162, 182–183
  see also Hayek; Keynes
linguistics 11, 71, 97, 99–100
  see also philology
London 11, 17–24, 28–34, 40–41, 45–46, 81, 117, 150, 213
Lovecraft, H. P. 1, 19, 201, 204, 207–212
Lovelace, Ada 164–165
Lubetkin, Berthold 11, 40, 46, 59–60, 63–65, 67, 70–71, 111, 113, 213
Lucas, John 174–175
Lugosi, Bela 56, 59

Macdonald, George 79–80, 107n.44
Macfarlane, Helen 75–76, 101–103

Index

machine for living in *see* cyborgs; Le Corbusier
machine for thinking *see* artificial intelligence; computer
MacNeice, Louis 65
Madin, John 113, 148–149, 212
Mad Scientist 1–4, 5–7, 59, 70–71, 198, 206–208
  see also Frankenstein, Victor; Freud; magic; magician; Zuckerman
magic 10, 20, 26, 28, 33, 35, 40, 86, 87–88, 104, 138, 160, 207
magician 6, 10, 40, 50, 71, 77, 86–89, 104, 147, 161, 198–199, 202–205, 215
  see also necromancer
Magnus, Albertus 5, 207
Mandeville, Bernard 136–137
Marcuse, Herbert 146–147
Marlowe, Christopher 8, 192
Marr, Nikolai 11, 97–101
Marx, Karl
  on the commodity fetish 78, 103–104
  as culmination of the Hegelian tradition in western philosophy 70–71, 204
  on the eighteenth-century Robinsonade 37, 39
  forms part of the mid-century synthesis effected by Keynes 12, 104, 143, 146
  on the goblin or spectre of communism 75, 78, 88
  on the magician 77, 88–89, 139, 145–147
  on philology 89
  as unable to account for 'Democratic Industry' in Birmingham 80–83
Masons *see* Freemasons
mass-production 46–47, 120, 128, 141, 143–145, 147
  see also industrial revolution

matter (a.k.a nature) 2–4, 7, 9, 6, 124, 133, 161, 165, 198, 202–203, 205–209, 213, 215
  see also fetish; spectre; spirit
Mechanical Turk 161–164, 169, 174
  see also automatons; computers
memory palaces 16–18
Mesopotamia 93, 95–96, 214
mimesis 11, 26, 34, 40, 49, 56–58, 77, 171–174, 176, 184, 190
  see also Imitation Game; Mechanical Turk
mind *see* spirit
Mirowski, Phillip 183–184
Mitchison, Naomi 79, 84, 88
Modulor Man 127–130, 132–133, 134
Moholy-Nagy, László 46, 127
Mok and Moina 45–46, 67, 69
Modernism
  Classical or High (roots in phenomenology) 11–12, 45–47, 64–71, 97, 104, 114, 152–153n.4, 214
    see also Marx
  late or mid-century 12, 71, 104, 112–115, 117, 120, 124, 128, 136, 148–151, 199, 213–214
    see also Keynes
  Romantic (roots in philology and psychology) 11–12, 70–72, 89, 97, 104, 152–153n.4, 214
    see also Freud
  post 11–13, 40–41, 71, 104, 112–115, 122, 128, 133–136, 147, 149, 160, 162, 200–201, 204, 209
    see also Derrida; Haraway; Hayek
Moore, Alan 9, 11, 18–24, 27
Moore, Henry 113, 121

Morgoth (a.k.a. Melkor) 84–85, 91
Morlocks 79–80
Moxon's Monster *see*
   Mechanical Turk
Mumford, Lewis 30, 114, 120–122,
   126, 160, 181, 188
mummies (Egyptian) 3, 27
   see also cyborgs; Egypt

Nation, Terry 118, 120, 125
necromancer 10, 40, 88,
   199, 205
   see also magician
necromancy *see* magic
Necronomics *see* extinct
   ecosystems; fossil fuels;
   spectre
neoliberalism *see* liberalism
Negarestani, Reza 13,
   201–205, 298
Nemirovsky, Alexandre 94–96
Neumann (von), John 183–184
New Linguistic Doctrine *see*
   Japhetic theory
Niemeyer, Oscar 113, 118, 120
Nietzsche, Friedrich 70–71, 204
Nieuwenhuys, Constant 135

occult 5, 16–17, 20–22, 27–28,
   39–40, 76, 202, 207
   see also magic; magician
Okorafor, Nnedi 13, 209–212
orcs
   etymology of the name 87–88
   fictional origins 84
   precedents in the Victorian
      goblin tradition 79–80, 90
   relationship to sorcerous
      practices 84–89,
      103–104
   significance 77, 81, 88–89,
      100, 103
   ubiquity within twenty-first-
      century media 76–77
   see also Black Speech;
      goblins; spectre
Orwell, George 99, 140, 143–147

Pandora's Box *see*
   Promethean, gifts
Paolozzi, Eduardo 121
Paracelsus 5–8
paranoia 27–28, 40, 116, 203–204
Paris 30, 46, 50–52, 57–58, 130,
   132, 135, 167
Penrose, Roger 172
Persia 46, 187, 201–203
petroleum *see* fossil fuels
phenomenology 70, 161, 204, 206,
   209, 215
philology 71, 89, 91, 93–94, 98,
   100–101
   see also linguistics
planning 13, 16, 18, 22, 2, 28–34,
   66, 116, 119, 127–128,
   132, 134–135, 139,
   180–181, 183, 185–186
Pliny 69
Poe, Edgar Allen 57–58, 163–168,
   173, 191
Polo, Marco 200–201
post-modernism *see* Modernism
Pound, Ezra 11, 68–70, 112–113,
   152–153n.4
Priestley, Joseph 205–206, 213
Promethean
   ambitions 1, 11, 13, 29–31, 48,
      60–65, 71, 97–99,
      122–124, 138, 183, 190,
      211, 213, 180–181
   foresight or prediction
      (Promethean liver) 13,
      180, 214–215
   gifts 46, 111–113, 118, 123,
      126, 135, 149, 151, 182,
      211, 215
   horror 8–9, 11–12, 46, 52–56,
      58–59, 71, 116, 152,
      187, 199–200, 205–206,
      207–209
   illusions 32–33, 56–59, 67,
      88–89, 121–122, 126, 147,
      173–174, 178, 182,
      187–188, 191, 207,
      209, 212

origins 200–201, 213–214
  see also magicians; mimesis
prosthetics see cyborgs; fetish;
  spectre
Proust, Marcel 70
Prynne, Jeremy 114, 136, 153n.4
psycho-geography 10–12, 17,
  18–21, 23, 27–28, 35,
  39, 41, 59, 63, 70,
  111–112, 114–117, 127,
  133–136
psychology 10, 17, 20, 39, 70,
  117, 120, 123, 134,
  143–114, 183, 204, 214
Puck see goblins
Púkel-men see Drúedain; fetish;
  golem; totem
pyramids 26–27, 88, 138–139, 144

Radcliffe, Anne 9
radical empiricism see Modernism
RAND Corporation 183–185
Read, Herbert 121
revenant see necronomics; spectre
revolution 9–10, 23, 29, 34, 46,
  76, 78, 83, 88–89, 97,
  99, 130–131, 135,
  142–143, 158, 161, 190,
  205, 213, 215
Ripper murders 19–24
Romanticism 8, 10, 11, 70–71,
  112, 152n.4
Rogers, Richard 148
Rossetti, Christina 80
Rushdie, Salman 126, 146
Russia 77–78, 88, 97, 100, 168

satirical misrepresentation see
  shame totem
Savage, Thomas Staughton
  49–50
Sauron (a.k.a The Necromancer)
  12, 78, 85, 88, 90, 91
  see also necromancer
Searle, John 172–173, 176–178
Schiller, Friedrich 10, 39
Schlegel, F. R. W. 71

Schopenhauer, Arthur 12, 70–71,
  204–206, 212
Shackle, G. L. S. 182, 184,
  186–187, 191, 214
Shakespeare, William 8, 102–103
shamanism see magic; magician
shame totem 11–12, 71, 79–80,
  104, 198–199, 205
  see also détournement; totem
Shelley, Mary 1, 3–5, 7, 9–10, 192
Shelley, P. B. 158, 201, 215
simulacra / simulation see
  mimesis
Sinclair, Iain 10–11, 18–19, 21–23,
  27, 35, 40
Situationist 104, 114, 123, 134
Skidelsky, Robert 142, 181
socialism 80, 83, 88, 140,
  145–147, 160
  see also communism; social
  liberalism
sorcery see magic
sorcerer see magician
Soviet Union 11, 77, 100, 183
spatial triad 133–134
spectre 9, 75–78, 83, 85, 88–89,
  102–103, 201
  see also artificial body; fetish;
  goblins; matter; orcs;
  prosthetics
Speiser, E. A. 95–96
Spicer, Nicolas 135
Spielberg, Steven 187, 189, 190
spirit 7, 10, 26, 39, 48–49, 75–78,
  86, 89, 91, 102, 104, 124,
  130–133, 151, 158, 161,
  198, 201, 203, 205–206,
  208, 213, 215
  see also matter; spectre
Stalin, Josef 78, 99, 100
Stein, Gertrude 70, 112
Stirner, Max 70

Thatcher, Margaret 11, 40–41,
  140, 145–146
theme parks 51, 187–189
Thing-in-Itself 205, 207–209, 212

Tolkien, J. R. R. 12, 71, 75, 77–81, 83–97, 99–101, 103–104
totem (pole) 16–17, 25, 31, 36, 38–39, 54–55, 65, 84–86
see also shame totem
Tschink, Cajetan 10, 40
Turing, Alan 165, 167, 169–179, 191, 193n.30
see also Imitation Game

uncanny, the 11–12, 18, 34–35, 39–41, 71, 77, 86, 116–117, 124–126, 135, 152, 169–170, 199, 205–206

Vanbrugh, John 23, 34
Vedic Hinduism 201, 206, 213
Venturi, Robert 40, 115
Vico, Giambattista 98–99
Vidler, Anthony 34, 41
Voodoo economics *see* Keynes

Wall, Cynthia 33, 38
Walpole, Horace 9, 19, 200
War on Terror 186–187, 202

Webb, Sydney 83
Westermarck, Edvard 61, 86
Wiener, Norbert 9, 122, 162, 167
Wizard *see* magician
Wood Jnr., Edward D. 54
Woolf, Virginia 70
Wren, Christopher 18, 21, 27–30, 32–34, 36, 38
Wright, Frank Lloyd 114, 117, 119, 120
Wyndham, John 125

X-Men 125

Yakub myth 199, 206–207
see also Mad Scientist
Yeats, W. B. 112, 124

Zedong, Mao 135
Zola, Emile 80
zombie 149–150
zoo 45–46, 51, 59–66, 68, 187–189
Zoroastrianism 201–204, 213
Zuckerman, Solly 60–63, 66–67

EU authorised representative for GPSR:
Easy Access System Europe, Mustamäe tee 50,
10621 Tallinn, Estonia
gpsr.requests@easproject.com